Volunteering

for the GENIUS®

D1520293

Discover how to live your
most rewarding volunteer life!

FOR THE GENIUS IN ALL OF US™

Helen B. Arnold, CFRE

Volunteering for the GENIUS™

One of the **For the GENIUS**® books

Published by
For the GENIUS Press, an imprint of CharityChannel LLC
424 Church Street, Suite 2000
Nashville, TN 37219 USA

ForTheGENIUS.com

Library of Congress Control Number: 2017936823
ISBN: 978-1-941050-49-1

Printed in the United States of America
10 9 8 7 6 5 4 3 2

Publisher's Acknowledgments

This book was produced by a team dedicated to excellence; please send your feedback to Editors@ForTheGENIUS.com.

Members of the team who produced this book include:

Editors

    Acquisitions: Linda Lysakowski

    Manuscript Editing: Stephen Nill

Production

    Layout: Jill McLain

    Design: Deborah Perdue

Administrative

    For the GENIUS Press: Stephen Nill, CEO, CharityChannel LLC

    Marketing and Public Relations: John Millen

Helen B. Arnold, a Certified Fund Raising Executive, is President of Arnold Olson Associates, a firm that provides fund development consulting services for nonprofit organizations. In addition, she is the nonprofit advisor of Clearly Compliant Inc., a company that provides third-party state registration services for nonprofits. Helen has a fifty-five-year (plus) history, both as a volunteer and a professional, in the nonprofit world. As a volunteer, Helen has worked for numerous charities and has served on sixty-two nonprofit boards in the Chicago, New York, Eastern Iowa, and Las Vegas areas.

Helen has served clients across the United States in all aspects of fundraising and organizational excellence. She has served as speaker for the Association of Fundraising Professionals International Conference on Fundraising and the Grant Professionals Association as well as faculty and speaker on a wide array subjects related to philanthropy. She is a certified AFP Master Trainer, and has received the Certificate of Nonprofit Management from Iowa State University. Helen is a contributing author to *YOU and Your Nonprofit* and *The Nonprofit Consulting Playbook* from CharityChannel Press. She is a member of the Association of Fundraising Professionals, Grant Professionals Association, the Eastern Iowa Planned Giving Council and the National Association for Charitable Gift Planners. She has received several honors recognizing her volunteer and professional achievements, including the AFP Eastern Iowa Outstanding Professional Fundraiser Award.

For my son Andrew R. Olson, who is the sunshine of my life.

For my father Duane Arnold, Sr. and my grandfather Sutherland C. Dows, who inspired and encouraged my passion for philanthropy and volunteering.

Dedication

Author's Acknowledgments

They say life happens when you make a plan. When I first committed to writing this book I had no idea that seemingly nonstop life crises would get in the way, repeatedly extending the publication date. This has taken a few years of fits and starts, highs and lows to get this book written. I am so grateful to Linda Lysakowski, ACFRE, my editor and friend, who first actually believed I could do this, and then waited patiently while I actually got it finished. I am in debt to Stephen Nill, my publisher and friend, for having faith in me to finish the job, and for having the persistence of a saint.

Abiding and heart-felt appreciation is due to Dawn Svenson Holland, Pam Marvel, Sarah Else, Anita Lappe, and my sister Mary Arnold for listening to me, holding my hand, kicking my behind when necessary, and making sure I didn't quit. And I can't forget my o-dark-thirty walking partner and sounding board, Sharon Perovich.

Editors, writers, and cheerleaders Jessica Reeder and Christine Whitmarsh from Christine, Ink got me to the finish line and made the writing better. Bless you!

And thank you my dear friend Laura Fredricks, for taking the time and giving your talents to contribute the Foreword! You're the best!

Contents

Summary of Chapters

Chapter 5
Volunteer Culture in the United States Today

Volunteers are important today not only for the nonprofit industry but for a wide array of other industries including community governance, politics, and education.

Part 2—Know Yourself

To have the most successful volunteer partnership between you and the charity, you will need a clear understanding of yourself, your skill sets, and your involvement preferences.

Chapter 6
Your Personal Retreat

Take the time to learn about yourself: what you like, what you're able to do, and what you're interested in doing.

Chapter 7
Investigate Your Local Nonprofit Community

Local community nonprofits and governing entities are generally in need of volunteer support, and may be easier to approach.

Chapter 8
Investigate International, National and Regional Opportunities

Don't limit yourself in your research for the best fit. Look beyond your local community. International and national organizations can have widespread opportunities. Several online sources are provided.

Chapter 9
Investigate Fraternal and Business Organizations

You may be a member of a professional or fraternal organization. Most of these offer volunteer options to support community causes.

Part 3—Your Choices: Places to Volunteer 109

Chapter 10
Faith-Based Organizations 111

Places of faith offer the longest history of formalized volunteer programs. In most situations there are several opportunities to become involved.

Chapter 11
School or Educational Organizations............................ 118

If you have children or grandchildren or simply enjoy being with kids, schools can always use your help.

Chapter 12
Direct Programs for Nonprofit Organizations 127

When you think of volunteering, helping with actual program service delivery for nonprofit organizations may be the first thing that you consider. This means you will be in direct contact with clients served.

Chapter 13
Organizational Governance 139

If you're particularly interested in serving on boards, you may want to look into governance opportunities. All nonprofits require boards. There are legal obligations and risks in serving on boards, and you should have a high passion for the mission of the organization if you're serving at that level.

Chapter 14
Special Events 149

Special Events are often big and always exciting. Special events have a beginning and an end, so you aren't signing up for life. In addition, special events often provide the volunteers a wonderful social activity and involvement with the larger community.

Chapter 15
Government and Politics...................................159

There are many opportunities to get involved with your local, regional, or national political party. Many volunteers even travel to participate. In addition, cities, counties, and states have committee and board service opportunities.

Part 4—Volunteering Abroad 171

There is literally an entire world for you to discover in volunteering. Volunteering in a foreign country takes significantly more time and preparation, but the experience is well worth it.

Chapter 16
Identifying the Right Opportunity 173

Volunteering in a foreign country is a tremendously exciting option. However, there are more advance concerns and requirements of which you need to be aware. Identifying the right fit for you when volunteering in a foreign country is the most important step.

Chapter 17
Requirements and Applications................................183

Know exactly what is required of you, including contractual obligations.

Chapter 18
What to Expect: Be Prepared 193

Unexpected challenges while abroad can range from inconvenient to dangerous and frightening. Try to plan for any eventuality.

Chapter 19
Travel and Medical...203

If you prepare in advance to be healthy you're in generally good shape. Not all countries have the level of sanitation or clean water that the United States does. And there may not be a drug store down the street where you're going.

Chapter 20
Make sure you plan for as many contingencies and situations as possible.

Clear and complete communication between volunteers and nonprofits is critical. You have expectations of the charity, and the charity has expectations of you. Make sure these are understood by all parties before you begin.

Chapter 21
It is imperative that you understand what you can expect from the organization. Get it in writing if possible.

Chapter 22
It is essential that the organization understands what it can expect of you, the volunteer. You're serving as staff, albeit unpaid.

Chapter 23
You will certainly enjoy making friends with people whom you would never know if not for volunteering. At the same time, the nonprofit is depending on you to do your job at a professional level.

Chapter 24
The clients are the reason you're there. You're making a difference in their lives in a way that may not be obvious to you, but means everything to them.

Chapter 25

Volunteers are in the unique position to be the best advocates for the organization, whether in a formal or casual setting. You represent the organization in the community, and your passion and enthusiasm will encourage others to support the mission of the organization.

Ethics, morals, good business practices, and fiduciary duties are serious, impactful standards for any nonprofit organization. It is good to have a clear idea of how these standards work.

Chapter 26

When all is said and done, working as a volunteer does have ethical and legal obligations.

Chapter 27

Policies and procedures should be a part of every organization's governance structure. What they are may affect your volunteer involvement.

Chapter 28

No matter how well intentioned, occasionally there are disagreements in a volunteer situation.

Chapter 29

Most volunteering opportunities will go smoothly. Sometimes however, you may want to be a little more careful.

Foreword

You have such a gift in your hands. Never before has such an off-the-charts comprehensive book been written about the personal journey of *selecting* the right volunteer opportunity for you and then *serving* as your way of giving back.

Most of us say to ourselves, "I have some extra time. I should do something meaningful for people who do not have what I have," or, "I was helped along the way. It's time for me to give back." That *give back* is the universal reason why people volunteer, and it's priceless.

Helen takes the topic of volunteering and puts structure to the process, *before, during, and after you volunteer.* The themes I love in this book are:

- *Be proactive.* Do your research, ask great questions, and probe your WHY. *Why* do you want to volunteer for this group?

- *Know expectations.* What you want out of this unique experience and what do they expect of you?

- *Stay ethical.* We pride ourselves in philanthropy on holding the highest standard of ethics in all our charitable work, so monitor the group you're working with and learn about your ethical obligations as a volunteer.

- *Know the law.* Charitable organizations are regulated by state charitable bureaus, so it is important that you hold your volunteer organization accountable.

- *Share the love.* If you have an amazing volunteer experience, spread the word and encourage everyone you meet to volunteer. We need you and our most deserving groups need you.

As a volunteer board member for three organizations, and a proud volunteer for over three decades, let me give this recommendation: savor every bit of advice Helen packs in this book. *Volunteering is a personal journey and will fill your life in ways you never imagined.* Trust me, every volunteer needs to read this. She is a dear friend of mine, I love her, and I'm so proud of her work. Welcome to your new personal journey to personal fulfillment. On behalf of the organizations that you will *serve—THANK YOU!*

Laura Fredricks, JD
CEO and Founder, THE ASK

Introduction

Welcome to the world of volunteerism! Volunteering offers you a world of opportunities for experiences, including meeting people and learning skills to which you might never otherwise be exposed. The prospects of working hard to help others are boundless and astonishing.

You may be the go-to neighbor who everyone depends on when food, or transportation, or babysitting, or tools, or hand-holding are needed (crisis or not). You may be a person who has a lifelong involvement in volunteering in your local community, throughout your region or state, or nationally. You may be a person who has helped in a local crisis but has not investigated a more formalized volunteer commitment. You may be a person who is interested in helping out but has no idea how to go about finding what you want to do or how to do it. Or you may be a person who has not given any kind of volunteering much thought. This book will help you if you're at all interested in giving back, learning the history of volunteerism, understanding the motivations of volunteers, and figuring out how to find the best fit for your volunteer energy and time.

You will discover your personal roots and passion as a volunteer. You will go on your own internal journey to find what you want to do as a volunteer and where you might want to do it. You will explore history and the current state of volunteerism in the United States as well as in other countries. You will learn about the benefit to you—the volunteer—and, of course, the remarkable difference it will make in the lives of those you touch.

You will learn the various definitions of volunteering, along with the history of volunteerism both globally and in the United States.

You will learn detailed information about different kinds of volunteering, how to research to choose the right nonprofit for you, and the steps to take to get involved. You will discover how to volunteer in your neighborhood and community as well as in your region, the United States, and around the globe.

Once you have analyzed what you're looking for, you will investigate what kind of specific "job" you're interested in and where to find it: governance/board service or tutoring first graders; teaching religious studies or working in hospice care; a youth activity leader, or any of a myriad of other options. You will learn about regional and national opportunities as well as local charities, fraternal and business possibilities, church and religious organizations, school or educational entities. Are you a highly social person? Special events may be your specialty. And you can't forget the highly charged political and governmental choices which are always fun and challenging.

Are you fascinated by travel? How about discovering where to volunteer in Europe? Or maybe Africa, South America, Southeast Asia, Australia are places of interest to you? Are you a student interested in learning about combining study and travel abroad? You will learn how research for and how to participate in these programs. You will also discover what you need to know to be safe and healthy when volunteering in another country. You will know what clothes to pack, how to prepare medically, and what to do in case of a crisis.

Importantly, you will understand what you can expect in the way of support, training, and information from the organizations for which you're volunteering. It is critical to make sure that you understand exactly what you're agreeing to. More importantly, you will come to fully realize what the organization for which you're volunteering will expect from you. Know that you're making a commitment to show up and do what you say you're going to do. These organizations depend on you. In addition, many nonprofit organizations may require fairly in-depth training, medical testing, background checks, or references, particularly if you will be working with an at-risk population. You will gain an in-depth understanding of what that process may look like.

Volunteering for the GENIUS will also discuss a variety of reality-based issues. First is volunteer ethics. Most ethical situations will be fairly obvious to you, but sometimes ethical challenges may be subtler. We will help you recognize ethical questions and how to deal with them. It's important for you personally as well as for the nonprofit that ethical awareness is top-of-the-mind.

In your volunteer career, you may run into situations that call for understanding of the legal environment. It is critical that you have a grasp of legal issues that may come into play with the volunteer position you're filling. We will talk about how to be aware, and how to ensure you have the knowledge you may need.

Finally, you will need to understand your choices when volunteer endeavors do not go as planned. Yes, sometimes the best laid plans do not work out as expected. You will discover how to identify possible conflicts and options for resolving them.

Throughout the chapters you will find sidebars. These are to give you an example of a point made in the text, or to supply a definition, or to tell a short story. Sidebars may include interesting facts, a noteworthy quote, or a highlight of what *not* to do.

Why am I writing this book? It's pretty simple for me: passion. Volunteering has been part of my DNA from very early childhood. My first volunteer 'job' was at the age of eight, stuffing envelopes for a political candidate. At thirteen, I volunteered as a teacher's aide all summer in the then-new Head Start program. That was only the beginning. My first major fundraising experience was at the age of twenty-one for the Junior League of Chicago. My résumé says I have served on sixty-two boards so far. That's true. But think of all the causes and charities for which I have volunteered *not* as a board director over nearly seven decades. In reality, my volunteer life has consistently run parallel to my paid professional life. I have spent equal time on both; sometimes even more on volunteering. (I will note with humor here that, in part due to times-out for volunteer commitments, this book took quite a while to write.)

I don't remember a time when I was not volunteering for something. Why? Volunteering is truly interesting. I am an information addict and want to learn as much about 'stuff' as possible. It is fun. It is full of adventures and new horizons. And you get to feel good about doing it. I have had the opportunity to become lifetime friends with amazingly talented and wonderful people. I have had chances to learn tons of new talents and expand my skill sets in real time. Volunteering even led me to join the nonprofit world as a professional.

Working for something without the pressure of earning a paycheck, and knowing it is changing the lives of people you will never know, brings spiritual color and emotional satisfaction to living. It is compelling. I can only hope that you experience the same wonderful return that I have.

When all is said and done, I believe volunteering is the purest form of personal philanthropy: absolute altruism. You're truly giving of yourself, with no expectation of receiving remuneration. There is no requirement to be rich, or influential, or famous to be able to bring significant change to the lives of people you may or may not ever meet. All you're obliged to bring to the table is a desire to make a difference, a quantity time, a goodly amount of energized passion, and the intentional focus to find the volunteer job that brings *you* inspiration and satisfaction. It is out there, waiting. You only have to look around, make a decision, and show up. *Thank you* for what you have done in the past and for what you will be doing in the future to make our planet a better place. It is by giving of yourself that you will be blessed with a rich and rewarding life while building a better world—one person at a time.

VOLUNTEERS
WANTED

79th Regiment of New York
Cameron Rifle Highlanders

AN ATTACK UPON WASHINGTON ANTICIPATED!!

THE COUNTRY TO THE RESCUE!

A REGIMENT FOR SERVICE
UNDER THE FLAG OF THE UNITED STATES

PATRIOTISM AND LOVE OF COUNTRY DEMAND A READY RESPONSE FROM EVERY MAN CAPABLE OF BEARING ARMS IN THIS TRYING HOUR, TO SUSTAIN NOT MERELY THE EXISTANCE OF THE GOVERNMENT, BUT TO VINDICATE THE HONOR OF THAT FLAG RUTHLESSLY TORN BY TRAITOR HANDS FROM THE WALLS OF SUMTER.

SAMUEL McKENZIE ELLIOTT
COMDG. 79TH REGT N.Y. VOLS
(HIGHLANDERS)

NOW IS THE TIME TO BE ENROLLED !

History and Definition of Volunteerism

Volunteering is as old as time. For most, it's human nature to want to help someone out. In this part of *Volunteering for the GENIUS,* the focus is on the historic background of volunteering. We'll begin by looking at your personal life and where you're likely already volunteering, whether you're aware of it or not. We'll define the current and historic meanings of the word *volunteer,* including different philosophies about volunteerism. We'll look at diverse historical roots of volunteering in various countries. Finally, we'll investigate the current status of volunteering in these countries, including, of course, the United States.

Chapter 1

You're a Volunteer

In This Chapter...

- You volunteer in your family and neighborhood
- You volunteer in your faith
- You volunteer in your schools
- You volunteer in your community

Your time and talents are incredibly valuable to charities or individuals that you're helping.

It may surprise you, but you already live the life of a volunteer. You may not look at it that way, since for you it is simply the way things are. Whether or not the word *volunteer* is used, people helping people are all around you. *You* are helping people all around you.

In this chapter we're going to take a snapshot of what you do every day. We'll talk about how you give your time and talents to your family, to your neighbors, in your place of faith, in your schools, and in your greater community. Take a minute and visualize what you do now or what you have done in the past. You might be amazed.

You Volunteer in Your Family and Neighborhood

Ah, living in a family is the best—and sometimes the worst, right? But whatever your family unit looks like or how it interacts, it is where you first developed the understanding that helping out was expected (or maybe required).

As a youth, you learned to do chores. Did you ever cook meals, finish the laundry, mow grass, help clean the house, or maybe even paint the fence?

You were doing what you could, with the skills you had at the time, to help others, even though the others were your family. Hopefully, you had a personal sense of satisfaction that you not only did the job, but did it well.

Sound familiar? Ideally, your whole family is helping with all of these jobs. But, whether or not your family members participate with a positive attitude, everyone benefits from the work done. No one submits an invoice for payment for their services. They, and you, are volunteering for the greater good.

Do you ever help your neighbors by shoveling their driveways in the winter? Or by taking them chicken soup when they are ill? Or by driving them to the grocery store when their car is not working? Have you loaned tools, or fixed an appliance, or painted a fence, or changed your neighbor's light bulbs? You help your neighbors without expectation of being paid—you're a volunteer. You make a difference in your neighbor's life.

I live in a neighborhood full of people with amazing generosity. One of our neighbors was recently diagnosed with multiple cancers. Not only that, her husband has Parkinson's disease and is disabled. With no fuss or fanfare, many neighbors stepped up to help. They are cooking meals, taking the couple to medical appointments, and helping with upkeep of the home. This will be a constant for the foreseeable future, until our friend is recovered. There is a need—the need is being filled. The neighbors are *volunteering*.

Another concept of neighbors helping neighbors being important and effective is shown through some community grassroots support organizations that have used "neighbor" in the title. Examples:

🔦 Neighborhood House (Seattle, WA)

🔦 Neighborhood Centers (Bellaire, TX)

🔦 Neighbors, Inc. (St. Paul, MN)

When you decide how you want to spend your volunteer hours and energy, you may want to consider one of these "neighborhood" agencies.

The concept of neighbors volunteering to help neighbors is the basis of human culture. Humans succeeded because we banded together and created social structures to help each other. These would include functions ranging from sharing community child care to helping with the care of elderly or infirm, as well as protection and hunting or gathering food in groups.

There is an African proverb that says "It takes a village to raise a child." Expanded, this means to me that everyone in the "village" is proactively committed to the welfare of all, and volunteers contribute whatever time and labor deemed necessary for the common good. (Yes, Hillary Rodham Clinton used this as a title for her book in 1996.)

You Volunteer in Your Faith

In your life, have you been part of a community of faith? Historically, places of faith have been at the core of asking for

You Volunteer in Your Neighborhood

A prime example of neighbors volunteering to help neighbors can be found in the traditional Amish community. In Amish or Mennonite societies, it is not unusual to see volunteers come together for a single family's barn-raising. A new barn may be needed to increase farm capacity or to replace an old or destroyed barn. The entire community participates (it can be as many as one hundred volunteer builders plus families)—children through adults. They volunteer their time and labor to complete the barn in one day, prepare and serve food to the people present, and then celebrate the event as a community party.

Another traditional Amish event is the making of a quilt for a young bride-to-be. The volunteers come together to contribute time and talent, stitching together the quilt. They bring refreshments and make a party of it! The end result is a beautiful quilt that will last through generations, plus a fun time!

Pure Genius!

and generating volunteer support for the needs of the community. All faiths of which I am aware have a strong moral belief that helping others is part of our obligation as caring citizens of our world. It is found in virtually all religions: from the *Golden Rule* to the *Principle of Reciprocity*, the philosophy is *to do unto others as you would wish them to do unto you*. Most organizations of faith have well-structured community volunteer opportunities in which their members can participate. These programs make a difference.

You Volunteer in Your Faith

The Church of Jesus Christ of Latter Day Saints has an intensive missionary program, generally for youth nineteen to twenty-one years old, who volunteer eighteen months to two years of their lives in support of their church. Volunteers are posted throughout the world, and accept this service as a statement of their faith.

Example

Your community very likely has a wide array of churches, synagogues, mosques, or other houses of worship. Have you taught Sunday school or other religious classes? Maybe you enjoy singing in the choir, or making costumes for liturgical performances. Have you given your time to decorate for religious holidays? Maybe your church or synagogue houses a food bank or a second-hand shop. Have you helped hand out food or sold last year's winter jacket to a child with no coat? Have you helped with a soup supper, or participated in or acted as a chaperone for a youth mission trip? Have you served in the institution's governance structure: maybe the board or council? Are you an ordained elder or deacon? Have you participated as a celebrant? Then you're a volunteer.

You Volunteer in Your Schools

Whether or not you're a parent or grandparent, an aunt or an uncle, a sister or a brother, a niece or a nephew, are you interested in helping teach children? Volunteering in your child's school, whether elementary, secondary, or high school, is a wonderful way to stay closely involved with your child's life and help at the same time. For me, the unexpected side effect was that, by being involved as a volunteer, I enjoyed my son's childhood and teen years much more than I did my own.

As a parent of an elementary-age child, you may have experienced being a room parent, or chaperoned a field trip, or helped with administrative tasks in the school office. You may have joined the PTA/PTO, or organized the annual Celebration Day, or tutored first-time readers. You're a volunteer.

As a relative of a student, or if you simply in want to help all kids, you may read aloud in the classroom, encouraging students to develop a lifelong love of reading, or help coach football or soccer. You make a difference to these children.

Volunteering in schools is fairly consistent whether public, private, or parochial schools. Middle schools and high schools may demand both higher volunteer support and more interesting activities for volunteering. Are you a band, choir, or orchestra parent? Are you involved with transportation to and from the debate club competitions? Do you volunteer for the cheerleading squad practices or coach the baseball team? What about science or robotics competitions for your student?

Many high schools have multiple parent boards: athletics, performing arts, sciences, visual arts. Have you devoted your time to any of these? And then there is everyone's favorite—the constant volunteer oversight of ensuring homework is done.

You likely think that all of this is just what life looks like for a family or friends with kids in school. However, if you're donating your time and talent, you're a volunteer.

So far we have been talking about mostly adult views of their volunteer involvement. But youth—tweens and teens particularly—have made a huge difference when it comes to volunteering. Generally, middle and high schools offer and encourage getting involved in clubs, school senates, and community fundraising projects—lots of opportunities! If you're a student and are filling out applications to colleges, you will find that your community and cocurricular activities are just as important as your grades.

For high school, I attended The Masters School in Dobbs Ferry, New York. Volunteering was very much integrated into what was expected of the students. Masters still considers volunteering so much a part of a full educational and team-building experience that it is included as a graduation requirement. If you go to the website *mastersny.com,* you will see that the school considers volunteering a signature program: "Community Service is a unifying experience at The Masters School. Formally, the school calls it MISH (Masters Interested in Sharing and Helping). Across every grade and subject area,

You Volunteer in Your High School

While in high school a student decided to get involved and implemented a large volunteer project. In her own words:

I will never forget when I was in high school and went on a family reunion. I chatted with one of my older cousins, a teacher in a small community in Zimbabwe, Africa. She told me about her experiences and about the many children in her school who were in great need of clothing. I wanted to help, but wasn't sure how. Then, I started to think about the many kids I knew locally in Iowa who had so many T-shirts that they couldn't possibly need or wear them all.

I knew I couldn't travel to visit my cousin in Zimbabwe, but I realized I could help the children she was teaching. I got a group of students together and we started a T-shirt drive called "T-Shirts for Africa." We made posters and hung them around our high school and community. People from all over our area donated and we collected almost a shipping container full of T-shirts.

However, I realized we had no cost-effective way to ship them to Africa. I had recently heard about another volunteer organization that was going to ship medical supplies to Africa. I suggested a plan where we could help each other. Instead of using nonreusable packing material for the medical supplies, we could use T-shirts! We organized a packing day and our organizations came together to pack a container. After the shipment arrived, the medical supplies would be removed and distributed to the local clinics and then the T-shirts would be given away to anyone in need.

This project meant a lot to me because it showed me that I could make a difference by thinking and acting locally and globally. It might take a bit of creative spirit and some hard work, but by working together I learned I could identify problems and solve them in innovative ways. I have always felt strongly about being a local and global citizen and this project helped my friends and me make a difference in the lives of others—no matter where they are in the world.

Frances Vernon, George Washington High School, Cedar Rapids, Iowa, 2004–2005 school year project service-learning opportunities are rich and varied. From tutoring individuals to sponsoring a grade-wide Hoops for Hope to the annual all-school Special Olympics, community service opportunities bring Masters School faculty and students together." All students, all years of study, participate. As a note, the program was called MISH in the 1960s as well.

There are exciting examples of students both initiating and participating in volunteer opportunities. If you're in high school, are you involved in activities for a cause? Have you raised money for a team or club?

The students in some schools collect clothing and send it to orphanages or homeless shelters. Have you put together a team of friends to participate in a charity fishing event? Have you traveled with classmates to help with cleanup or rebuilding of homes in New Orleans after Hurricane Katrina? While all of these activities take effort, they are also fun, right? Everyone experiences rewards: if you make a difference in someone's life—you have a great time working with a team—you're a volunteer.

In recognition of the effect and reach of philanthropy by young people, the Association of Fundraising Professionals established the International Youth in Philanthropy Awards more than ten years ago. The awards honor youth ages ten to twenty-three "who demonstrate outstanding commitment to the community through direct financial support, development of charitable programs, volunteering, and leadership in philanthropy."

The 2013 AFP Youth In Philanthropy Award recognized Marli Overgard, this is her story:

> In November, 2011, Marli Overgard's world changed forever when her family suffered a terrible loss when her twelve-year-old cousin, Hunter Biermeier, died from injuries sustained in an ATV accident. While her grieving family gathered at Gundersen Lutheran Medical Center (La Crosse, WI) at Hunter's side, Marli noticed how her youngest cousins were affected. They had nothing to distract them from the frightening circumstances around them, and that experience gave Marli an idea.

> Marli, age fourteen, along with her best friend, Molly Young, were inspired to turn the tragedy into something positive. As part of their High School Key Club and Faith Formation Project for Confirmation, they began raising money to provide stuffed bears and blankets for children at the hospital where Hunter died.

The original goal was humble: raise $500 to purchase twenty-five bears and blankets and deliver them personally to the hospital. But three months later, they had raised $2,000, resulting in one hundred bears and blankets being delivered over the next eight months. Marli realized her work could be a permanent memorial to Hunter's memory.

Marli, along with Molly and Hunter's parents, Teresa and Kyle Biermeier, cofounded a charity called Hugs from Hunter Foundation. This charity promotes Hunter's positive spirit and carries out his dream of reading books to sick children in the hospital. Currently Hugs provides thirty bears and blankets each month to the La Crosse Children's Miracle Network Hospital, Medlink AIR flight and Tri-State ambulance crews serving La Crosse County. Association of Fundraising Professionals; afpnet.org.

If you're a youth involved in either Boy Scouts or Girl Scouts, you're required to actively volunteer to qualify for advancement in ranks. You may have been involved in projects sponsored by your place of faith, such as serving food at a meal center or providing childcare during services.

Are you in college? Does your college have short-term volunteering opportunities in other countries or in other parts of the United States? Many colleges offer class credit to participate in work/travel volunteering. Maybe you're a member of a fraternity or sorority that sponsors events in support of charities or causes in the community.

You Volunteer in Your Community

What a huge canvas your community is. You may have volunteered formally or informally in the past. You may have helped with an immediate community crisis like cleaning up after a tornado, a flood, or a hurricane.

Immediate- and longer-term volunteer support after a natural disaster is critical to community recovery. In 2008, Cedar Rapids, Iowa suffered a "thousand-year" flood. There were massive losses requiring significant cleanup and rebuilding. Volunteers, both local and from all over the United States, participated in the recovery.

Recovery would not have happened without expansive volunteer support. Knowing how important volunteers were to the process and that those volunteers needed to eat, sleep, and have amenities like showers while

You Volunteer in Your Community

A massive flood hit eastern Iowa, specifically Cedar Rapids, in June of 2008. It required countless volunteer hours to clean up and recover.

From Dan Baldwin, President/CEO, The Greater Cedar Rapids Community Foundation, 2002–2010:

Even in the best of times, volunteerism is vital to a healthy community. Whether it's driving for Meals on Wheels, coaching soccer, or sitting on the board of your favorite nonprofit, citizen involvement is the heartbeat of community life. It is our most common, and often most overlooked, act of philanthropy.

When disaster strikes, volunteerism may mean the difference between a partial or complete recovery. In the wake of the flood of 2008, community contributions took many forms. Even as the floodwaters were cresting, a call went out that the last functioning city well was at risk. One thousand, five hundred people showed up to sandbag. After the waters receded, exposing literally thousands of homes and businesses as severely damaged or destroyed, volunteer teams began showing up from across the country, working with locals to go house by house, tearing out water-logged siding and removing debris. This went on for months. A redevelopment corporation was formed, led by local businessmen and women willing to utilize their expertise to develop strategies for garnering funds and visioning a new city. It's hard to specifically quantify the numbers of people and hours who volunteered before, during, and after the flood, but one can say with certainty that Cedar Rapids would not have made its stunning recovery if not for volunteerism.

And people gave. Millions of dollars flowed into the community foundation's flood fund. Volunteers, again, worked with foundation staff to decide how the money should be deployed. In many ways, the flood fund became a foundation within the foundation. The first act was to restore the nonprofits who themselves were in the flood's path.

It is often said that disasters don't create character, they reveal it. In the case of Cedar Rapids, what was revealed was a community ready to work hand in hand to do what it took to recover and rebuild.

The Greater Cedar Rapids Community Foundation was recognized as the National Philanthropy Day Outstanding Foundation in 2012 by the International Association of Fundraising Professionals for its work in response to the catastrophic flood.

they worked, The Greater Cedar Rapids Community Foundation went to extraordinary lengths to support the volunteers. The foundation developed a grant process to underwrite those needs, recognizing that the volunteer demand would be fairly long term.

You might prefer participating in how your community is governed. You may want to make a difference in the longer term and choose to run for the city council, or you may devote volunteer time to the Chamber of Commerce or Red Cross. You may have participated in a neighborhood cleanup project, or helped build a house with Habitat for Humanity. Have you participated in a fitness event or attended a black tie event to support a charity?

There are likely more charitable organizations that need your help than you may be able to list right now. If you think about it, you're very probably both a donor and a volunteer. And with your time and attention, you have made a difference in someone's life.

Now that we have taken a look at your life, what do you think? Have you been more of a volunteer than you originally thought? My guess is yes, and I hope you're smiling with the discovery. As a child in your family, as a youth and student growing up, as a college student, as an adult, you have very likely been involved in many ways in the act of volunteering.

As we move on, and in order to help you with a more global understanding, we're going to take a look at some of the definitions and examples of different ways volunteering has been defined and how volunteerism has been exercised.

To Summarize...

- You're already a volunteer, even though you may not realize it.
- You volunteer in your home and neighborhood.
- You volunteer in your place of faith and schools.
- You volunteer in your community.

Chapter 2

Definition of Volunteerism

In This Chapter...

- Definitions of volunteering and volunteerism
- Philosophies of volunteering and volunteerism
- Cultural differences in volunteering

ere we are investigating the root meanings and historical background of the word "volunteer." We take for granted how the word is commonly used today. But through history, the concept of volunteerism has been the subject of differing intellectual and philosophical opinions.

What exactly does the word *volunteer* mean? How was the older word "voluntar(ism)" originally used? In this chapter we will discuss common dictionary definitions as well as some interesting historic philosophies of volunteerism that may be a little more obscure to you.

There are many formal definitions of volunteer and volunteerism. Some definitions have nothing to do with philanthropic volunteering, so for our purposes, we will focus on charitable volunteering.

Volunteer/volunteerism comes from the Latin *voluntas*, which means the will, the desire. The Latin *voluntarius* meaning voluntary, of one's free will. (Remember this definition when you read about philosophies in the next section.)

The word volunteer is a noun, a verb, and an adjective. The noun and verb have evolved to include both the person involved in and the act of community service. But has that always been true? Has the act of volunteering always been viewed the same way that we see it today?

Definition

Volunteering and Volunteerism

There are a million dictionary and organizational definitions of volunteerism. Over the last several decades, I have developed my own personal definition and set of standards. These seem to work for me. Feel free to develop your own personal definition as your volunteer experiences widen.

Volunteering:

◆ Can be formal or informal

◆ Can be well planned or spur-of-the-moment

◆ Is intentional—an individual, proactive decision

◆ Is given from the heart

◆ Fills both organizational and personal needs

◆ Is not financially compensated

◆ Is a way to actively participate in the greater communities

◆ Fills human, societal and environmental needs

◆ Respects the human rights, equality, culture and dignity of all

◆ Is an integral component of a rich personal life

◆ Is crucial to a healthy society

◆ Makes an enormous difference! Never underestimate the long term and wide ranging benefit of the work you contribute.

Philosophies of Volunteering and Volunteerism

The focused, intentional acts of volunteering did not suddenly explode into civil society. That approach developed over time. In our civilization today, the philosophy of volunteerism may appear pretty simple and self-explanatory and is tied to specific activities. But if you delve deeper into the psychological roots and evolution of the concept, it can become a little more nuanced. There are actually several different theoretical ways to understand the concept of volunteerism.

Historically, the older version of the word voluntarism was used in reference to exhibiting high moral and ethical behavior. Differences among scholars arose in arguing whether or not choosing to exhibit this excellent behavior was the will of God, or the intellectual will of the individual. It had less to do with active acts of kindness than with general honorable conduct.

Philosophers have long discussed whether or not we as individuals act morally of our own free will versus being driven by an outside force (a Greater Power). Are our choices voluntary or involuntary? Are they emotional or the result of intellectual reasoning?

If you are anything like me, sitting in a philosophy class in school is probably not your favorite learning memory. I was always looking for a task based solution instead of just an intellectual discussion. But for some, having a glass of wine and discussing the various theories of volunteerism may be wonderfully entertaining. Here I am going to summarize some of the different esoteric opinions about what really constitutes the essence of volunteering. While this discussion is more of an intellectual exercise than a practical application, a quick look will tell you how expansive the concept of volunteerism really is, and how many very smart people over history have pondered it. I am summarizing in very general terms. I will also add the names of philosophers for each sample, so you can do your own in depth investigation. Please understand that my summary is from a laymen's point of view.

- Medieval Voluntarism

- Theological Voluntarism

- Metaphysical Voluntarism

Medieval Voluntarism

Theory: This theory, generally based in Christianity, says that an individual's determination to act ethically, morally, or philanthropically comes from God's will being bestowed directly on that individual by God. It infers that the individual's intellect, knowledge or choice is sublimated to God's will.

Philosophers: John Duns Scotus (thirteenth century) and William of Ockham (thirteenth through fourteenth centuries).

Theological Voluntarism

Theory: Also based in Christianity, the theological approach believes that the individual chooses to believe or have faith in God. Responsibility for choosing moral, ethical and philanthropic actions stems from that faith, but is still the individual's choice. Each individual is in control and is accountable.

Philosophers: Scientist Isaac Newton (1642–1727), historian Francis Oakley and theologian James Luther Adams (1901–1994).

Metaphysical Voluntarism

Theory: This theory will require a bit of a redefinition of *will* and *intellect*. Here, *will* is viewed as irrational, unconscious, or possibly unreasonable. *Intellect* is viewed as conscious, deliberate, with considered choice. *Will* is considered to drive the actions of the individual. *Intellect* is considered controlled or directed by *will*. Confusing? So we can generalize that if *will* drives action, then the individual choosing to engage in ethical, moral or philanthropic action is likely acting in an irrational or unconscious way, with little control over those actions. Controlled *intellect* may be involved, but emotional *will* is still the driver. In metaphysical volunteerism, *will* and *intellect* seem like they may be in constant conflict.

There are several other philosophical approaches to the essence of volunteerism, so do some of your own research if you are curious.

Regardless of which philosophy makes sense to you, understand that whether or not you

🔦 are compelled by some outside force or faith;

🔦 have a deep internal motivation to act;

🖎 act from an involuntary or voluntary emotional drive; or

🖎 simply made a rational list of pros and cons or are curious;

your individual decision to be a volunteer is intentional, deliberate, and proactive.

Cultural Differences in Volunteering

In this section I am going to give a short synopsis of several different cultural approaches to volunteering. In **Chapter 4** I will go into more-detailed discussion of cultural differences based on geographic regions, religions, governmental, and historical information. For now, I am going to talk about the genesis of volunteering in the following areas:

Family Culture

As we discussed in **Chapter 1**, the volunteer seed is planted at home. The family culture is to help each other, with deep loyalty to the family unit. Over time the volunteer generally attitude expands to include your immediate environment, your community, and the larger world. However, in some traditional or tribal cultures, volunteering may be strictly limited to the family, and helping outsiders may be discouraged. As society has progressed, the tradition of helping family has expanded. However, historically public volunteer and charitable largesse, from Asia to Europe, was often provided by both religious orders and the wealthier, more highly educated levels of society. The community's large wealthy and influential families were the patrons of charitable support.

Our family experience generally guides all of us in how we approach volunteering. For some families that may look like getting involved in every activity imaginable. For some families, the loyalty of volunteer time belongs solely within the family circle. Some families consider volunteer involvement a priority. For some families it is not feasible. Whatever your family experience the ultimate decision for volunteer participation is yours.

Religious Culture

Religion, regardless of country or culture or time, has historically been the core around which society has operated. Religion is powerful. If you have traveled, you may have noticed that in most towns and cities, religious buildings are architecturally central to the communities. The religious centers are the spiritual and often the social heart of the community.

Religious teachings, regardless of which faith, are the basis of formalized volunteering as we understand it today. Particularly before the time when education of the average citizen was a standard, the church was the center of power and influence in any community. During time periods when the populations were functionally illiterate and had no access to wider education, codes of behavior were, and in many countries still are, dictated by the clerics.

Understanding the power that religions had and have in daily lives, it is easy to see that any religious teachings are the standard by which people lived their lives. Originally, religious centers were the only formal institutions that assumed responsibility for whatever charitable or volunteer needs there were in the communities. Typically, these options were basic and included orphanages, homeless shelters, or food and clothing for the poor. Individual incomes during the preindustrial time period were so low, working for free to help high numbers of those in need was just not feasible for the average family.

Organized charities, and the opportunity to support them with volunteer labor, were fairly limited prior to the Industrial Revolution. With the advent of the economic growth of the middle class in the Industrial Revolution, more people, particularly in Europe and North America, became involved in more charitable endeavors.

Prior to the middle seventeenth century, tools and equipment were manufactured in homes. After the advent of iron and building of huge transportation systems, factories produced these goods. And while more people earned more money, at the same time more societal challenges developed, and the need for charitable and volunteer support grew proportionately.

Today, religious institutions offer countless opportunities for local and regional volunteer involvement. Additionally, religious organizations have also been crucial in delivering services in many countries that lack a comprehensive independent charity structure. For instance, nearly all NGOs (nongovernment organizations; or charities) in Cuba are established and maintained by religious organizations.

Governmental Culture

In some countries, the government gets directly involved with providing support for those in need in their communities. As societies have become less religion-oriented and more secular, and governments have become more centralized over the last few centuries, governments have taken on some of the charitable work formerly done by the churches.

For example, in the United States, the volunteer Peace Corps is a government agency. Volunteers can go to the centralized resource *volunteer.gov*, sponsored by the US government. This government-sponsored site is a huge source of volunteer prospects. All charities in England and Wales are centrally registered and regulated with the government Charity Commission. The Australian government also has a centralized focus with the Australian Charities and Not-For-Profits Commission. Canada offers country-wide volunteering through *imaginecanada.ca*.

Pure Genius!

Governmental Culture of Volunteering

I saw first-hand an example of direct government involvement to address a specific need when I visited Cuba with a group of American nonprofit professionals. (Please don't construe this as an overall value statement about the government in Cuba. It is simply an example.)

In Cuba, infant mortality was a huge problem in the 1950s: ninety-one infant deaths per thousand births. The Cuban government established maternity homes where higher-risk pregnant mothers can live during their pregnancy, free of charge, and receive good nutrition and medical and dental care as well as parenting training. Our group visited a maternity home in Havana.

Once the baby is born, the mother and child stay in the maternity home until both are determined to be recovered and healthy from the birth. Additionally, all pregnant women in Cuba, in a maternity home or not, receive food support, vitamins, and free medical care during their pregnancies, and immediately following the child's birth. As a result of this program, the infant mortality rate has been reduced to five per thousand births according to our group's government guide during the visit.

Even with government assistance, in most countries, states, provinces, and communities, support of community causes cannot happen without volunteers. Governmental entities acknowledge that they simply cannot afford to support food, shelter, clothing, and medical care for those in need. Therefore, governments are often willing to partner with private charities to meet the community needs.

Many governments help these charities with logistics and managing regulations. (In some situations, however, logistics and regulations can still be a challenge.) Governments generally recognize that volunteers contribute significant economic value and impassioned support to the communities in which they work.

Social Culture

The Industrial Revolution (circa 1760–1820) brought about a boom in volunteering. With the lifestyle changes brought on with the building of factories, the improvements in travel and the availability of products and services that had never before been part of daily routine, involvement with charitable works increased.

Initially, there was an increased set of needs to be met in the ever growing society. An easier lifestyle increased available leisure time—time that could be given to other interests. Becoming involved as a volunteer with public causes of all kinds became standard. Some of the causes were of course political in addition to charitable. But the collective willingness of citizens to publicly work together for a common cause was locked into social life at all levels.

In the last few hundred years, the number of causes—the opportunities for involvement for the public good—have exponentially expanded. Today, there are approximately 1.5 million 501(c)(3) charities in the United States, plus schools, governments, political causes, environmental organizations, and religious institutions all of which have needs for volunteers.

In today's culture, volunteering for charitable causes has become totally integrated into our social activities. It is impossible to open a newspaper or watch a television or open your mail without seeing an invitation to join a gala or a fitness event or a hot-air balloon festival, or a duck race or... all for a good cause. Volunteering for the social opportunities offered is a huge reason many people become involved. People love the parties. They love the public recognition. They love being associated with the famous people who also support the purpose. There is so much from which to choose, and folks just plain love having fun!

To Summarize...

🖋 *Volunteer* in today's world is defined as a noun, a verb and an adjective and refers to acting for benefit of others without expectation of remuneration.

🖋 *Voluntarism* is historically academically based in various philosophies that discuss whether or not moral and ethical individual action is based on emotional will or intellectual reasoning.

🖋 Volunteering can be approached across various cultural avenues: through family, religion, government, or social channels.

🖋 With approximately 1.5 million nonprofit charities in the United States today, the options for individual volunteerism are vast.

Chapter 3

Historical Roots of Volunteering

In This Chapter...

- Asia: China and Japan
- Middle East: Israel
- Europe: England/United Kingdom
- United States

We have talked a little bit about the general roots of individual volunteering. As we discussed in **Chapter 1**, the actions of helping each other are as old as man.

But when did volunteering become more structured, more expanded? Has the process been the same in every country or culture?

In this chapter we're going to look at an overview of the history and cultural background that were the beginnings of formalized volunteerism in a few parts of the world. We will look at select examples that show how differently volunteerism can evolve. In the United States we take for granted that all countries view volunteering as we do. This isn't the case. Different countries and different cultures may value volunteering and volunteers quite differently.

In some cultures, volunteering is heavily integrated into society. In some others, formalized or organized volunteerism is more incidental. Only a few examples are included, but they are demonstrative of how volunteerism can differ from country to country.

Asia

Asia includes a massive collection of countries and cultures. The United Nations divides Asia into five major regions: Central Asia; East Asia; Middle East; and South Asia. The UN also divides these regions into numerous subregions, but for our purposes, we will limit our discussion in this section to the examples of China (East Asia) and Japan (East Asia).

Each of these countries represents very old world civilizations. Each of these countries has a rich heritage and both have made centuries of significant contributions to world culture. The two countries are located in fairly close proximity, but the practice of volunteerism in each country developed quite differently.

China

China is one of the oldest world civilizations. The written history in China dates back to the Sheng Dynasty, c. 1700–1046 BC. Overall, Chinese history is a story of successive semifeudal ruling dynasties ruled by emperors, empresses, and warlords through ancient, imperial, and modern time periods up to the twentieth century.

The precursors of the value of volunteering in Chinese Society date from 722–476 BC. It was during this Spring and Autumn period that the Hundred Schools of Thought of Chinese philosophy developed. The religious theologies of Confucianism, Taoism, Legalism, and Mohism were established, and became mixed in daily life. The philosophies became combined in practice, assimilating what was considered the best of each of them into common use. Eventually Confucianism became predominant and is considered the cultural origin of Chinese philanthropy and volunteerism. This evolved much like the faith-based genesis of volunteerism in other parts of the world.

While the Confucian spirit of caring for others by each individual was part of societal belief, beginning during Imperial China overall philanthropy and good works of substance were generally considered to be the responsibility of regional wealthy families or warlord rulers as proof of their influence and power. This top-down charitable support, in the form of money or labor, was based on the immediate needs of the local citizenry: food, shelter, illness, or recovery from a crisis. This philanthropy was limited to the influential family's geographic area. Can you see a parallel in the family/neighborhood/community origins of volunteerism in **Chapter 1**?

Over the centuries, Chinese dynasties and empires were both centralized and decentralized, depending on the political strength of the emperors or the waging of regional wars. From time to time China was broken up into separate smaller independent kingdoms, each with its own warlord ruler.

China was a huge, primarily rural, area which made it difficult and expensive to rule from a central seat of government (the emperors). Most of the population lived lives of subsistence. To a large extent, much of the country

Chinese Philosophy of Volunteerism

Confucianism formed the basis for the social order in China since 200 BC. It provided the working rules and ethical precepts for Chinese to follow. Even today the majority of Chinese still behave according to these rules.

Confucianism views the individual as social creatures obligated to each other through relationships. These may include the relations between sovereign and subject, parent and child, elder and younger, husband and wife, or even friend and friend. Confucianism defined the rules in the engagement, action, and responsibilities in all these human relationships and interactions. Proper conduct proceeds not through compulsion, but through a sense of virtue and self-consciousness achieved by learning, observing, and practicing.

Definition

was ignored by the central rulers unless war was being waged. If the regional warlord or ruling family was unable or unwilling to help in time of need, what did poorer, common people, and remote communities do to help each other when there was a significant challenge? The answer was that the common citizenry began to develop a grassroots system of a community civil society or a social association to address daily societal needs. Over time, these civil societies evolved to offer all kinds of support to its members: philanthropic to banking, crisis support to communal socialization.

Western missionaries had a presence in China beginning as early the seventh century. The predominant religion of the missionaries was Christianity, and eventually all denominations were represented. As Western religious concepts were introduced and expanded, acceptance by the Chinese was sometimes problematic, as it was seen as competitive with already accepted ancient philosophies. There was some acceptance of the message of the missionaries, and some rejection of them by the Chinese population. As the imperial form of government lost power and eventually ended following the World War II defeat of Japan in 1945, the communist party took power in China.

By 1949, the People's Republic of China was established under Mao Tse-tung and China became a fully communist society. When the Chinese Communist Party took power in 1949, those who professed to be Christian were censured. Belief in or public support of any Western cultural ideas, including philanthropic volunteering, were not allowed by the communist military regime. Concurrently, already established civil and social societies were either eliminated or were assimilated directly into the communist government and were operated as part of the communist party structure.

Under the communist People's Republic of China, the Chinese lived in a systematized society subject to the authority of the state. However, by 1970 reforms began to take place. By 1989 there was a grassroots democracy movement beginning. Social organizations were slowly allowed to reorganize but were somewhat more regulated than originally conceived under the emperors. Non civil society/social organization volunteerism was still state controlled and relatively structured.

Chinese Volunteer Structure

Chinese civil or social associations are not structurally parallel to Western nongovernment organizations (nonprofits). While the Chinese civil associations volunteer financial and physical support for community needs, the associations are primarily membership-based public interest organizations connected by family, social views, intellectual connection, business, or political positions. They are broader in scope and activity than simple volunteer support, and closely related by personal affiliation of the members. These groups may be identified as guilds, charity groups, trade groups, kinship organizations, and chambers of commerce.

Understanding these differences will be important to you if you choose to volunteer abroad or within the Chinese culture in the United States.

IMPORTANT!

Japan

Japan is less than 1,100 miles away from its neighbor, China. Japan has a history that shares some elements of China's history, as well as some details that are very different. Through much of its long history, Japan was a feudal society, ruled by an emperor and warrior-class shoguns. The country was self-dependent and essentially closed to world trade. The average Japanese had little contact with or knowledge of other cultures beyond early Christian missionaries (who were banned from the country by the mid–1600s). Eventually, Japan was forced by its citizens to become open to other countries. By the nineteenth century, the Japanese merchant class started challenging the feudal system and demanding the opening of Japanese ports.

Chinese Anthem "March of the Volunteers"

As a point of interest, the national anthem of the People's Republic of China is "March of the Volunteers." It was written in 1934 by Nie Er to a text by Tian Han. It was debuted in a Chinese film in 1935, and is in Frank Capra's film, *The Battle of China*. It was introduced as the national anthem in 1949. It appears that this song refers to people "volunteering" in a socialist context, e.g., "volunteering" to serve the state as a soldier, teacher, etc. One can only surmise that these 'volunteers' were not given much choice in how they served, and philanthropic volunteerism was not much of a reality.

Observation

In 1853, US Commodore Matthew Perry sailed to Japan and negotiated (ultimately by military threat) the opening of two ports to international trade. Increased knowledge of European and American cultures was introduced to Japan through this expansion of commerce.

Unlike China, Japanese society historically did not see a need to organize in its communities to address the needs of its people, and had no civil association-like structure. If there was any problem, the regional ruling shogun or his military followers took care of it. Like Imperial China, philanthropy in Japanese society, if necessary or appropriate, was dispensed by the emperor or members of the Shogunate class, primarily as a tool for social and political influence gain, with the side effect of helping those in need.

Japan was by choice and nature isolationist for much of its long history. There was deep control of daily lives by the ruling government. Interestingly, there is little record of deliberate volunteerism in Japan until the 1995 Kobe earthquake. This earthquake registered at 7.2 on the Richter scale, reported six thousand deaths, and generated a massive call for volunteers to aid in recovery and rebuilding.

Since the Kobe earthquake disaster, volunteerism in Japan has grown exponentially, along with the number of nongovernment organizations (or nonprofit organizations). Volunteering in response to disaster was reinforced following the tsunami that destroyed the Fukushima Daiichi nuclear reactors in 2011. Volunteers who were called to respond to the reactor destruction were the specialized Skilled Veterans Corps: two hundred volunteers aged sixty or older. These volunteers were engineers, doctors, cooks, even singers. The reason for this older corps was the opinion that at their ages, there would be less likelihood that nuclear exposure would affect their lives. Negative health from nuclear exposure can take fifteen years or longer to appear.

The Dawn of Modern Volunteerism in Japan

The Kobe Earthquake was a hallmark moment for the institution of volunteering. It is considered to be the beginning of formalized volunteerism in Japan. In the year following the event, over one million volunteers stepped up to help those in need. This push for volunteerism was key to the implementation of the 1998 Law to Promote Specific Non-Profit Activities which made the creation and maintenance of small-scale NGOs more manageable.

IMPORTANT!

Middle East—Israel

While we're going to specifically discuss volunteerism in the country of Israel, it is also important to understand how volunteering fits into the general culture of some of the other countries of the Middle East. Some of these countries might include Afghanistan, Iran, Iraq, Saudi Arabia, Turkmenistan, and others. The majority of these Middle Eastern countries are tribal in structure and primarily Islamic in religion. The general populations are economically challenged, and the countries are limited in infrastructure, educational, and medical opportunities, and have been in a war status for decades, sometimes centuries. There are some exceptions to this, such as the Hashemite Kingdom of Jordan, but not many. Due to these situations plus the Islamic restrictions against the societal mobility of women, volunteerism is limited and struggling. Most volunteer needs are staffed by groups outside the countries, through foreign NGOs such as Médecins Sans Frontières (*doctorswithoutborders.org*). There are a few organizations that are working hard to make a difference, however, including the Afghan Peace Volunteers (*ourjourneytosmile.com*).

For an in-depth look at volunteerism in the Middle East, the Jewish State of Israel is a unique example. The history of the organized State of Israel is short. The history of Palestine, out of which Israel was established, is long, but we're going to focus on the unique volunteer situation in Israel since its formation in 1948.

Israel was partitioned out of Palestine in 1948 by the United Nations, following the end of World War II. Palestine is of course one of the oldest areas of civilization and the birthplace of several religions, primarily Judaism, Christianity and Islam.

Due to massive immigration mostly from Europe post-World War II, the Israeli population grew by seven hundred thousand between 1948 and 1952. It was with this population growth that volunteerism became a way of life in Israel. Israel's initial government was Socialist-Zionist. The country had no cash resources and very limited infrastructure (roads, municipal water and sewer, transportation, or defense). A large percentage of the new population came into the country with no money, no possessions, and no idea how they were going to survive.

Initially the Sabras, or native-born Israelis, provided free food, clothing, shelter, medical care, and protection. But the need soon became overwhelming, and the supplies were limited. With pleas for support by the new country, volunteers traveled from all over the world to help this newly born, war-weary country. As more people gathered, the original volunteers, those who traveled from abroad, plus refugees who had been helped when they first arrived, continued to provide volunteer labor for people who kept immigrating. Out of necessity, everyone, men *and* women, were expected to volunteer for military service or in some other way to protect and build this new country. It was a total community effort.

Israel is distinctive, as volunteers virtually built the country: homes, Kibbutzim, cities, public services systems, infrastructure (roads, sewers, etc.)—

whatever was needed. Volunteers, both Sabra and from other countries, continue to be a major part of life in Israel today. Israel is an extreme example of the power of working together for the public good—volunteering. This is a country that may not have survived its birth without the unreserved volunteer support it has received.

Europe: England

The history of volunteering in Europe varies somewhat by country. However, like most areas of the world, volunteering in Europe was originally founded through religious tradition and teachings. These might have come from ancient Norse traditions, the Gallic mythology, Druidism, or Celtic traditions. For our purposes, the focus will be on the specific example of Britain.

Britain (England), or now the United Kingdom, is a great illustration of how peoples and cultures can be historically influenced by being occupied by foreign powers. From early times (BC), Britain was invaded and occupied by other countries (Norse, Romans, Gallic). The very British term Anglo-Saxon refers to the mix of Irish, Scottish (Celt/Anglo), and German (Saxon) peoples. Roman, Viking Danish, French, and German cultures became combined and ultimately blended on these small islands. Diverse folkloric traditions became integrated into daily living. Also, following centuries of invasion and occupation, the Britain learned its lessons about colonization and eventually became the

Israel— Volunteer Army

There was an international corps of military volunteer soldiers called Machal that traveled to Israel to fight in the Israeli Army. Mahal is the Hebrew acronym for "Overseas Volunteers." In 1947–9, more than 4,400 overseas volunteers (Jewish and non-Jewish) came from fifty-six countries to defend and fight for the new State of Israel during its struggle for survival and independence.

At the time, Israel had neither adequate time nor the financial resources to build a sufficient native army for defense. This foreign volunteer army made all the difference in the success of the fighting force that was critical during the establishment of the country. The Machal are honored in a memorial near Tel Aviv, Israel. In that tradition, the IDF (Israeli Defense Force/Israeli Army) still accepts soldier volunteers from all over the world today.

mahal-idf-volunteers.org

Pure Genius!

most widespread colonizing country in history, adding to its global exposure and awareness.

From early history Britain was primarily an agrarian economy ruled by a variety of kings and queens through regional nobility. These nobles held hereditary titles originally given by the crown, usually in recognition of support through military service and monetary funding. Typically, these members of the peerage held onto their castles and land holdings by formally pledging, or "volunteering," their local men as soldiers to fight for the crown in times of war. These dukes, marquises, earls, viscounts, and barons held authority over the daily lives of the citizens in their regions. On a local level, and similar to the beginnings of volunteerism in China and Japan, volunteering was much less formalized and much more on the neighbor-to-neighbor level. In time of famine or other crisis, the local ruling noble families were left to manage the challenges both financially and physically, with little support from the centralized monarchy. Systematized, though still limited, volunteering on a more extensive basis during these times was generally driven by religion and its associated clergy.

Scope of Influence of Volunteerism in the British Empire

At its peak, the British Empire was referred to as "the empire on which the sun never sets." By 1922, Britain ruled over more than 13 million square miles and more than 450 million people worldwide. British thought and societal standards, including volunteering to care for those in need, are still part of many global cultures.

IMPORTANT!

The later seventeenth century saw the beginnings of secular volunteerism in England. This included the formation of fraternal societies, friendship societies, and other kinds of membership groups. These groups helped their members in time of crisis, shared resources such as private libraries, and offered private places (clubs) for entertainment and relaxation. Some of these changes were influenced by the gradual move from a one-religion country (Anglican) to the spreading of alternate religious views, including the Dissenters (Protestants).

The economy and functioning of British life changed with the Industrial Revolution, which was 1760–1840. The economy transformed from agricultural to manufacturing with the invention of iron, use of steam power, modernization of textiles and manufacturing, and development of the railroad. During the Industrial Revolution, and due to colonization, the British Empire controlled the majority of trade with most foreign countries, ensuring access to abundant and varied resources and raw materials. Incomes of investors increased. The economy exploded. The agrarian-based life style started moving into manufacturing work in the larger cities.

There still was a definite class structure in Britain. The government remained a now-constitutional monarchy, ruled by the king or queen. The peerage still held authority over the daily lives of most of the population.

While the economy improved overall, the living standards of the average common person saw little improvement until later, during the late nineteenth and early twentieth centuries. Institutional philanthropy, including volunteering, and with exception of the private societies and clubs, remained primarily the province of the wealthy, the government, and the church, and was often regulated under British law.

Volunteering started to become more institutionally widespread and more a part of common British life in the nineteenth and twentieth centuries, although privately funded institutions still required governmental approval.

With the Industrial Revolution as well as the growth of the British Empire, England saw huge changes. Britain had

England—Early Volunteerism

Early formal voluntary giving or organized volunteer programs in England were heavily controlled, even regulated, by the state. One example is, reflecting the close connection between the church and the ruling regents, approved religious giving was greatly restricted to the Anglican Church. Another was asking (expecting) local citizens to volunteer for neighborhood militias to protect the country from foreign invasion (The British Volunteer Corps). The Corps was overseen by the British military. This volunteer militia was extremely important during the Napoleonic Wars and through World War II. During much of history, for an entity to become established as an independent charitable organization approval was required by the Crown or by Parliament.

Observation

defeated Napoleon. The population focus had changed from agriculture to manufacturing. People moved, in huge numbers, from rural to city living.

With the changes and the population increase in the cities there was an amplified demand on civil and communal assistance. Political reforms gave more people representation, which in turn became a demand for social and economic equality. Abuse of women and child labor in the factories and mines caused the passing of labor laws. Trade unions were legalized. In the cities, housing for the lower classes was appalling. New cheap homes for the increased city dwellers were unregulated and unsanitary, with no paved roads, sanitary sewers, or building standards. Too many remained poor. Being a poor person was actually declared to be a crime, and workhouses came into being. Civil unrest and labor strikes were common. Amidst all of this transformation, England experienced an increase in organizations specifically structured to help those with the increasing medical, housing, food, and life-safety needs of the changing population.

Pure Genius!

European Volunteerism in Practice

The Crimean War (1853–1856) was waged between Russia and the Ottoman Empire. To keep Russia from defeating the Ottoman Empire and controlling the Black Sea, Britain and France joined the conflict in support of the Ottoman Empire. The fighting on the Crimean Peninsula was fierce, and a huge percentage of British soldiers were dying. Florence Nightingale and thirty-eight other nurses (including some nuns) volunteered to travel to the war zone to provide medical aid for the wounded. The volunteer nurses arrived at the Crimean hospital to discover horrifying sanitary conditions. More soldiers were dying from infection and diseases such as typhoid and cholera than from battle wounds. Nightingale changed how they were being medically treated. In addition to treating the wounds and diseases, she instituted proper diet for patients and installed adequate cleanliness practices and sanitation systems, including forcing the British government to send a Sanitary Commission to the region to repair the sewers and the ventilation systems. Florence Nightingale's work is considered to be the beginning of national public health systems.

Organized volunteering expanded beyond it being the sole historic responsibility of the wealthy class. Independent groups formed to help widows and orphans and veteran soldiers as early as the end of the war with Napoleon. Homes were established for unwed mothers. Hospitals were established for the mentally ill. Many of these were staffed primarily by volunteers. However, charitable organizations still required approval of and financial support by the government, and were resultantly closely controlled.

A famous example of volunteering and its long-term effect was Florence Nightingale and her contributions to the Crimean War. Florence Nightingale (1820–1910) was a nurse, founded a college of nursing, and is considered to be the founder of modern nursing. An excellent example of how volunteerism worked at that time, Nightingale was a volunteer, was funded by a nobleman, and got the British government to support her cause.

United States

Originally, North America was explored by and to some extent settled by the Vikings, the Spanish, and the French. Italian-born explorer Christopher Columbus, representing the Spanish crown, is noted for having landed in the West Indies in 1492.

The beginning of the seventeenth century the outset of the flood of immigrants from the British Isles and Europe to North America began. These initial groups from England, France, and Germany were searching for religious and economic freedom. These people were demanding individual independence, self-determination with no ruling class, and less government control of their daily lives. The social personality of the immigrants guided the way the country was settled, ultimately affecting the forms of government and the approach to daily life in what would become the United States of America.

The first permanent English settlement was established in 1607, mainly as a trading settlement by the Virginia Company of London in Jamestown, Virginia. A second British colony was established by the Pilgrims who sailed from the Netherlands and England. They arrived at Plymouth Rock in November of 1620. With the initial struggles in establishing themselves in the new world with very limited resources, colonists discovered that their best chances of survival were to volunteer to help each other wherever and however possible.

As the individual colonies continued to establish themselves, different forms of government evolved. Most choices were based in the various forms familiar to the settlers, reflecting the countries they came from. The evolution of volunteerism was different among the colonies as well. While the life style of the colonial settlers encouraged freely organized volunteerism, some colonies (Massachusetts Bay Colony) were most comfortable working within what was allowed by the government, similar to English system. In other areas where and how volunteerism was encouraged was dissimilar. For instance, in Rhode Island, government support of churches was not allowed; churches had to be completely supported by their members. Thus, volunteerism was organized by the churches without any state support.

In order to survive and thrive in the new world, the people had to depend on each other. In some of the early colonies, government control over volunteering for public benefit carried over from England, while at the same time independent religious doctrine drove a lot of volunteer participation. Overall, volunteerism was crucial in the building and defense of the new country, as there were no other resources and no initial infrastructure. Everything had to be built from the ground up. Church attendance was often required, particularly in Pilgrim settlements. Thus the theology of mutual support was reinforced. All men were required to volunteer to serve in the militia (similar to Israel). Citizens were

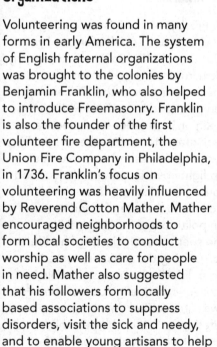

United States Early Volunteer Organizations

Volunteering was found in many forms in early America. The system of English fraternal organizations was brought to the colonies by Benjamin Franklin, who also helped to introduce Freemasonry. Franklin is also the founder of the first volunteer fire department, the Union Fire Company in Philadelphia, in 1736. Franklin's focus on volunteering was heavily influenced by Reverend Cotton Mather. Mather encouraged neighborhoods to form local societies to conduct worship as well as care for people in need. Mather also suggested that his followers form locally based associations to suppress disorders, visit the sick and needy, and to enable young artisans to help each other.

Pure Genius!

expected to donate labor to build roads or other public structures. Volunteer local militias and the new national volunteer army were critical to the success of the American Revolution in 1776.

There was a period called the Great Awakening in the 1730s and 1740s which created a nonreligious, nongovernmental consolidation of networks consisting of political, social, and economic groups that wanted independence. It was during this time that religious or civil volunteerism moved clearly away from governmental oversight and regulation.

Volunteering through Religion in America

A Presbyterian minister, leading revivalist and social reformer, Lyman Beecher (1775–1863) helped formally structure the organizations that became known as the "benevolent empire" and is credited with giving religion in America its distinctive voluntary stamp. Beecher originally became enmeshed as a volunteer in fighting intemperance (liquor and public intoxication). Teaching his followers the role of volunteerism in political and institutional life, he spent the remainder of his life organizing the voluntary system in political movements, schools, colleges, and religious crusades. He was able to find time in his very busy lifetime to father thirteen children, one of whom was author Harriet Beecher Stowe.

IMPORTANT!

By 1776, the American Revolution was happening. The volunteer militias and independent fighting citizenry formally self-organized to both protect the local communities and to advance the drive for independence.

After dealing with British aristocracy and governance, Americans were frightened of too much governmental power. The organizational documents of the United States reflect independent thinking and individual responsibility for the whole as well as the separation of church and state. This independent thinking helped with the establishment of voluntary associations or organizations formed to put forth specific issues or needs that citizens wanted to see addressed. There was no waiting for the government or the wealthy class to address the situation. People were coming together for the common good. With the new nation, they were no longer subjects—they were self-determining citizens.

The eras of the Civil War through the mid twentieth century saw the exponential growth of volunteerism in America, in spite of the strengthened centralized government following the Civil War.

Volunteer soldiers, doctors, workmen and -women on both the Confederate and Union sides were essential in the four years of fighting. Following the war, volunteer membership associations flourished: educational, veteran, sanitary, civil. and religious. The aftermath of the Industrial Revolution in America encouraged the organizing of labor unions, fraternal organizations, professional associations, and national trade unions. By the beginning of the twentieth century (World War I), there were two clear and fundamental volunteer paths. One was public, including municipal services like fire departments, government boards, and commissions, and was supported by government funding. The other was private, such as social welfare and health care, and was supported by private contributions and labor.

It is following World War II that the construction of volunteerism in America expanded. There was a much more pervasive awareness, by both the government and the individual citizens, of filling the need for global reconstruction and recovery. And the modern era of volunteering has developed.

To Summarize...

- Volunteerism has developed at different levels and with varying success in different parts of the world.

- Historically helping those in need has been modeled by the wealthy ruling classes, theology and spiritual doctrine, government, and individual people.

- The Industrial Revolution in Europe and the American Revolution in America helped develop widespread secular volunteer initiatives.

- Volunteering has advanced, but not consistently, on a global scale.

Chapter 4

Volunteerism in Current World Cultures

In This Chapter...

- China
- Japan
- Israel
- United Kingdom

We have looked at the history of a few countries' evolution in volunteerism. Clearly not all of the countries we have discussed have had the same experiences or look at volunteering in the same way. In our current world environment, nations are more connected than ever before. We have better and faster communications systems, a highly mobile citizenry that travels easily all over the globe, and we are better informed and aware about how dissimilar life patterns can be in different cultures.

While the world is shrinking, philanthropy and volunteerism is expanding. There are global nonprofit organizations, generally human service oriented, with branches in many countries. Various organized religions establish remote clinics, schools, or low-income housing in countries that may not have the ability to provide these services locally. Individual countries are building and increasing their nonprofit and volunteer infrastructure. People from some of the cultures we have examined have immigrated to other lands, bringing their unique approach with them and integrating it into their new society. All of these initiatives offer volunteer involvement. This chapter will look at the same countries we have talked about, and how volunteering is implemented today.

China

Remember that under the eras of imperial rule the Chinese developed localized civil societies and social organizations to support the needs of its citizenry. Under post-World War II communist rule, these organizations were generally controlled by the government, and were less independent. However, by 2007 these societies and social organizations saw resurgence in number and in independent operation. By 2007, legally registered civil/social associations in China grew to nearly four hundred thousand, 174,000 of which were public service agencies and 1,340 were foundations. The rest of the associations were specific-interest and professional associations.

Some of these associations in China are small, local, grassroots organizations and may not be legally registered. There are approximately eight to ten million Unregistered Social Organizations (USOs) in China today. Conversely, by 2012 there were approximately 460,000 registered nonprofit organizations, which include a) registered civic associations, b) private nonenterprise organizations such as schools, hospitals, and human service organizations, and c) foundations, both public and nonpublic fundraising foundations.

While currently there is a basic level of independent nonprofit organizations

Volunteering in China

China is moving into twenty-first century volunteerism. As China becomes less culturally isolated, volunteering options and involvement are increasing. A significant example of this was the sheer number of volunteers who participated in the 2008 Beijing Olympic Games. The Beijing Organizing Committee for the Olympic Games reports seventy thousand games-time volunteers (primarily Beijing University students), 2,640 administrative volunteers, four hundred thousand city volunteers, one million societal volunteers, and two hundred thousand cheering volunteers participated in the Beijing Olympic Games.

Observation

in today's China (460,000 for 1.35 billion in population), the fundamental volunteer and support of community needs is still accomplished primarily in the context of the civil and social associations (eight to ten million in 2012). This is true not only in China, but in other countries with localities where there exists a high concentration of Chinese residents. In some areas with a concentration of Chinese immigrants (such as San Francisco), Chinese civil and social societies actively serve their cultural population.

With the public relations opportunity and visibility of the 2008 Olympics in Beijing, the Chinese nonprofit sector grew quickly and exponentially. With the growth of global communications and social media as well as travel becoming commonplace in today's society, nongovernment organizations are increasing in China. Chinese citizens are being educated in other countries and are bringing back new ideas about organizing and giving back. Multinational companies are establishing offices in China, with more available financial support to develop a strong charity infrastructure. Numerous international charities are establishing offices and operating in China, offering more options for addressing community issues.

The current internal nonprofit/volunteering opportunities are a combination of government, social/civil associations, and student organizations. While there are political and economic challenges with the independent or foreign NGOs (nongovernment organizations), there is still growth, and with the increasing number of organizations, volunteer options are expanding. There are multiple organizations that currently offer volunteer participation in China, including those that emphasize teaching English to the Chinese (International Volunteer Headquarters, *volunteerhq.org*). As a volunteer from another country, advance understanding of and sensitivity about the Chinese culture is critical.

Japan

Japan has been slower to see improvement and expansion in volunteerism or philanthropy. In fact, volunteerism is not considered to have been fully established in Japan until the end of the twentieth century. Japan's unwillingness to adopt what it considered the Western standard of volunteer involvement held strong until the Kobe earthquake disaster in 1995.

On January 17, 1995, a 6.9 magnitude earthquake in Kobe, Japan left 6,434 dead, three missing, and 36,896 injured. Up to that time, it was the worst disaster in post-World War II Japan: 248,388 structures holding 446,485

Beginning of Formalized Volunteering in Japan

The fact that volunteers from all over Japan converged on Kobe after the earthquake to help victims of the disaster was a crucial event in the history of volunteerism in Japan. The year 1995 is often regarded as a turning point in the emergence of volunteerism as a major form of civic engagement.

In December 1995, the government declared January 17 a national "Disaster Prevention and Volunteerism Day," and the week from January 15 to 21 a national "Disaster Prevention and Volunteerism Week," to be commemorated with lectures, seminars, and other events designed to encourage voluntary disaster preparedness and relief efforts.

Pure Genius!

households either collapsed or burned and 316,678 people were displaced. The sheer numbers and scope of destruction are nearly impossible to comprehend. But for the Japanese, this disaster was the genesis of what they now refer to as "the start-year of volunteerism in Japan."

Following the earthquake, the Japanese government was totally overwhelmed and unable to effectively deal with the destruction. Citizens and voluntary organizations from Japan and around the world gathered to help. Rescue and recovery, medical, food and clothing, shelter, transportation, debris removal as well as psychological counseling were only some of the services that volunteers provided.

During the first month a daily average of twenty thousand volunteers worked. The estimated volunteer days provided the first month following the earthquake was 620,000. For the first two months, an estimated one million volunteer days were provided.

Following this drastic total-immersion approach to volunteering, Japan passed new laws to support volunteering. In 1995, the Government Agency Coordinating Committee on Volunteering was formed. By 1998, the Civic Activities Promotion bill was passed, providing a path for the establishment of independent nonprofit organizations. Up to this time, there was no legal framework to incorporate an independent nonprofit in Japan. This law was the foundation of the Japanese nonprofit infrastructure.

Currently, Japan, like China, hosts several foreign-incorporated nongovernment organizations as well as increasing numbers of Japanese nonprofits. The nonprofit sector is influenced by Western culture as well as Japanese culture, and is displaying a more global approach to volunteerism. Positions are available to both Japanese-speaking and non-Japanese-speaking volunteers. As an example, Second Harvest, a national American food distribution nonprofit with localized chapters, has an affiliate in Second Harvest Japan (*2hj.org*). Hands on Tokyo (*handsontokyo.org*) and Foreign Volunteers Japan (*foreignvolunteers.org*) offer international volunteer connections.

Israel

Israel continues to be a country that depends heavily on volunteerism from both its citizens and from foreign visitors. Volunteerism in Israel in the twenty-first century is just as important as it was in 1948. Thirty-two percent of the Israeli people are active volunteers. Thousands of volunteers emigrate every year to work with Israeli programs. Specialized areas for volunteers include one-on-one teaching and tutoring; immigrant associations; security needs through the Civil Guard; national Rescue Teams, and with special requirements, the Israeli Defense Force (IDF).

While some original Israeli volunteer organizations still exist today (e.g., Magen David Adom, or Israeli Red Cross), many of the volunteer organizations created following the 1948 partition eventually were taken over by the government. This included even the volunteer fighting unit Haganah. In 1972, and in recognition of the critical value of volunteers, Prime Minister Golda Meir approved the founding of the government-funded Israel Voluntary Service.

Today, volunteerism is an integral and active part of life in Israel. Volunteer initiatives are coordinated by The National Council for Voluntarism as well as local volunteer groups. Numerous international charitable organizations send volunteers every year to help in all areas including traffic control, education, hospitals, social services, environmental needs, or security. All major volunteer organizations participate in the nationwide "With All My Heart" project by collecting and distributing food, household goods, clothes, school supplies, etc. to those who are in need.

Israel works closely with many international volunteer groups including International Association of Volunteer Effort (IAVE), Association for Voluntary Administration (AVA), World Alliance for Citizen Participation (CIVICUS), European Network Agencies for Voluntary Action (VOUNTEUROPE) and L' Association pour le Volontariat Européen (AVE). For many Jewish youths around the world, spending time working and volunteering in Israel or working

on an Israeli kibbutz (a farm or communal settlement in Israel) is an important part of their life commitment.

United Kingdom

Today the United Kingdom today is a constitutional monarchy, and no longer holds the extensive protectorates or colonies it once did. The elected Parliaments (this includes the House of Commons and House of Lords) of the country governs, but the head (queen or king) of the royal family is the figurative head of state. Countries in today's United Kingdom include England, Wales, Scotland, and Northern Ireland. The United Kingdom does not include countries that are closely tied to the United Kingdom as prior colonies or protectorates.

The charitable nonprofit sector, including volunteerism, in today's United Kingdom is complex, sophisticated, extensive, and an integral component of British life. In the United Kingdom, this sector is called civil society. In the World Giving Index of 2015, the United Kingdom places sixth overall (57 percent) in the combined ratings for helping strangers, giving money, and volunteering time.

In the United Kingdom, there are both public (e.g., universities, National Health Service) and private (e.g., social services, general charities) organizations. There are Volunteer Centres that offer a Volunteer Centre Quality Accreditation credential. The NCVO's mission includes improving the "external environment on behalf of the voluntary sector." It shows the approach to philanthropy is substantially through the volunteer component, instead of the general tendency to assume philanthropists are solely monetary donors.

An estimated 15.2 million people volunteer in the United Kingdom at least once a month, out of a population of approximately sixty-four million. That is a huge number of volunteers working in countless nonprofit organizations and projects across several countries. There is even a Community Life Survey and a Citizenship Survey completed each year by the citizenry to keep accurate track of volunteer participation and effect.

Voluntary Organizations in the United Kingdom

Voluntary organizations and the philanthropic sector in the United Kingdom are considered to be a positive partnership between government, business and voluntary participation. There are currently more than 195,289 registered charities in the UK. Resources to connect with volunteer options include the Big Project: thebigproject.co.uk and the National Council for Voluntary Organisations: ncvo.org.uk. Volunteering in the United Kingdom is considered essential for an excellent society.

Definition

Hundreds of organizations in the United Kingdom actively recruit volunteers for service at the local, regional, national, and international levels. Likely due to the economic climate, volunteer participation has remained stable, but not grown the last several years. Working families appear to have less time to devote to volunteering. The only currently growing volunteer sector in Britain is those aged sixty-five years and older, although young adults have a strong presence as well.

The relatively small islands of the United Kingdom currently boast nearly two hundred thousand nongovernmental organizations. Volunteering and support of these charities is thoroughly integrated into daily lives, from the monarchy to the average person on the street.

To Summarize...

- China continues to deliver volunteer initiatives through civil societies and social organizations. The independent volunteer sector in China is growing.

- Japan did not prioritize volunteering until the late twentieth century, in response to a significant natural disaster.

- Israel is a country originally established mostly by volunteers and continues to depend on a deeply rooted national and international volunteer culture.

- The United Kingdom has a long standing and fully integrated volunteer culture.

Chapter 5

Volunteer Culture in the United States Today

In This Chapter...

- Why people volunteer
- Volunteer statistics in the United States
- Economic and business impact of volunteers
- Overview of volunteer opportunities

Volunteering in the United States is an integral part of the social culture. In this country, more than most, it is taken for granted that a life well lived includes giving back. Volunteers willingly almost eight billion of hours annually at a value of nearly $200 billion to the national economy.

French diplomat, historian, political scientist, and writer Alexis de Tocqueville visited America in the early 1800s to study, in part, the reality of democracy in operation. His book with his research is entitled *Democracy in America* (1835). One of his observations about common volunteer support among the people was, "I have seen Americans making great and sincere sacrifices for the key common good and a hundred times I have noticed that, when needs be, they almost always gave each other faithful support." That is still the reality today.

How do we identify and value of all this unpaid work? This is the chapter in which we're going to consider what a commitment to volunteering looks like emotionally, professionally, and economically.

Why People Volunteer

We have talked a lot about you as a volunteer and how volunteering evolved from your daily life. We have also looked at a lot of history and how organized volunteering grew roots in different cultures. Later we're going to talk about how to plan and implement your future volunteer involvement in great depth. But before we go any further, let's take a minute and talk about the wide array of reasons *why* you may choose to volunteer and *what difference* it will make to charities when you give your time, energy, and talents away for "free."

Have you ever heard any of these reasons why someone did something nice for someone else? Have you ever had these thoughts yourself?

- "It was the right thing to do."

- "Because no one else was stepping up."

- "I had nothing better to do that day." (Said with humor.)

- "I didn't really do anything that monumental."

- "I couldn't ignore the situation, could I?"

- "I wanted to learn something new!"

I would guess that some of these statements sound familiar. Over the years I have heard these statements quite often from many people who do so much for others. A few of the statements are self-effacing and nearly shy. People sometimes seem almost embarrassed that they were caught doing good. The reasons people volunteer are many, and at the end of the day each and every person who volunteers has their own personal reasons for getting involved.

The motives for volunteering time and talent are very similar, and occasionally identical, to the purposes for giving a cash gift to a charity. In fact, most volunteers are also cash donors. The reasons for choosing to volunteer are usually multiple and complex, just like individual human beings! Let's talk about some of the more common responses.

Someone (I Know and/or Trust) Asked Me to Get Involved

You participate simply because you're asked. And if you're asked by your best friend, or your pastor, or by someone you have a tremendous amount of respect for, it is nearly impossible to refuse!

The invitation from a person may be a direct request, "Will you please help us by (insert the task here)?" However, you may not be actually asked by a person—it may be an indirect invitation. An indirect request might be seeing a special program on television about an organization doing amazing work, and you're so excited you just have to get involved! Another indirect request might be listening to your friend talk about how much of a difference an organization made when it provided child care, or food, or housing in the friend's time of need. It touched your heart, and you made the call to join the cause.

Volunteering Makes Me Feel Good

You have volunteered, and you know this: there is no amount of money that can buy the feeling you get when a child gives you a smile and a hug to thank you for helping them. Conventional wisdom believes that the endorphins generated by

Volunteering Makes Me Feel Good

Yes, volunteering makes you happy!

If you have volunteered, then you know intuitively that what I am going to say is so true. Volunteering leaves you feeling happier, more content, more satisfied, and more rewarded than sitting at home on your couch. Numerous studies have been done assessing the positive emotional and physical rewards to volunteers for the work that they do. Results indicate that the more often you volunteer, the higher the personal wellness return. Your enhanced sense of accomplishment and well-being would be similar to having your salary increase overnight from $15,000 a year to $150,000 a year. Medical science says that if you are happy and fulfilled, you may even have more longevity! So, volunteering can add years to your life! Just think about that for a minute.

IMPORTANT!

these good feelings will lengthen your life. Really. Those who volunteer tend to be physically healthier and have lower early mortality rates. Volunteering also combats depression because of the opportunity to be with other people and to develop interpersonal support systems.

My Religion or Faith Requires/Expects/Encourages Volunteering

We have explored the fact that religions—of all kinds—have been the sources of the philosophy and practice of volunteerism. No matter what your religion might be, helping your fellow man is a constant theme. Most places of worship have community outreach initiatives, such as food banks or child care. They also have internal governance volunteer possibilities if that is your interest. Religion is a very major driver in volunteer participation.

I Want to Pay It Back by Paying It Forward

You may have had the experience of becoming homeless. Your past may include visits at midnight to a hospital after being beat up by someone close to you. You may have a child who was born with physical challenges. Or you may have a parent who needs daily special care. A particular organization has helped you so much. That great volunteer helped you through paperwork and hard times; someone was there for you. You want to make sure that the people who follow you and are facing similar life problems have the same support you received when you needed it. You have a special commitment and understanding because you have lived it. You have a lot to give to the next person.

I Want My Name Connected with the Cause

We have all watched fabulous special media events with famous stars in attendance that support a huge array of causes: eradication of autism or HIV/AIDS; cancer and Alzheimer's research; saving wildlife; or stopping climate change. The needs and missions are endless. It is energizing to participate with an organization that is excitingly high profile! On a more local level, there may be a prominent business person or philanthropist that you may want to meet or with whom you want to work. Volunteering for a charity with which they are involved may be a great way to do that!

I Believe in the Mission/the Good That This Organization Does

There may be something that you care about passionately. Maybe you love your pets, and you want to help at the local animal shelter. You may want to make sure every child has an equal chance for a quality education. Or you may want to make sure that dance, music, and art are alive and thriving! You pick your spot to volunteer, and you will make a difference.

My School (Either Current or Future) Requires Volunteer Involvement

Any high school student applying for college entrance knows how important extracurricular volunteer involvement is in ensuring acceptance at a college of their choice. Many high schools in fact require community volunteer hours by students as a graduation requirement. College sororities and fraternities, clubs, and affinity groups often have very active volunteer initiatives.

I Love the Special Events!

Have fun! Make new friends and develop new contacts! Special events can create a busy and full social life. (I actually had a friend tell me that she served on boards—nineteen concurrently—solely because of the social life around the special events.) Even if you tend to be a little shy, get involved in a special event. You will be with people who have common interests (the organization or mission) so you will always have something to talk about. Special events usually mean that you will be interacting with lots of different people, so it can lead to some unexpected experiences. It will certainly increase your social skills and your relationship skills. And, shy person, once you do your first special event, the next ones will be much easier. Promise.

I Want to Learn a New Skill and Help My Career/Build My Résumé

As a volunteer, you get to learn and do new things that you may never have thought of before. And you don't have to get a college degree in order to do the job. You may want to try something new to see if it is a good fit for a full career. You may just want to do something very different from your day-to-day job. Many volunteer positions provide in-depth training in skills such as crisis management, museum docent tasks, sales and marketing, communication, and public speaking. You may even learn about accounting or horse training. Who knows? For every interest there is an opportunity. And the skills you learn you can put in your professional tool belt and take with you wherever you go!

I Want to Make a Difference

I have long maintained that every person born wants to make a difference in their lives, without exception. No one at the end of their life says, "Whew! I am so glad no one noticed my existence." Each of us needs to find the best way to make our own personal difference—in a way that makes us feel productive and fulfilled. The net results to you are that you will have higher self-esteem, increased self-confidence, a sense of accomplishment, and emotional satisfaction in your life. The net result to others is that you will make a big difference in the lives of people you may or may not ever meet. Good for you!

I Volunteer Because My Employer Expects It

Volunteering is often either encouraged or required by employers. Corporations believe it is a visible corporate commitment to their communities, and publicly serves their customers. As a company volunteer, you increase the visibility your employer and the other employees at the same time you're helping someone else. It also can be a wonderful way to develop teamwork and a sense of loyalty within a company. If you're rolling up your sleeves and serving mashed potatoes alongside the company president, it creates a whole new level of feeling like you all are working together toward a common goal. This translates well into intraoffice relationships.

Volunteering is an excellent way to get career experience or enhance job skills. If you're looking for a job, it always helps to volunteer. It shows that you want to learn and are willing to work. If you're a high school or college student, and are successful in securing a volunteer internship in your chosen field, the experience will emphasize your qualifications on your employment applications.

Volunteer Statistics in the United States

Globally, the United States places second of the top twenty most charitable countries, at an overall score of 61 percent, in the World Giving Index for 2015. This is based on three categories: "Helping a Stranger," "Donating Money," and "Volunteering Time." Interestingly, Myanmar holds first place, New Zealand third place, Canada fourth place. *cafonline.org*. You can see that size or location of country has little to do with the national attitude toward philanthropy and volunteerism.

Volunteering is a big number in economic impact in both labor and dollars. For those who are a little analytical, I am now going to dive into some of those numbers and what they mean. There are many sources that will tell you how many people give volunteer hours, but for clarity I am going to use the most recent information available from the Bureau of Labor Statistics, US Department of Labor. My resource is the "Volunteering in the United States 2015" press release dated February 25, 2016. This report, in summary and in detail, can be accessed at *bls. gov*. The statistics were gathered through the Current Population Survey (CPS) which is a monthly survey of sixty thousand households that obtains information on the nation's noninstitutional populations age sixteen and older. Another resource that I am using is the Corporation for National and Community Service (NNOC) at *nationalservice.gov*.

Volunteer Statistics in the United States

Economic Impact: According to the Independent Sector (*independentsector. org*), following are the Trends and Highlights of Volunteering and Civic Engagement and *volunteeringinamerica.org*, in the United States in 2015:

◆ There are 62.8 million active volunteers who provide 7.9 billion hours of service at a cash value of $184 billion.

◆ In 2015, the average volunteer hour had a cash value of $23.56.

Think of how much it would cost the nonprofit community if these volunteers were paid.

IMPORTANT!

The two messages that are very clear in this report are that for 2015:

🖋 Volunteer rates have declined slightly (likely due to the economic downturn and uncertain unemployment rate).

🖋 A staggering number of people are still giving an astonishing number of volunteer hours in the United States.

The reporting period is for September 2014 through September 2015, the most recent available. During this time period, approximately sixty-three million people volunteered an average of fifty-two hours. People sixty-five years old and older donated an average of ninety-two hours of volunteer time during this year. Nearly sixty-three million individuals volunteer an average of fifty hours each during a given year in the United States. An approximate total of 7.9 billion hours of time and labor were donated in 2015.

Both men and women seem to spend about the same amount of time volunteering. However, more women appear to volunteer than men. This is across all ages and education levels. The most likely age group to volunteer is the thirty-five- to forty-four-year-olds. The least likely to volunteer are the twenty- to twenty-four-year-olds, presumably because this is the peak time to establish a career and start families. As older folks retire, about half of seniors turn the avocation of volunteering into a second vocation. About a quarter of all teenagers are active volunteers.

Most volunteers limit their participation to one or two organizations. Individuals with higher educational levels tend to be the group that volunteers for multiple organizations.

More people volunteer for religious organizations than any other kind. Following that, educational, youth services, social, and community service organizations are the most frequent recipients of volunteer service. More mature volunteers (sixty-five+ years) do more of their primary volunteering with religious organizations than do other age groups.

Types of activities performed by volunteers vary by educational level. Individuals with a bachelor's degree or higher tend to provide management or professional services or tutoring. Those with less than a high school diploma tend to provide general labor such as an usher, direct client program service, or general clerical.

Most often performed tasks include food service, fundraising, and tutoring or teaching. Men tend to engage in general labor or sports activities. Women tend to engage in food service, fundraising, or tutoring and teaching.

Rural and suburban areas show about the same rate of volunteer involvement, cities slightly less involvement.

Finally, the surveys report the statistical reasons how respondents become engaged in volunteering:

🔍 Forty-two percent volunteer after being asked by an individual and/or organization.

🔍 Forty-two percent volunteer by approaching an organization on their own initiative.

Economic and Business Impact of Volunteers

I know you loved the numbers so far! We're going to continue a bit in the same vein as we investigate the real economic impact of volunteers. Unfortunately, the general perception of volunteers too often is that since the labor is "free," it is not worth too much. Or, since volunteers are not paid, their stature in the organization is somehow less than paid staff. Nothing could be further from the truth.

What does it mean that around eight billion hours were donated to all of the organizations and communities in the United States? It means that $184 billion in services were given—*for free*. What would have happened to all those charities if they were required to issue paychecks for all of that volunteer work? Or pay benefits for volunteers as employees? Most charities would be out of business. If that happened, how would necessary services be provided? By individuals? By government? Not provided at all?

Each and every volunteer hour actually has a quantifiable dollar value for the charity (*independentsector.org*). In 1980,

Economic Impact

There are approximately 1.5 million active nonprofit organizations in the United States. According to *independentsector.com*, the overall nonprofit community in the United States provides approximately 5.4 percent of the nation's entire GDP.

The nonprofit sector employs approximately eleven million people, or approximately 10 percent of the paid workforce. This figure does not include any unpaid volunteer support.

Seventy-five percent of the nonprofit sector reports less than $500,000 in annual expenses. You can see how paying volunteers to do the work they do would bankrupt the nonprofits.

IMPORTANT!

that average national hourly value was $7.46. In 2015 that average national hourly value was $23.56. It is safe to assume that each year will see an increase in the value of an average hourly compensation rate.

Each state has a different hourly rate value for volunteers ranging from less than $20 to more than $38 per hour. As reported by the Independent Sector, in 2015 an average volunteer hour in Washington, DC was worth a high of $38.77 while in Arkansas an average volunteer hour was worth a low of $19.14.

Volunteer hours are reported in many ways. Nonprofit organizations keep track of volunteer hours and report the hours and value on the annual IRS 990 form. Additionally, individual charity annual reports generally highlight the volunteer hours and value to highlight the importance of volunteer support in the community.

The type of work or services provided by volunteers can often be valued at different levels within the same nonprofit. Professional legal, medical, or public relations support may be valued a higher per hour rate, while general clerical may be valued at a lower hourly rate. This kind of statistical volunteer record keeping can be labor intensive for the organization, but it gives a more accurate snapshot of the volunteer work actually provided along with its dollar value.

Overview of Volunteer Opportunities

Let's take a look at the general categories of the nonprofit world in the United States. We will be going into a lot more detail in later chapters, but for now, take a look and see in what area you might like to get involved.

According to *Giving USA* 2016 (reflecting statistics for 2015), the kinds of charitable organizations in which US donors and volunteers are involved are:

🔍 Religion, 32 percent

🔍 Education, 15 percent

🔍 Human Services, 12 percent

🔍 Foundations, 11 percent

🔍 Health, 8 percent

🔍 Public Society Benefit, 7 percent

- Arts, Culture & Humanities, 5 percent

- International Affairs, 4 percent

- Environment/Animals, 3 percent

- Individuals/Other, 2 percent

- Unallocated, 1 percent

Do you see any areas that appeal to you?

The number of hours worked, the number of people working those hours, the economic value of volunteers in the United States is almost overwhelming. But the real value is in the work volunteers do—the difference they make—one hour, one person at a time. What kind of organization speaks to you? What kind of work do you think you might want to do? What will fill your needs and goals? What needs and goals do you want to fill for others? Your opportunities are virtually limitless.

To Summarize...

- People volunteer for a wide array of individual reasons and volunteers make a profound difference.

- What volunteers do is real, critical work delivered by millions of caring, committed individuals for billions of hours every year.

- Nearly 30 percent of the population of the United States actively volunteers in a large number of interest areas.

- Actual dollars contributed to charities totaled $373.25 billion in 2015. Nearly eight billion volunteer hours were contributed in 2015 for a value of approximately $184 billion in "free" labor.

Part 2

Know Yourself

Now you have some historical perspective. You have a new appreciation of just how valuable your time and efforts can be. You're excited to get going! Where do you go to find information? There are so many volunteer adventures you want to have! How do you get started? We're going to discuss understanding your skills and preferences, as well as how and where you might want to become involved. You will discover how to research big-picture and more-detailed volunteer opportunities. Then you can plan for success in your volunteer partnership with your charity of choice.

Chapter 6

Your Personal Retreat

In This Chapter...

- Know yourself and your history
- Build your résumé of skills
- What are your personal preferences?
- What are your personal restrictions?

This chapter is all about you. We will help you figure out how to be the best volunteer you can be. If you know yourself well, you will pick the right volunteer role that will best fill the needs of the charity and at the same time satisfy you personally.

Think before you jump. If you're going to spend your precious time, efforts, and passion making a difference in the lives of others, make sure that you're doing the kind of job that you like—one that fulfills you, too. To help make sure you will find exactly what you want to do, we're going to take you on your own personal retreat. Hopefully, you will get to know yourself better than you ever thought you would. Then when you're investigating all of the resources at your fingertips, the right job will grab your attention when you see it!

Before you start out to commit to a volunteer cause, take some time to think about who you are, what you want to do, as well as any possible questions you might have. For some people, getting involved as a volunteer can be impulsive. It may be a reaction to another person or to a particular experience. Or, a lot of time and thought may have gone into the decision.

You will ultimately spend a lot of time and effort fulfilling your volunteer hours, so make sure you actually think about it in advance. There is a saying, "Plan the work, work the plan." Just ask yourself, would you look for a new job without a résumé or without planning for what kind of job you're going to apply? In this chapter, you will do some self-discovery.

Know Yourself and Your History

Find a quiet place and an hour or two block of time—maybe more. Make this appointment with yourself a priority. Do yourself a favor and write it on your calendar.

You have found your place. You have scheduled your time. Do you have your paper and pen? Do you have your beverage of choice, maybe a few snacks? Good. Take a deep breath and blow it out. Clear your mind. Now let your awareness drift while thinking about what cause or world/local need raises passionate feelings for you. What might be your personal goals in volunteering; maybe in your life? What have been your personal experiences? Take a little time and try to write a short personal mission statement, at least in regard to your volunteering: who are you, what do you (want to) do, where do you (want to) do it, for whom do you (want to) do it? Your only limit right now is your imagination.

Make a Proactive Decision

Before you start, have a good idea of where you want to end up. As a professional fundraiser, I never go into a meeting with a prospective donor without having a clear idea of the commitment I am looking for before I leave. Having that focus in mind helps avoid getting sidetracked by too many nonrelated conversational tours. Once you think about your time, interests, and skills, you will know generally which volunteer path you want to take. Try not to get too distracted by a bright, shiny object.

Inspiration

What Is Your Personal Volunteer History?

Have you volunteered in the past? I know you have. Get your paper again and list what you have done as a volunteer. It doesn't have to have been a big major project. It can be what you might consider a small action, done on the spur of the moment. Write down where you have done it and for whom you did it. Don't be shy. It's okay to toot your own horn here. Be completely honest.

- You may have personally helped neighbor or a member of your family.

- You may have helped with or participated in a special event.

- You may have tutored at your child's school.

- You may have helped after a natural disaster in your community.

- You may have served on a board for a community organization.

- You may have made fundraising calls or sent postcards to friends for a charity.

- You may have been elected to your city council or the PTA or your church's board of deacons.

What other times and places can you add to your list? Are you surprised to see how long your list is?

How did you feel when you did these activities? Are there tasks or adventures that you liked a lot? Or some that you would prefer not to repeat? List those as well, and keep them in mind. You will be using this information in a few minutes.

Build Your Résumé of Skills

This list of skills is going to have two sides. The first side is what you think your skills are. You don't have to be an expert in anything on this list, just have a little experience. The second list will have the skills you may want to learn or about which you want to become more expert.

List what you do in your work. Include skills you may have acquired at former positions as well as current work. Have you learned things while working that could be helpful in other ways? These proficiencies could include just about anything: computer, organizational, mechanical, legal, financial, food service, teaching, counseling, construction, changing the oil in your car, tuning a piano, or any of a myriad of other skills.

List what you do for fun. Do you run for fun? Do you like to work with wood or cook or read in your spare time? Do you scrapbook or teach your dog awesome tricks? Do you play on a basketball or softball team or play pick up football games on the weekends? How are you with video games? Do you sew Halloween costumes? Do you sing in a choir or play in the Christmas tuba band? Do you hike and build fires and pitch tents with your family? Don't be shy about this list. If you focus and think about it carefully, you will be able to list a lot more talents than you expected to when you started this process.

List the skills that you have particularly used in your volunteer experiences. What did you seem to do the most? Are there any talents you discovered as you participated? Don't leave anything out!!

What Are Your Personal Preferences?

It is very important that you are completely honest with yourself when you're thinking about what you prefer to do as a volunteer. There is no right or wrong with your list here. You're not obligated to like any volunteer role because it is expected of you, or because your best friend says you should do it or because you have always done it. This is your chance to write your script the way *you* want it.

If you're a professional, do you think you would want to contribute that kind of work? If you're a CPA, do you want to help a nonprofit with its accounting? If you work

---

What Are Your Personal Preferences?

Choose a job you actually want to do. If you become unhappy or frustrated in the volunteer tasks you have chosen to do, it could end up not being a good state of affairs. Proactively communicate. If you want to keep serving that particular nonprofit, talk with the volunteer coordinator or the executive director. Investigate other resolutions; maybe find another way to be of service, or another job to do. Volunteering should always be a win-win situation. Be flexible. Do not feel like you have failed if you need to change what you're doing. Sometimes the best laid plans simply don't work—for a wide variety of reasons. Being open to options is hugely important.

WATCH OUT!

for a public relations firm are you interested in providing marketing services? Or, since you work at your profession all day, would you prefer to do something completely different, like tutoring high school kids or cooking for community meals, or holding an exercise class in a senior center?

Would you feel better doing something that you already know how to do? Or would you like the opportunity to learn something totally new? Is your preference working directly with clients of the charity, or would you be more comfortable serving administratively or on a board?

Think about special events! Most communities have lots of special events and organizations from which to choose. Black tie galas, telethons, motorcycle rallies, hot-air balloon events, food and entertainment festivals, marathons/runs/walks, and the Special Olympics all are fun, entertaining, and a super way to meet lots of people.

Think about how much time you want to devote to your volunteer endeavors. Are you interested in a few hours a week? More? Do you want to get involved only occasionally or steadily? Special events are very busy and demanding before the event date, then the work disappears after the event and wrap-up meeting. Serving on a board will demand recurring monthly board and committee meetings. Tutoring will likely take at least a couple of hours a week during the school year. Be sure to be comfortable with the time you're planning on giving.

If you want to learn new skills, are you willing to set aside the time to become trained or certified? If you want to volunteer for disaster relief organizations, you may be interested in traveling during times of regional or national catastrophe. Will your life accommodate that kind of commitment?

What Are Your Personal Restrictions?

Understand that when you make a commitment to an organization to do a particular job, they are depending on you to be there and do it. So make sure you understand, to the best of your ability today, what you're interested and willing to do, and what you're unwilling or unable to do.

There can be large general barriers to successful individual volunteering. These conditions are universal in the nonprofit world, so know that you're not alone. While we need to take these into consideration, here we are trying to focus on you on a personal level.

Personal Restrictions

A survey was done in Ireland to find out what barriers volunteers thought existed that impaired their ability or willingness to volunteer. Barriers to volunteering complied by the Community and Health Network, Department of Social Development, Northern Ireland (2007)—unedited:

What are the barriers that stop people from volunteering?

◆ Time gap between applying and doing!

◆ Formal process tedious and puts people off

◆ Matching volunteers and their skills to opportunity

◆ Does the community organization provide the resources to support volunteers fully

◆ Time challenges

◆ Other personal commitments

◆ Lack of confidence (self- or in others)

◆ Lack of detailed information about what job entails

◆ Being accepted by covolunteers

◆ Lack of awareness of what volunteer work entails

◆ Lack of support by organization staff

◆ Transport and travel, especially for rural residents

◆ Is it beneficial to getting on in career?

◆ Accessing adequate information about volunteering opportunities available

These are issues that you may see either from the charity toward you, or from you toward the charity. Are any of these a mental STOP sign for you?

The most immediate priority on personal restrictions is often physical. Is there anything in your life that may physically prohibit your choice of activities? For instance, if you're allergic to dogs or cats, you probably want to avoid volunteering for the animal shelter. For many undertakings, you may need to be able to lift heavy items, including lumber for Habitat for Humanity or instruments for the marching band. Or you may simply not want to do heavy lifting of any kind. Make sure this is part of your considerations.

If you're working with small children, you will need to be able to run around the playground to make sure they are safely supervised. If you're camping with youth outdoor groups, you will probably need to be able to do some hiking or swimming or canoeing. If you're helping in a community kitchen, you may need to be able to lift large pots and pans full of food, unless there are others in the volunteer group who can perform those tasks.

If your intent is to volunteer in another country, do you have any chronic physical conditions that may be a barrier to serving in more remote locations? Also, if you're intending to volunteer abroad, are you ready to undergo the physical evaluations and inoculations that might be required for that kind of travel?

Any physical situations must be considered and resolved. I don't mean to say that you must automatically limit yourself, but you must be honest about how to manage any physical limitations that may affect what you want to do.

You also may want to consider jobs or tasks you just plain don't like and don't want to do. There is absolutely no reason for you to be unhappy in your choice of volunteer involvement: you won't do your best work and both you and the charity will end up losing. If you don't like to stuff envelopes, by all means don't volunteer to do it. If helping to manage a huge special event makes you uncomfortable, decline the opportunity. If direct contact with clients makes you nervous, get involved in the administrative side of the organization.

Now think about any life issues that may have to be taken into consideration. Where do you live? What is your job? What is your family structure? What are the primary daily-monthly demands of the different areas of your life? How do you see blending what you're doing now with what you want to do as a volunteer? Is your intent to involve friends or family as well, or embark on a more solo adventure? Write it all down.

Some volunteer opportunities cost money. If you plan to volunteer in another country, travel and housing could very well be your personal expense. Participation in special events may require that you purchase a ticket or provide some level of sponsorship. Simply paying for gas to get to and from your volunteer job may be a challenge for you. All of these cost considerations should find their way to your list. We will investigate how to determine any costs to your volunteer involvement in later chapters, but you should be aware now of the possibility.

Do you need to connect your volunteer involvement with your job? Your employer may ask you to help staff a community fundraising event. You may be expected to represent your employer on a board of directors. Your involvement may be short term or longer term. Hopefully your employer let you know about any expectations when you were hired.

In the case of representing your company or employer, you have the added expectation of showing the community that your employer cares, that it is serving its community's customers as well as the company expectations. It is public relations at its best. A positive note is that customarily the employer gives its volunteers time off to do volunteer work.

Now that you have thought about all these facets of volunteering, make sure that the expectations of your involvement still fit into your passions and the patterns of your life. Travel or no travel? Arts and teaching but no sports? *Yes* to senior citizens but *no* to children? A few hours a month or only a few hours a year? Is volunteering important for your career? Make more lists: activities you would love to do, activities that would be okay but not necessarily be your first preference, and activities that are a total no-go. Again, there's no right or wrong about these lists. They're just for you. They're going to help you find the most perfect volunteer fit for you and your life. Take the time now to think this through. It will save false starts, frustration, and disappointment down the road. Volunteering is all about you getting as much satisfaction from your endeavors as do the clients of the charities. It should always be a winning circumstance for all concerned.

You have taken a new look at yourself. You have some idea of what you might like to do as a volunteer. You may actually have several volunteer journeys you would like to take. Outstanding! Now is the time to do your research for specific engagement. Take enough time to do good research into opportunities. Don't be impulsive at this point, or you might end up in the wrong spot.

You're excited and want to get going! Take the time and do the investigation required to become fully informed, or you will end up confusing activity with accomplishment.

To Summarize...

Q Understand yourself and your personal history.

Q Assess your skills and be honest about your personal preferences.

Q Recognize your personal restrictions.

Q Start your research.

Chapter 7

Investigate Your Local and Regional Community

In This Chapter...

- How to access opportunities
- Volunteer jobs you might want to investigate
- Kinds of organizations
- State and Regional Volunteer Resources

I am going to provide an overview about researching how to find the perfect volunteer fit. Volunteer involvement begins where you are now. We're going to stay close to home to find the best fit for how you want to become involved.

You've heard the old saying, "grow and bloom where you're planted." We're going to discuss how to find your volunteer fit in your immediate community. Take a look around you. See what is going on in your close area, town, or city. The vast majority of the volunteering you will do will be in your local vicinity.

We will investigate the different ways you can find the best prospective situation for you. Then we will go on to help you discover how to become involved, how apply, and how to get trained if necessary. We'll discuss different kinds of involvement you might consider. Finally, we will touch on several different kinds of local organizations. Some of these organizations we will discuss in more depth in the next chapter.

How to Access Opportunities

Let's explore some of the ways you're likely to access opportunities:

Being Asked by a Friend

Unlike international or national volunteer engagement, you have the choice of becoming involved with a more local nonprofit in your community in several ways, all of them fairly easy. It is likely that if you have a history of volunteering, you have been personally asked by a friend to help out at one time or another. It may never have occurred to you to take that leap without your friend asking you to lend your support in a specific project. Merely being asked was the trigger for your involvement.

Personal Request

My son is an Eagle Scout. His involvement started at a school scout recruiting event when he was starting first grade. I remember from my own experience as well as watching the parents of other scouts, it takes a significant level of parent volunteer involvement as well as scout leader volunteer hours to get the youth to any level of accomplishment. Where the scouts went, the parents naturally followed. It all began with that first meeting, when parents were personally asked to become involved along with their child. Little did the parents realize at the time how many years of involvement would result from that first "little" request.

Example

Have you become involved with any local charities only because someone you like, or someone with whom you want to become connected, has picked up the phone, or taken you aside at a party and asked you? A personal request is by far the highest-rated compelling reason that most people decide to serve, particularly when the involvement is requested by someone you know, like, or respect.

So far in my life, I have served on sixty-two boards of directors: one for-profit and sixty-one nonprofits. Virtually each time I was asked to serve by someone I know. (Conversely, I have friends who have also encouraged me over the years to learn the word *no* when being asked.)

A personal request for help may come from your school or church or your next door neighbor or your best friend. It is hard to say no to someone you know. In these instances, you have likely been a student or a church member, or have had children or grandchildren involved in the organizations, or have watched your friend participate. There is a fun understanding in the school volunteer world that if you get the children involved in an activity, the parents and grandparents naturally follow. So when the PTA or PTO president calls and asks you to help, you as a parent are likely to do your best to be involved.

Sometimes you may be contacted out of the blue: you do not know the person or the organization asking you to participate. You may or may not be familiar with what they do. It is flattering to be asked, but don't say yes simply because you are complimented. If you have been approached by a charity that you don't know too much about, take a little time and learn about what it does. If and when you're comfortable, get involved. Your time and talent are valuable. Spend them wisely.

Personal Connection to Mission

What a charity does and who a charity serves are important, to the clients and to the community. Remember your retreat? What causes touch your heart? Is there a nonprofit in your area that fits your interest? Has a charity become important to you because of help you or your family has received? Do you feel that you want to give something back to it?

There are many local places you can access that will have lists of charities and volunteer opportunities in your area. Contact your Chamber of Commerce or your United Way, or your community foundation for information. Do a search online with your interest and the word "volunteer" and your city, and the opportunities will appear.

Special Event Participation

We have talked a little about special events earlier. If you love social interaction or are amazingly organized, this may be an excellent choice for you.

The purpose of special events is to increase public awareness of an organization or cause, raise money to support it, and bring new donors or volunteers into the fold. They are also a great way to thank current donors and volunteers with public recognition. They can also be just a terrific way to have fun! Many people become aware of a cause or a charity initially through special events.

Most entry-level donors give their first gifts through participation in a special event. These events are the most public of the volunteer options. Special events can take concentrated time, many overall volunteer hours, and sometimes financial support.

Special events are great because they have a definite schedule. You can plan on how to fit the event into your busy life, and you know it will be over on a certain date. Special events are also known for offering something different that isn't a part of daily life. Events can include activities from a black tie gala to a fishing competition. You may want to note that special events can be all about details and keeping deadlines. If you personally are somewhat relaxed about schedules and still want to do an event, you may want to volunteer to do the event tasks that are not quite so time-exacting.

Many volunteers become involved in special events through their workplace. Often a corporation selects one or two charities that fit the focus of that company's charitable giving. Employees are encouraged to participate in events that benefit the selected charities. Generally, employees get paid time off to do the events (and have a lot of fun with their coworkers), the company benefits from the positive response from the community, and the charity benefits from the support of the corporation. Again, win-win-win.

Volunteer Jobs You Might Want to Investigate

In this section we're going to take a look at the general types of volunteer positions that you could consider in your local area. You may have already thought about many or all of them. Our goal is to stretch your brain a little bit to look beyond where you might have looked so far.

Administrative Service

Administrative volunteers are folks who would not generally work directly with clients of the nonprofit organization, although they may have some contact. This type of work is typically behind the scenes, and volunteers could be recruited for a long-term set schedule or on an as-needed basis.

Administrative tasks for nonprofits can vary from organizing files, moving offices, preparing mass mailing projects to setting up and cleaning up special events. In schools, volunteers are often asked to staff the front office and help with wrangling student and parent requests throughout the day. Libraries often need volunteers to shelve books, staff the check-out desk, or manage the audio-visual equipment. Free medical clinics may require volunteers to help patients check in and complete medical histories, as well as managing the records and phone follow up of the patients. A community theater may need volunteers to staff the ticket sales desk or manage the beverage station during intermissions.

If you deeply support a particular charity but are not comfortable with the personal pressures of direct client service or special events, administrative tasks may be perfect for you. Organizations are deeply grateful for this kind of service, as paid staffing seems to always be insufficient due to limited funding. Also, you will be in a position to learn a lot about the inner workings of the organization. It will give you a comprehensive understanding of the successes and challenges the charity faces every day. Be warned however that all that you see and do as a volunteer in a job like this requires absolute confidentiality. You can't go home and talk about what you see and hear behind the scenes.

Direct Program Service

Do you like working directly with people? In being a direct-service volunteer, you're a public face for the mission of the organization to the client. Some jobs may take specialized training; all take dependability, honesty, and a real affection for meeting new people. Direct-service volunteering also takes commitment to a schedule: weekly, monthly, whatever is appropriate for what you're doing. The nonprofit will be depending on you doing what you agree to do. Again, make sure of the details of what you're taking on, in fairness to both you and the organization. Here, too, confidentiality is expected.

Maybe you're interested in reading to elementary-age children once or twice a week. Maybe you would like to provide companionship to or participate in activities with the elderly who are living in a retirement home. Possibly tutoring high school kids after school is your cup of tea. If you like carpentry or painting, you may want to help renovate or build affordable housing.

Get out your list of talents and interests you wrote earlier. Look at it. Then think about the nonprofits around where you live. If there is a job that you think might be of interest to you, I am confident you will be able to find a place to do it in your volunteer world.

Board Service

Boards of directors or boards of trustees (their purposes may differ, but boards function the same way) for any charity can make all the difference in how successful the organization is in the fulfilling of its mission.

Normally, a volunteer is invited to participate on a board for one of several reasons. You might be asked because:

- Of your past and future public and financial support the mission of the organization.

- You're in a position to advocate for the organization: legal, political, etc.

- You have a position of public influence and name visibility, which will attract others to support the organization.

- Of your professional skills that are needed to support the work of the board and organization.

A One-Stop Volunteer Opportunity

The Special Olympics is a global example of several kinds of volunteer involvement. You can participate as a direct program volunteer, an administrative volunteer, an intermittent service volunteer, or a board volunteer in areas including health, human services, education, and culture. You can get everything in one place!

Pure Genius!

Every board has legal obligations including financial, regulatory, and ethical oversight. The board establishes policies and does long-range planning. It does not get generally involved in the daily operation of the programs of the organization. If you can understand these conditions, you will find board service very rewarding, and certainly educational. Again, confidentiality is an absolute requirement.

Intermittent Service

Intermittent service is really volunteering from time to time, with no set schedule month to month or year to year. This can consist of occasional special events to weather disasters. You generally wouldn't plan ahead for this kind of volunteering. It's typically a response to something that has happened unexpectedly, or with little notice.

Hopefully, you're finding ways to volunteer that will fit your needs and your life. The more you consider your options, the more option choices come to mind.

Kinds of Organizations

We have taken a short look at kinds of volunteer jobs. Now let's look at just a few examples of nonprofit organizations that you might find locally:

Religion

By far, religious organizations host the highest level of both donor dollars and volunteer time in the United States. Within the congregational family of each church, synagogue, mosque, temple, or meeting house there are multiple volunteer openings. Assignments might include administrative, direct service, board, or intermittent roles. Speak with your clergy or members of the nominating committee to find out where you may be interested in becoming involved. Writing the newsletter, teaching religious classes, singing in a choir, mentoring youth groups, coordinating weddings, serving on the governing board, or visiting shut-in members may become part of your involvement.

Education

Schools are a huge part of our lives: preschool, elementary, middle, high schools, then possibly colleges are all likely part of your experiences. Direct service is the most probable involvement at the preschool and elementary level in the forms of tutoring, room parenting, and special event participation. Other kinds of volunteer tasks could include parent boards, or office administrative help.

Human Services

As the name infers, human service organizations serve the life needs of its clients. These may include safe and affordable housing, quality child care, drug treatment and counseling, adoption, social services, aging services, emergency shelters, food banks, veterans' needs, or youth development. The list can be long, but the bottom line is that these organizations strive to help individuals find a better quality of life on a fundamental level. There are consistently places in administration, special events, board service, and certainly direct-service volunteerism in human service organizations.

Providing direct service to clients may require specialized training by the nonprofit, so be prepared to invest that kind of time.

Health

Health nonprofits can include organizations that are primarily direct service such as hospitals, nursing homes, or free medical clinics. Hospitals and medical facilities use many direct-service volunteers as well as board

Arts and Humanities

A really unique arts destination is the Neon Museum in Las Vegas. The Neon Museum collects, preserves, studies, and exhibits the iconic neon signs from historic Las Vegas hotels, businesses, and landmarks. Trained volunteer docents conducted tours for nearly seventy thousand visitors to the Neon Museum and Neon Boneyard in 2015.

Example

volunteers. Most of the hospitals and clinics have a well-developed volunteer participation program. Just pick up your phone and call. Hospital boards may include both governance boards and foundation boards for the same facility.

Arts, Culture, and Humanities

Arts, culture, and humanities organizations can include ballet companies, local or regional theaters, art galleries and programs, or symphonies or orchestras. Programs may be targeted for performance or display or for participation. Volunteers are critical to ensuring that tickets are sold, audiences are seated by volunteer ushers, costumes and scenery are made, music is played, or that special fundraising events are successful.

State and Regional Volunteer Resources

State and regional volunteering is the in-between area of volunteering: not next door, but not across the country or on another continent, either. Let's explore:

Nongovernment Nonprofits

There are nonprofits, some national, that deliver their missions and do their work via a regional or state presence. While regional or state-wide options might include a little travel, it will not be as expensive and time consuming as fully national or international travel. Organizations that work regionally typically have extensive volunteer needs because they are delivering services across a larger geographic area but still with limited budgets.

More localized organizations may offer more hands-on involvement than a national organization may can. An example of this kind of organization is Trees Forever (*treesforever.org*), which implements conservation projects across the state of Iowa. Volunteers plant trees, work with community conservation planning groups across the state, provide education to groups and schools, and advocate with the state government.

State, County, or Local Government

Each state, county, and town or city has boards and commissions that ask for volunteer citizen service. Typically, the board members must apply and are appointed by the governor or county supervisors or mayor. These boards might be responsible for the oversight of areas such as nursing, accountancy, cosmetology, engineering and land surveying, contractors, medical, dental, education, utilities, or many others. Are any of these areas your specialty or of interest to you? Are there issues facing your state legislators that you want to influence? Are there county initiatives you want to influence? Are there city governance issues that you think should be addressed? This kind involvement may be a great choice for you.

Typically, the state or county or city website will have the application process posted. You may have to link to the specific department to obtain the application information. Don't be shy! You may think that if you don't know anyone in government you won't have a chance, but most of those who are in charge of the decisions prefer a wide range of representation on these boards. In some situations, some boards may pay a stipend, so make sure you find out all the facts before you apply. Update your résumé, as you will probably have to submit it with your application.

Virtually every state and county needs volunteers to help staff the state parks or outdoor state-sponsored special events. You can link through the state websites (remember that government websites are *.gov* or *.state.gov*) or, for parks, through the National Park Service at *nps.gov*. If you prefer seasonal outdoor endeavors, these choices might be perfect!

Occasional Opportunities

This is the option for you if you want to volunteer once in a while but not necessarily on a particular schedule. It is also the choice you might make in response to some kind of emergency or immediate need.

Do you live a region that has been affected by a natural disaster? Have you experienced a tornado, a hurricane, a flood, or a wildfire? Following disasters, volunteers are critical to managing food, shelter, clothing, medical attention, and reconstruction. The commitment may be a few hours to a few months. After Hurricanes Katrina and Sandy, teams of volunteers traveled from all over the country to help clean up and rebuild.

For immediate response to catastrophes, look at the websites for your city, your county, or your local United Way. Most of these will have information to get you connected to wherever the volunteer need is the greatest. You can also check with your local human service charities or any of the local places of worship.

To Summarize...

🔍 You can access volunteer opportunities through friends, special events, or a personal connection to the mission.

🔍 There are volunteer opportunities available for all interests and skill sets.

🔍 Investigate different kinds of organizations.

🔍 There are volunteer-specific local, state, and regional resources to guide your search.

Chapter 8

Investigate International and National Opportunities

In This Chapter...

- International volunteer opportunities
- National public-sector volunteer organizations
- National private-sector options
- Service-learning approach to volunteering

International, national, and service learning are much broader in scope than local, regional, or state volunteering.

In investigating these opportunities, there is a huge amount of information available. Again, I strongly recommend that you do your research online. You certainly can do research by telephone and by standard mail, just be aware that it is significantly slower. Another source might be your local library. Many libraries offer whole sections devoted to the nonprofit sector.

We will start with a few big-picture options of international volunteer organizations. We will work though sample national public-sector and national private-sector options for your consideration in becoming involved.

Finally, we'll take a foray into the service-learning approach to volunteering. Read this chapter as a starting point and continue the research process on your own. Quite a lot of background detail has been included to give you an idea of the scope of where you can look and what options you may want to consider.

International Volunteer Opportunities

If you're open to some fairly high adventure, volunteering in another country may be in your future! We will get into *how* to do this in detail in a later chapter. Right now we will look at a sampling *where* you can look to volunteer abroad.

There are countless choices in volunteering beyond the borders of the United States. But before you make any impulsive decisions about where you want to go, there are some preliminary decisions you will need to make.

How much time do you want to spend volunteering in another country? Just your vacation time? A few months? A year or two? A high school or college semester? When you plan, include a little extra time for leisure travel because you will want to see as much of your destination country as possible.

A core consideration is cost. What is your budget for travel and volunteering? Some options will pay you some kind of minimal stipend, but many will ask you to pay for your adventure. Start by developing a preliminary budget based on where you might want to go. Travel (to and from the country plus within the country), food, clothing, housing, sightseeing, and unexpected expenses are all important.

You need to know what you have in spending cash to know what will best fit your goals. Be as accurate as you can here. I have found that no matter how much you plan, there are always unexpected expenses, so you will want to include some budget flexibility. If cost is a barrier, there are organizations like Cross Cultural Solutions (*crossculturalsolutions.org*) that will help you organize fundraising for your personal trip, or many programs have suggestions about how you can raise funding to support participation in their programs.

Find out if language or special skills be required. Organizations will tell you if they recommend that you speak a language. Generally, programs will have multilingual leaders. Even if speaking the language is not required, you may want to become familiar with the language of the country you will be visiting. Learn at least a few basic phrases if you can. There are numerous English/

(choose language) phrase books and audio programs available from bookstores or online.

Plan ahead. It takes time to apply, fulfill the requirements and obtain your passport and visas, as well as any other required paperwork. When choosing a destination country, use your common sense. Check with the US Department of State (*state*.gov) and find the list of countries that are not currently recommended for travel. You will want to try to avoid a country that is on the State Department don't-go list, is involved in a war, or has a major medical epidemic.

Keep Good Records

The expenses of your volunteer work may be deductible as a charitable contribution on your tax return. Consult your tax advisor to understand your own personal situation.

IMPORTANT!

As a side note, if you're interested in a nonprofit career, it's good to understand that starting as a volunteer with an organization can eventually lead to a paid position with that organization.

Peace Corps

The Peace Corps (*peacecorps.gov*) is likely the most well-known of the foreign volunteer programs in the United States. The Peace Corps was established by President John F. Kennedy on March 1, 1961 by executive order. The purpose was (and continues to be) to send trained American men and women to other countries to assist in development efforts.

To date the Peace Corps has placed volunteers in 139 countries and trained more than 215,000 volunteers. Currently volunteers are actively serving in sixty-five countries included in the geographic areas of Africa; Latin America; Eastern Europe/Central Asia; Asia; the Caribbean; North Africa/Middle East; and Pacific Islands.

There are four major groupings in the Peace Corps. They are Peace Corps (two-year commitment), Peace Corps Response (high-impact, three- to twelve-month assignments), Global Health Service Partnership (one-year assignment to train and grow health care capacity in medical and nursing schools), as well as graduate programs for volunteers (Peace Corps service can be combined with master's degree program or a returned volunteer may receive financial support for graduate school).

Peace Corps initiatives include Feed the Future, the President's Malaria Initiative, Let Girls Learn, and the President's Emergency Plan for AIDS Relief. Currently, Peace Corps volunteers tend to be younger (only 8 percent are over 50).

Go to the website *peacecorps.gov* and take the first steps to get informed about what is available, where you might want to go, and what steps you will need to take to get there. The application is online and all of the information is easy to access. For this program, you must be eighteen years or older and if you have a spouse or significant other in your life, you can volunteer as a couple. The Peace Corps is unique in that following two years' service, each volunteer receives a stipend and specialized training to help transition them into their new home lives. While serving, transportation, medical, and dental care is provided as well.

Portal Organizations

There are multiple international portal organizations that both offer their own programs abroad and online links to other overseas volunteer opportunities. Some are subject-specific, such as student exchange/volunteer programs, and some offer a large choice of ways to get involved. Here we are limited to just a few illustrations, but keep looking and you will discover so much more.

One example is Projects Abroad. Founded in 1992, Projects Abroad (*projects-abroad.com*) is one of the largest organizations to offer volunteer service projects and internships overseas. It offers placements in Asia, Africa, Europe, and Latin America. There are high school programs, gap-year options, and spring break and medical/healthcare choices. Subjects include business, environment, journalism, law, sports, teaching, and lots of other subjects.

Another is Volunteer Abroad (*goabroad.com*). Go to the site then pick a country, pick a cause, and pick a duration, and the site will send you online to other nonprofit overseas programs that fit your parameters. Some of other portal organizations include Cross Cultural Solutions (*crossculturalsolutions. org*) and International Volunteer HQ (*volunteerhq.org*). Once you start looking, you will be astounded at the variety available to you.

Volunteer Vacation

As a member of International Association of Fundraising Professionals, I participated in a trip to Cuba several years ago with other nonprofit fundraisers. The purpose of the trip was to encourage Cuba to allow more nongovernment organizations (NGOs) from other countries to establish a presence in Cuba. To that end, our group met with government officials and the Cuban judiciary. The relationship-building trip was planned and implemented by People to People International. Since travel to Cuba was prohibited at that time, special travel visas were issued by the US Department of the Treasury.

We had special guides that took us to all of the tourist highlights you would expect, but we also got to visit farms and outlying towns as well as charitable enterprises led mostly by religious entities. While in Cuba, our group launched and completed a small capital campaign to replace roofs on a facility for elderly homeless women. It was an excellent volunteer vacation!

Pure Genius!

Volunteer Vacations

Did you know that there is something called a volunteer vacation? Have you ever wanted to hike Yosemite Park or take a Mediterranean cruise on your vacation? Have you made plans to photograph the Serengeti or go fishing in the Indian Ocean? You can see the world and do good at the same time.

You can choose to go for a week—or a month. You can go with yourself, your friends, your family, your sorority, your church group, anyone! On a volunteer vacation, you can tailor your experience to your age and physical considerations.

You can go to an amazing number of countries and focus on a purpose that is important to YOU. We are talking about international travel here, but you can go lots of places within the United States as well. You can sightsee without being a tourist. At the same time, you will have the opportunity to contribute to a local community and get be able to really learn about their culture in-depth.

Teach English, dig wells, build a house, and meet with artists and musicians. There are a lot of offerings available for volunteer vacations. Be aware of two things: these cost money and you truly need to do your homework to make sure that the organization is reputable and dependable.

When you participate in a volunteer vacation, you will often stay with a host family in the community where you're working. There are also more custom trips such as trips for donors sponsored by the charity to which the donors contributed. These charities are generally focused on international initiatives.

School Options

If you're a student and want to combine study and volunteering abroad, check with your college registrar or with the International Student Exchange Program (*isep.org*) to find out what programs are open to you. Most colleges and universities have options to study abroad for a semester or for a year, and the study term can often be combined with a volunteer project. On the high school or community college level this volunteer and study option may be for only a matter of weeks, or for a shorter school term.

You may also want to volunteer to host a student coming to your area from another country. You would be expected to provide a home environment as well as assistance for the student's work and volunteering. The time commitment is generally a school term or summer term. Often these relationships become lifelong. Sometimes, basic knowledge of a second language is helpful. Your willingness to volunteer your time, effort, and home to a foreign exchange student will make a life-changing difference to that student.

The best place to begin your research might be with your high school or college registrar's or advisor's office. Your school may also have information and application forms online with approved programs for your school. Or of course you can begin by going online. Your family may even want to volunteer to

Sample Student Exchange Programs

School Student Exchange Programs are a more specialized and structured option for youth who wish to combine study with volunteering. There is generally a cost attached to this option, as well as a time commitment.

◆ American Institute for Foreign Study (*AIFS.org*)

◆ People to People Ambassador Programs (*peopletopeople.com*)

◆ International Student Exchange Programs (*isep.org*)

◆ AFS-USA (*afsusa.org*)

◆ National Student Exchange Program (*nse.org*)

As a comprehensive list, visit the US Department of State website for all kinds of foreign study options, including the Fulbright Scholar program at *exchanges.state.gov*.

Example

be a host to a student traveling from another country. But if you are at all interested, take the initiative and apply.

Professional Volunteering

Do you have a special skill? Are you an engineer or a dentist, a teacher, or veterinarian? Have you done urban planning or small business development? Would you be willing to share those skills to help communities be healthier, or develop a way to be economically self-sufficient? Do you have an agricultural background in crops or livestock? Then professional volunteering may be for you. Programs of this sort generally demand significant time and work commitment. You may be giving several months a year for more than one year. Also you must qualify for professional volunteering.

While almost all organizations such as the Peace Corps and Projects Abroad have professional volunteer options, probably the most famous is Doctors Without Borders or Médecins Sans Frontières (*doctorswithoutborders.org*). This is a French-founded international humanitarian charity devoted to solving the problems of world health. Its headquarters is in Geneva, Switzerland, but it has offices worldwide. It was awarded the Nobel Peace Prize in 1999. This organization is always looking for all kinds of medical and dental professionals. Additionally, volunteers who specialize in logistics, transportation, security, and support of the medical personnel and clinics are critical.

It may seem overwhelming just looking at the international choices. Just take your time, ask all the questions you have, and find the best fit for you. In a later chapter we will talk about the practical details of volunteering in another country. This kind of volunteer option is an exciting road to travel so prepare and make sure it is the journey of a lifetime.

National Volunteer Organizations

At the national level, there are numerous public-sector, faith-based, and private-sector options for you to investigate. I am going to summarize only a few here, but you will see when you go to the websites that you will be able to link with many other options.

Corporation for National and Community Service

Presidents throughout history have established their signature volunteer initiatives and agencies. The Corporation for National and Community

Corporation for National and Community Service

1201 New York Avenue, NW
Washington, DC 20525
nationalservice.gov

The Corporation for National and Community Service (CNCS) is a big, comprehensive, informative website (*cns.gov*). The mission is "to support the American culture of citizenship, service, and responsibility." CNCS is an umbrella agency that offers both programs and initiatives that connect more than five million volunteers annually. The focus areas include hunger, health, poverty, environment, human services, and education.

Example

Service is one of them. The Corporation for National and Community Service is a public service agency of the Federal Government of the United States. It is both a source of connections to volunteering plus a grant making agency for volunteer initiatives. In effect it operates much like a foundation as it is the largest annual grantor supporting service and volunteering initiatives.

The original agency was developed beginning with the National Community Service Trust Act of 1990 by President George W. Bush being signed into law. This law created the Commission on National and Community Service.

Specific initiatives of the CNCS have expanded under every president. CNCS was expanded in 1993 by President Bill Clinton when he signed the National Community Service Trust Act, which merged the federal offices of ACTION and the Commission on National and Community Service to form CNCS. At this time, AmeriCorps was folded into the CNCS tent. Presidents George W. Bush and Barak Obama each added their own projects. The agency simply keeps growing.

There are many operating programs under CNCS supervision. Each of them can be contacted directly for volunteering or there is a place on the *cns.gov* (or *service.gov*) website where you can list your interests and skills and start to find the right volunteer place for you. Some of the more familiar CNCS core programs include: AmeriCorps, VISTA—Volunteers in Service to America, FEMA Corps, and Senior Corps (includes Foster Grandparents, Senior Companions and RSVP-Retired Senior Volunteer Program); the Social Innovation Fund and the Volunteer Generation Fund. I should point out that among all these initiatives there are some paid positions available.

There are hundreds of ways to become a volunteer through the Corporation for National and Community Service. There are links on this portal website that will even take you to Federal Civil Service, the Peace Corps, the military, state, and local government opportunities, the US Public Health Service, and Veterans Affairs.

CNCS also links to *volunteer.gov* which is a portal for volunteering at America's natural and cultural resources. If you want to work at a campground or a national monument or a national park, this is an excellent way to find the perfect place. You should plan on spending a fair amount of time investigating the *cns.gov, nationalservice.gov*, and *serve.gov* websites.

Volunteers of America

I want to give you an example of a national volunteer organization that is faith based. I chose this one because of its longevity. Volunteers of America (*voa.org*) is a nongovernmental, Christian organization focusing on one issue: the betterment of society through faith-based volunteerism. It was established in 1896, and currently has approximately sixteen thousand employees in addition to its volunteers.

Volunteers of America

1660 Duke Street
Alexandria, VA 22314
(703) 341–5000
voa.org

VOA's organizational impact statement says:

> *We provide services that are designed locally to address specific community needs. Our common areas of focus include promoting self-sufficiency for the homeless and for others overcoming personal crises, caring for the elderly and disabled and fostering their independence, and supporting positive development for troubled and at-risk children and youth. We look at the whole person and address both urgent and ongoing needs, with the goal of helping people become as self-reliant as possible.*

If you think this fits with what you're looking for—being connected to a faith-based organization—this might be the place to investigate.

Example

Beginning its national effectiveness following World War I, Volunteers of America continues to provide local volunteers in communities across America in the areas of aging; children, youth and families; community corrections; community enhancement; emergency support; employment and training; homelessness; housing; intellectual disabilities; long-term care; mental health; seniors; substance abuse; and veterans services. There are a lot of choices here.

To find the local opportunities via this site, you will have to do a little searching. There is a way for you to search volunteer opportunities by state under the Volunteer link, or you can search by field of interest.

Volunteers of America is just one example of a faith-based, volunteer-focused organization. There are countless more. Find one that matches your values and works in your area or field of interest, then get involved.

Points of Light

I am using the Points of Light Foundation as an example because the name is so well-known. It is unique in that it is both national and international in scope. Points of Light is familiar to you if you are old enough to remember the inaugural address of President George H.W. Bush in 1989. In it, he emphasized the importance of volunteers being critical partners with the government in ensuring national health, safety, and progress: "I have spoken of a thousand points of light, of all the community organizations that are spread like stars throughout the nation, doing good. We will work hand in hand, encouraging, sometimes leading,

Points of Light Foundation

600 Means Street NW,
  Suite 210
Atlanta, GA 30318
404 979 2900
pointsoflight.org

Points of Light is the world's largest organization dedicated to volunteer service. In 1990, Bush established it as an independent, nonpartisan nonprofit organization, the mission of which is to empower volunteerism. In 1991, the foundation merged with the National Volunteer Center Network. To give you some context, it was in 1993 that President Clinton established the Corporation for National and Community Service, about which we have already talked. In 1992, a national organization was established as a network for sharing resources called CityCares. Eventually, the name of CityCares changed to HandsOn Network. The Points of Light Foundation and HandsOn Network merged in 2007 to become, simply, Points of Light.

Example

sometimes being led, rewarding." While started looking like public-sector initiative—and yes, it includes several government initiatives—Points of Light operates as a general charity (501(c)(3).

Today, Points of Light is the umbrella organization for three divisions:

🔍 The Action Networks include HandsOn Network which manages 250 local volunteer centers, GenerationOn which is the youth volunteer program, the Points of Light Corporate Institute which aids companies in involving their employees and customer in volunteering, and AmeriCorps Alums which is the national AmeriCorps service alumni network that develops the next generation of volunteers.

🔍 The Civic Incubator helps develop new forms of civic action. It is an international think-tank and support for entrepreneurial ventures and initiatives for volunteer actions.

🔍 Points of Light Programs builds and scales training for volunteers in local communities to meet critical needs and build stronger communities. The programs focus primarily on environment, education, economy, emergency preparedness, and veterans and military families. Points of Light provides volunteer training, education, and placement.

Points of Light initiatives have volunteer involvement available through national service, community based service, or civic engagement events (e.g., Martin Luther King, Jr. Day of Service). Go to *pointsoflight.org* to get connected in your area if you're interested in volunteer service.

Citizen Corps

Citizen Corps, while totally governmental (public sector), is an example of a single-issue agency. After the September 11, 2001 attacks, huge efforts have been made at all levels to ensure emergency preparedness, protection of the country against attack, and expanding and supporting first responders. These initiatives are based on local citizen responsibility for community safety. This is a national program implemented on the regional or local level.

Citizen Corps' mission is to train volunteers in all aspects of handling all kinds of emergencies to make communities safer and stronger. It is coordinated by the Department of Homeland Security/Federal Emergency Management Agency. FEMA works with the training and education of local, state, and federal entity staffs and volunteers. The volunteers join and are active through their local communities.

The Citizen Corps website (*ready.gov*) will connect you with your local Citizen Corps Council. If you have trouble finding any information, try looking at your city, county, or state emergency preparedness websites. They will likely be able connect you with training and volunteering for emergency situations. This can be a really fun, if sometimes physically demanding, endeavor.

National Private-Sector Options

National private-sector organizations have a focused central mission. While there is a national presence, the activity generally takes place on a regional or local level. There are a lot of these, and you're likely familiar with many of them. Examples of this kind of organization might include the Heart Association (*heart.org*), the American Cancer Society (*acs.org*), or the ASPCA (*aspca.org*).

You can access both national and more local information through the organizations' primary websites. Virtually all of

Citizen Corps

Years ago I served as a Boy Scout Den Leader. One of the badges scouts can learn is Emergency Preparedness. My family lived in a community near a nuclear power plant. Disaster preparedness drills were mandatory. All agencies participated: fire, police and sheriff, hospitals and airports, and local and county officials.

At the time the Citizen Corps volunteer exercises were called Project Impact. My scouting den was chosen to portray victims in a Project Impact stadium bleacher collapse disaster. They spent hours being made up with gashes, broken bones, burns, dismemberments. After extraction from the collapsed building, they all got a ride in an ambulance to a hospital, where they were triaged and treated. A few of them even got to play dead.

The boys loved the experience, and learned in real time in a realistic way how a disaster is managed. No amount of lecturing in a classroom would have given them the comprehension they received from this exercise.

Pure Genius!

these sites have a volunteer link to click on. Once you enter your location, the site will give you the closest organization contact. Finding an organization is as easy as typing in your interest, such as "animal" and the word "volunteer," and your search engine will take you to lots of organizations.

While we are talking about national organizations, you may be interested in serving on the national organization on the board or on a national committee. Generally, you would start with involvement in a local chapter, but not necessarily. Be aware that it may mean travel to meetings and national events, usually at your personal expense. It is really exciting to be involved at the national level, but be sure you're fully informed about what is expected of you in time, talent, and treasure.

Service-Learning Approach to Volunteering

Unless you have already been involved in service learning, you're not likely to be familiar with it. Service learning is actually a teaching plus work project. It combines receiving classroom instruction with doing significant volunteer work. It is targeted at students currently in school and is considered an experiential approach to learning.

This program was initiated under the Community Service Act which authorized the Learn and Serve America grant program. Generally, service learning is a cooperative effort between schools and community organizations that are in need of volunteer support. The students prepare for the volunteer work in a classroom setting and then do the actual service activity. They bring their experiences back to the classroom for discussion and analysis. The outcomes are the benefit to the nonprofits involved as well as a more informed, experienced, and civically aware future adult. It is a thoroughly win-win process.

If you're a younger volunteer, this might be a terrific opportunity! If your school does not offer this, maybe you could suggest it to school officials.

You have had a lot of information presented to you in this chapter. I trust it has not been too overwhelming, as it is only the tip of the iceberg. Hopefully, it has encouraged you to expand your notions about volunteering. Remember, you not only give a lot, you get a lot back in learning new skills, meeting new people, and making a difference.

To Summarize...

🔍 There are vast resources to identify national and international volunteer opportunities.

🔍 National volunteer organizations include public-sector, private-sector, and faith-based options.

🔍 Student exchange programs offer study plus volunteer choices.

🔍 Service-learning approach to volunteering is a distinctive and valuable approach to learning about volunteering.

Chapter 9

Investigate Fraternal, Business, and Political Organizations

In This Chapter...

- Fraternal organizations and societies
- Business organizations and associations
- Labor unions
- Political involvement

When we think about being a volunteer, we generally think about working for charities that provide direct services to constituents.

However, there are other interesting options that more indirectly support charitable causes or initiatives. Many of these alternatives are based on social affiliations, or business interests, or work unions, or collegial alliances or political concerns, instead of a charitable mission.

Here we will be investigating how you can become involved in groups that include fraternal organizations, business associations, labor unions, and political interests. These kinds of groups are typically membership organizations and typically charge dues to be a member. These groups gather because members have common interests based on a kind of business, a belief system, an economic situation, or educational direction.

Volunteer involvement in these kinds of groups is not generally the primary focus, but can be an important component or requirement of maintaining your membership. In some cases, members may not even be aware that volunteer involvement is available through groups such as these.

Fraternal Organizations and Societies

Fraternal organizations date back as far as ancient Greece and Rome. Fraternal organizations, business associations, and labor unions are formed based on common interests specific to a particular group and tend to be social, common purpose (such as a profession or trade), or a particular faith. Many of these groups have local, national, and occasionally international outreach.

The best part of becoming involved with any of these fraternal organizations, societies, or associations is the social aspect. These are wonderful openings to meet people with interests similar to yours, and have amazing fun working and playing together for a common objective.

While volunteerism is not typically the primary focus of these groups, the members are expected to be involved in whatever volunteer projects the organization supports. The types of fraternal groups might include lodges, fraternities, temples, societies, knights, shrine, masonic, sororities, and orders. Business organizations might include associations, societies, or groups. Labor unions are typically based on a single trade or profession, and would include the union name and possible local number. Political involvement is reflected by party

Fraternal Organization

The word "fraternal" means "brother."

A fraternal organization is a type of primarily collective organization whose members associate for a mutually beneficial purpose such as for social, professional, or honorary principles.

Definition

membership. For our purposes here I will discuss common elements in each category, along with a few examples.

Social Fraternities and Sororities

When we think about fraternal organizations, most of us immediately think of social fraternities or sororities connected with colleges and universities. Most of these groups have Greek names such as Sigma Chi or Kappa Kappa Gamma. Generally, these fraternities and sororities are perceived as being focused on the social aspects of attending college.

The original college-based fraternity established in the United States was the Phi Beta Kappa Society in 1776 at the College of William and Mary in Williamsburg, Virginia. At the time, it was considered a literary society. Its membership was generally limited to seniors or upperclassmen, and many members stayed affiliated and active as college or university faculty after graduation. The existing college fraternity/sorority movement evolved in the early 1800s, lost some momentum during the Civil War, and eventually the first nationally organized fraternity, Alpha Tau Omega, was established in 1865.

Today, social fraternities (generally male or mixed gender) and sororities (generally female) on college and university campuses recruit members beginning in the students' freshman year. If you're considering joining a sorority or fraternity on your college campus, you will be joining the "Greek Life." There are advantages and disadvantages to joining this kind of group.

Benefits to fraternity/sorority membership may include access to campus housing, a rich social life, opportunities for leadership within the group, the likelihood of making and keeping lifelong friends, and enhanced academic support. Most sororities and fraternities also participate in supporting various philanthropic causes, primarily through special events.

Joining a sorority or fraternity typically includes participating in rush week at the beginning of the school year. You visit the organizations that you like, and the members will, you hope, issue you an invitation to join. You then become a probationary member for a time to ensure a good fit between you and the organization. Once that time period is finished, you complete a pledge period and are initiated as a permanent member. You will be expected to pay dues and participate in the activities of the sorority or fraternity, including volunteering for charitable activities.

Social Fraternities and Sororities

College fraternities and sororities typically require members' philanthropic volunteer support as part of their "Greek" life. Often this is in the form of participating in fundraising events for the school or for a selected charity. The Greek organizations at the University of Iowa raise close to half a million dollars annually toward the Dance Marathon, which benefits the cause of pediatric cancer. Overall, the Iowa Fraternity and Sorority Community donates almost fifty thousand volunteer hours every year.

Example

The downside to becoming a fraternity or sorority member might include the hidden costs of membership, community event participation, logo-wear, living in the chapter's house, or other items. Notable negative group behaviors have occasionally become issues for a few chapters. Make sure you learn all of the facts of your target fraternity or sorority so you can make an informed decision about participation.

Common-Interest Fraternal Organizations

Common-interest fraternal organizations are also membership based, generally have dues, and provide social interaction. However, the members come together because of belief in a shared focus, interest, or synergy. These groups can also be referred to as service organizations, as they provide both volunteers and fundraising efforts for charities.

There are some fraternal groups that offer only a single activity goal, such as the Red Hat Society which promotes interpersonal relationships among women. These groups don't apply to our discussion. Some of the groups have a more global view such as Lions International which supports the "civil, cultural, and social welfare" of the community. *lionsclub.org*

Most of these organizations welcome anyone interested in becoming a member. Some ask that a current member propose your name. Go to their website, find a chapter near you, and contact them. Once accepted as a member, you will be expected to attend meetings, pay annual dues, and participate in any community service activities.

Faith-Based and Ethnic Fraternal Groups

Faith-based and ethnic fraternal groups are by their nature a little more restrictive on membership and, therefore, volunteer opportunities.

Common-Interest Fraternal Organizations

There are several examples of common-interest organizations that also get involved with supporting their communities through volunteerism. Examples, with areas of focus, are:

◆ Toastmasters International: Public speaking, community leadership (*toastmasters.org*)

◆ Kiwanis: Global volunteerism, children (*kiwanis.org*)

◆ NAACP: Ethnic equality and civil rights (*naacp.org*)

◆ Ecological Society of America: Climate change and ecological preservation (*esa.org*)

◆ Rotary International: Community business development; eradication of polio worldwide, world peace. (*rotary.org*)

◆ Optimists: Optimism: "Bring Out the Best in Youth," eradication of childhood cancer (*optimist.org*)

◆ Benevolent and Protective Order of Elks: Promote community welfare, patriotism, happiness, scholarships to youth, and support of veterans (*elks.org*)

There are fraternal groups for every kind of interest you might have.

Membership is restricted to you being a member of a certain religion or to you having a particular ethnic or cultural background. The two most identifiable faith-based fraternal organizations in the United States are the Freemasons (Masons, Masonic Shrine) (*freemason.org*) and the Knights of Columbus (*kofc.org*). Each organization's focus is based on religious tenants, and volunteer-based community service is strongly focused in that way.

There is also the Orthodox Church in America (*oca.org*). To gain membership in any of these, you would need an invitation from a current member. You would then be required to go through an educational process prior to being accepted for full membership. Again, there are continuing membership requirements including annual fees and community service.

There is an amazing list of ethnically based fraternal organizations that welcome you if you're African American or American Indian/Native American if you're Irish or Ukrainian; Hispanic or Croatian, or any of a hundred other cultural or ethnic backgrounds. From B'nai B'rith to the Daughters of Scotland, if you can think of it you can find it.

Business and Professional Organizations and Associations

There are all kinds of business and professional organizations and associations for virtually any kind of career, vocation, or business interest. Business and professional organizations and associations offer membership to those who are focused either on business in general (e.g., a Chamber of Commerce) or on a very specific profession (e.g., Appraisers Association of America). You would likely be interested in one of these choices if you're interested in community business development, or if you're already working in a certain profession and you would like to become involved with others in the same profession. Be aware as you do your research that not all business or professional member organizations offer volunteer involvement beyond possibly serving on a board. Take the time you need to get all the facts. Here are a few examples offering community volunteer options as part of your membership:

General Business

The most well-known general business association is the Chamber of Commerce. (Note that some communities may use a different name for its business alliance organization.) In any city or town, this business membership association is focused primarily on the economic and business success of the community. The people who serve on the chamber board, committees, programs, initiatives, or special events volunteer their time. Both nationally and locally, chambers offer a wide variety of programs and events in which you can become involved. Most chambers of commerce have websites where you can collect information on membership and look at options for your volunteer involvement. Most chambers, or area economic-development programs, also support community initiatives and special events that benefit their member businesses. You'll have a lot of chances to volunteer!

Specific Professional Organizations

The list of profession-specific associations can seem endless. If you're a banker or a restaurateur, a farmer or a printer, a physician or a boat builder, there is a

Specific Professional Organizations

Examples of the variety of specific professional membership organizations that proactively offer some level of volunteer involvement include:

◆ American Institute of CPAs (*aicpa.org*)

◆ National Association of Realtors (*realtor.org*)

◆ American Dental Association (*ada.org*)

There are even professional umbrella organizations such as the American Society of Association Executives. This society serves professional executives of membership organizations.

Example

professional membership association for you. Each association, society, or group has its application and dues criteria that you would need to satisfy. Certainly, an association that specializes in your exact profession will help you in your career. You will build professional and personal friendships. However, if you're looking for volunteer options, you will have to make sure that the group you are researching will offer them. Not all of them have volunteer choices.

Labor Unions

The final kind of fraternal or business organization we will talk about is labor unions. We are not going to deliberate the pros and cons of labor unions here; we are only going to look at how you can get involved as a volunteer.

Labor, or trade, unions grew out of the Industrial Revolution in the late nineteenth century. The purpose was to support its members in advocating for better working conditions and better wages and benefits, and to ensure the integrity of professional trade standards. Over time, labor unions have become highly organized, financially independent, and politically powerful. The two major umbrella groups are the AFL-CIO (1955) and the Change to Win Federation (2005).

Labor unions have also become an integral part of society in America. Like other fraternal organizations, labor unions mutually support their members. This support can often come in the form of financial help in time of need, volunteer support when necessary for a family, or stepping up when there is a community need. Many unions have foundations that give to causes in their communities, and often have a formal process that a nonprofit can access for grants. Often special events are organized for the membership, in celebration, or recognition, or on almost any reasonable basis.

Depending on the union, you may or may not be required to be a member if you're simply helping with a special event. So check that out in advance. If you're an electrician (International Brotherhood of Electrical Workers, *ibew. org*) or an actor (SAG-AFTRA One Union, *sagaftra.org*), or if you work for a railroad (Brotherhood of Railroad Signalmen), or if you're on an NFL team (NFL Players Association, *nflpa. com*), go to the union's website and click on "get involved." Then find a way to get your volunteer boots on!

Political Organizations

If you choose political volunteering, be prepared for a relatively short-term, intense experience. Being a volunteer in the political process is not quite like any other kind of volunteering. Political volunteering is, by its nature, always cyclical. It depends on the schedule of the campaign and election date of a candidate running for office.

Volunteers in political campaigns tend to be more passionate and engaged over campaign issues. Political campaigns demand a lot of time from volunteers: to canvas neighborhoods (door knocking), call constituents, staff special events, help with direct mail, register voters, or help manage

Political Organizations

Major political parties in the United States (those that have separate state organizations), listed alphabetically:

◆ Constitution Party: *constitutionparty.com*

◆ Democratic Party: *democrats.org*

◆ Green Party: *gp.org*

◆ Libertarian Party: *lp.org*

◆ Republican Party: *gop.com*

There are nearly thirty other comparatively minor political parties that do not have separate state organizations. A word of caution: do not confuse elected congress representatives who declare as "independent" with the Independent American Party. They are not necessarily the same thing.

Example

satellite campaign offices. If you work on a political campaign, you should prepare yourself to encounter others who, just as passionately, do not agree with your views. On the other hand, you may very well get a chance to meet a candidate who ends up being the next president!

As former US house speaker Tip O'Neill said, "All politics is local." The best place to begin your political volunteering is right where you live. Each state, and almost all counties in each state, has a well-organized political-party-specific organization, including a party chair and party committee. You can look for a website for your party of choice or go to the national party website and connect to your local group from there.

While like business, fraternal, and social organizations you're expected to become a member of a political party for which you're volunteering, political parties do not have a required membership fee, although all political parties appreciate donations, to put it mildly.

To Summarize...

- Volunteer opportunities are not limited to charities that provide direct service to clients.

- Membership-based fraternal, business, labor union, and political organizations offer volunteer involvement implemented through the purpose or activities of the group.

- Professional development and social interaction are significant reasons for fraternal, business, labor union, and political volunteering.

- Fraternal and business organizations can be business focused, faith based, offer social affinity, of common interest, or be profession-specific.

Part 3

Your Choices: Ways to Volunteer

Now that you have a thirty-thousand-foot view of where you might investigate volunteer opportunities, it's time to look more closely at for the best fit for *you*. In this section we'll investigate specific types of charitable organizations and the how you might choose to be involved.

Chapter 10

Faith-Based Organizations

In This Chapter...

- Program activities
- Committee work
- Administrative support
- Governance

Faith-based activities make up a large portion of many lives. One-third of all volunteers in the United States today are volunteering for their faith home.

As we have discussed in earlier chapters, spiritual and religious groups offer the longest history of structured volunteer involvement. If you're already a volunteer, you very well may have had your first volunteer experiences within your house of worship, regardless of what that faith might be.

Within organized religions, there are many ways to get involved as a volunteer. There are multiple levels of involvement in most places of worship. There are faiths that are more-formally organized and less-formally organized. Be aware that not all faith-based volunteer options are necessarily connected to a specific congregation or organized meeting place, so keep your options open. Each congregation or religion has its own way of practicing its faith, so be flexible if you choose a place that is new to you. The unique culture of faith-based volunteering is that those involved typically consider all members or attendees as part of their family of faith, providing an extra level of emotional commitment.

Program Activities

Program and occasional activities are typically where you will begin your involvement with your place of worship. You may not be too interested in attending meetings or managing administrative tasks. You may want to do things like weekly ushering or hands-on service in your place of worship. This

---

WATCH OUT!

Program Activities with Sensitivity

In working with and around OPKs (Other People's Kids), you need to be aware that you cannot offer opinions or act in a way that can be misinterpreted by the kids. Parents are justifiably very protective of their offspring. Sometimes the kids may appear to go through a personality change once their parents drop them off. Choose to be amused instead of offended. If challenged, try to use distraction instead of the threat of punishment to manage less-than-perfect behaviors.

Your job is to keep them safe, sometimes from the world and sometimes from themselves. Do this verbally and kindly. Only. If more is required in extreme cases, after notifying the adult in charge of the activity, call the parents first.

In a faith-based setting, make sure that you refrain from trying to teach the youth your personal views of your religion or ethics or morality, unless the parents have given specific permission. Generally, teaching occurs with an approved curriculum. Stick to that curriculum.

Keep your sense of humor. Don't offer an opinion to another adult in the vicinity that you don't want published in the newspaper. I guarantee you will be overheard, and it won't go well when the kids get home.

may include singing in the choir or teaching religious education classes (adult or youth), as mentioned before. It could also include staffing community outreach programs such as a food bank or a second-hand store. Does your church provide meals for homeless or near homeless in your city? You could cook or serve or help clean up for those meals. Maybe the church youth have a weekly activities program or an annual mission trip. Offer to serve as an advisor or chaperone. Does your church, temple, meeting house, or synagogue host weddings or baptisms or bar-mitzvahs or bat-mitzvahs, or funerals/memorial services after which a reception is held in the community hall? You might offer to volunteer to help manage those events.

The scheduling for this area of volunteering can be challenging to manage. There can be a significant time demand. For instance, being in a choir requires weekly rehearsal time, singing at one or more services every week, and singing at unexpected services at the last minute (e.g., memorial services). If a youth advisor, your time may be spent in additional activities (trips, car washes, etc.) in addition to the weekly gatherings.

If you're interested in this kind of volunteer service, contact the appropriate committee chairs or the staff in the office. Either should be able to tell you how to get started.

Committee Work

As with any kind of organization, committees in places of worship really drive the implementation of the programs set by the governing board. The ones that jump to mind are the music committee and the religious education committees. In most places of worship these programs are integral and well developed. However, they will need to be updated each year, thus the work of the committees. If these interest you, ask the committee chair if you might become involved. (A list of the committees with chairs and contact information should be available in the church office.) Each of those committees might supervise special holidays or events in the life of the church, so you might want to make costumes for a pageant or teach a summer program to children! The committees recruit the volunteer teachers for the religious education needs, but you may want to participate in that in addition to the committee work.

Other kinds of committees may be seated to provide management of other programs of the church. Examples would be a committee to manage a food bank, or one to oversee the youth programs, or another one to supervise a second-hand store. If your place of worship provides a preschool or day care, that is a major undertaking for a committee, due to the state and local laws and regulations that must be followed for those. Experience or training as an educator may be an excellent qualifier!

Volunteer committee members often become the implementing (working) volunteers. If you are a music committee member, you may also end up singing in the choir or directing the elementary kids in their choral adventures.

Other kinds of committees may really be interest groups. Often these groups focus on studying faith-based literature or film. Some may sew quilts or make clothing for charitable causes. You may even want to create a committee or group yourself if you see a need or interest within your congregation.

The caution for working on a committee is that when you say you're going to show up, show up. The others on the committee are depending on you. Again, be prepared for congregation members to occasionally share their passionate opinions on how to you might do the job better, even though they may be unwilling to do the actual work themselves. Just smile and thank them for their input. Or, if they actually have shared a good idea, take their advice to heart.

Administrative Support

In many organizations, the administrative offices are staffed by volunteers. Phones need to be answered, mail needs to be processed, daily problems that crop up need to be resolved. All of that takes immediate time and attention. A full staff that is paid, with salary and benefits, can be expensive, and not all churches can afford those expenses. Some churches mix paid staff and volunteers for the administrative needs. Then there are periodic demands such as the writing, printing, and distribution of newsletters or doing the weekly service bulletin. What happens when visitors want to ask about holding a wedding?

This kind of volunteering may be a great fit for you if you want to schedule exact times and hours each week, and work in a setting (your place of worship) that feels familiar and comfortable for you. This kind of job experience can also be a terrific way of learning if you're a younger person to starting out and looking for a working career. You can gain job skills that can translate into a great livelihood.

If you have any skills on the computer, or on the phone, or with filing, or maybe managing a cleaning crew, go to your church's office, ask if they need help and with what, and offer your assistance.

In this setting it's important to understand, even if it's not spelled out for you, that anything that goes on in this office is confidential. What happens there stays there.

Governance

Most faiths of the world have an organizational structure of some kind. Additionally, most groups have a designated place for the congregation to gather.

Most spiritual groups have a physical property and a congregation which must be managed on a day-to-day basis. Many places of worship have a governing body made up of volunteer church members. It might be called the governing board, or session, or church council, or something similar. The governing entity will be responsible for not only ensuring the delivery of the religious services, but of managing the activities that take place outside of those services.

The volunteer governing board will generally have positions of officers and committee chairs. This board will be responsible for the implementation of the congregational mission through the hiring of the faith leader; raising sufficient funding to pay for the programs, salaries, and operating costs; establishment of program content; or approval of church involvement in community outreach and social welfare. Programs might include religious education of children and adults, a music program, a food bank, a second-hand store, meals for the homeless, a preschool, etc.

Generally, a governance board of this kind will have, in some form, a nominating committee. You, as the prospective volunteer, will need to let that committee know that you're interested in contributing your skills and talents. A phone call may be fine, or you may have to fill out an application form. Most religious entities will expect you to already be a member, or become a member.

These governing bodies generally require multiyear commitments, with obligations for monthly meetings as well as meetings with any committees to which you're assigned. These tasks can take a lot of time, so be prepared. If your church or synagogue is engaged in a major project such as building a new building, the time and work commitment may be even higher. If your assigned task includes visiting home-bound members of the congregation, add that time expectation to your calendar.

Officers of the governing board will be expected to spend even more time and, in some cases, have additional skills. For instance, the treasurer may need an accounting or bookkeeping background.

Please, remember that you will be expected to be at services. Also, church members will feel free to call you at home with any complaints or suggestions, and you will need to listen to them. It is just part of the job.

Be aware that when it comes to personal faith, people are passionate about their individual beliefs. In the context of a governing board meeting, this can translate into conflict when trying to come to a decision. Your faith leader will help with the resolution of an emotional or difficult situation, but be prepared to not be surprised when conflict happens, because it will happen.

As always, ask questions and become fully informed *before* you commit.

Governance in a Faith-Based Congregation

Some places of worship may have additional governing boards with targeted tasks. In the Presbyterian Church, the session is the primary governing board and the board of deacons is tasked with the spiritual and physical support of members of the congregation. Members of both boards must become ordained in order to serve, but ordination is only a one-time event for an individual. It lasts for life.

In a Jewish synagogue, the governing entity might be a board of directors or synagogue board, led by a rabbi. For Quakers, the boards may be called Elders (in charge of spiritual matters) or Overseers (in charge of temporal matters). The Moravian Church may have a provincial board, or a Baha'i Temple may have an executive board or resident assembly. Faiths may also have different roles for the pastor, or rabbi, or elder, or congregants in the internal governance processes. Some faiths are led by the congregation in lieu of a single leader.

Example

To Summarize...

- Faith-based organizations can offer a wide array of volunteer options.

- Faith-based volunteering will typically include an extra level of personal emotional involvement.

- Major areas of involvement within a place of worship include program or occasional activities, committee engagement, administrative support, and governance oversight.

- Volunteering for a spiritual or religious organization can offer training for paid career alternatives.

Chapter 11

School or Educational Organizations

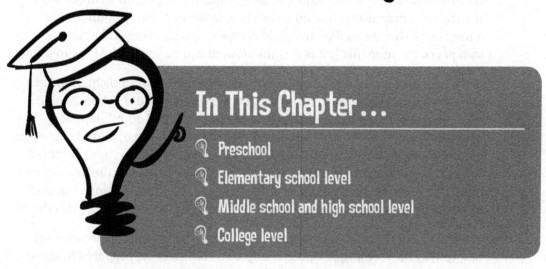

In This Chapter...

- Preschool
- Elementary school level
- Middle school and high school level
- College level

At all levels of precollege education, parental or adult volunteer involvement is encouraged in the strongest possible terms by school districts and teachers. In the eyes of teachers and school administrators, volunteers are viewed as indispensable in providing students with a higher degree of excellent learning during their school careers. Without volunteers, schools would have to limit some curriculums or activities due to budget and personnel constraints. So know that you're enriching these students' lives and making countless additional experiences available to them with your participation.

If you have, or have had, children or grandchildren, or if you just enjoy being with kids, schools can always use your help. Here we're going to look at volunteering with different age groups, since how you volunteer will change as the kids grow older. At every level, you are there to be a part of the child's life, and help ensure that each child is as happy and successful as possible.

Schools at every level, plus school districts, have websites that offer volunteering links. Most school districts have a district volunteer coordinator as well. Through those links you will be able to connect with not only individual schools, but also district-wide options. If you wish, feel free to simply call the schools or districts, too.

Preschool

There is a wide array of preschool or early-learning-level schools in our society. The students may attend one for a variety of reasons. The important reason to remember is that the earlier any child is exposed to learning and interaction with peers, the more likely it is that the student will be successful later in school.

If you haven't had the opportunity to spend much time around children ages one to five, you may need to be aware that the younger the children are, the more attention is needed from adults—and a lower child-to-adult ratio is necessary (more adults are necessary to manage the group of kids). Most states require ratios such as one adult for every four to nine children in a preschool setting, depending on the age of the children. When those requirements are in place, the school typically hires professional teachers. Your volunteer duties would have to work around state regulations and school operating procedures.

Preschool-age children are typically high energy but do not stay focused on one activity for very long. Consequently, as a volunteer, be prepared to move quickly from activity to activity to keep them engaged. You should be aware that your duties will likely include cleaning up each activity as you go. Put on your comfortable shoes.

Each preschool has its own criteria for engaging volunteers. Preschools may be public or private. They may be a nonprofit or a for-profit day-care situation. How you participate as a volunteer will be prescribed by the policies of the particular school setting. A Montessori school will likely have a lot of parent and other adult volunteer support, including a parent governing board much like a PTA. A for-profit day care may not offer the same opportunities.

If volunteering is allowed and encouraged in your child's particular situation, your volunteer duties will likely be limited to your child's classroom. If you do not have a child in the school, you will likely be assigned to one teacher and limited to specific activities such as reading at nap time or helping an individual student identify letters or numbers. As a parent, your preschool may or may not allow classroom parties to celebrate seasons or major events. If they are allowed, you could volunteer to supervise those parties with games and fun activities.

In asking to volunteer at a preschool, go to your child's teacher first. You may need to complete an application process, and some schools will do a background check prior to placing you with children. If you don't have a child in the school, make an appointment to meet with the principal or administrator. In both cases, find out what is and is not allowed, and what you will be able to manage with your interests and schedule.

Elementary School Level

Elementary school grade levels begin at prekindergarten or kindergarten and go through grade five or grade six, depending on the local school district structure. (Incidentally, in other parts of the world, these schools may be referred to as primary schools.) Elementary

Preschool and Kindergarten

Following two years at a Montessori preschool, my son attended an all-kindergarten public school. I was very active as a room parent. I did reading tutoring, class trip chaperoning, and field day activities. And I organized a lot of parties. Kids love parties.

Since it was basically up to me (his teacher was very flexible about allowing volunteers to be creative!) the class celebrated every single holiday during the year, from Columbus Day to Halloween, Thanksgiving, Christmas, Hanukkah, Kwanzaa, Presidents Day, St. Patrick's Day, Easter, Passover, May Day, and the End of School Picnic Day.

The End of the Year Picnic Day was the best. We grilled hot dogs and hamburgers outside, played games, and goofed off. The other classes were unhappy, as was the principal, because it made them hungry. But, it was the last day, after all, so we just smiled.

The teacher informed me she was passing my son to first grade, but was keeping *me* back to repeat the year.

Example

schools are normally smaller in size than middle schools (grades six through eight), junior high schools (grades seven through nine), or high schools. They tend to be tucked into residential neighborhoods in order to offer closer, less intimidating, access to the younger students. Conversely, larger middle and high schools may be located in a more commercial or business area.

Since elementary schools can be small, you may wonder what possible options they may offer a volunteer. The answer is—a lot. There are more than a hundred thousand elementary schools (public and private) operating in the United States today. That is a lot of schools with a lot of students.

Elementary schools always need volunteers for tasks such as tutoring or reading to the children, or help with chaperoning trips, or adding an extra set of hands in the school office. If your children or grandchildren attend the school, you can volunteer to be a room parent or a room grandparent. If you have no children, you can be an honorary room parent or grandparent. There are even foster grandparent programs that you can join through *nationalservice.gov*. You may be interested in establishing an informal before-and-after-school day-care program for parents who work. Possibly a coordinated shared ride system to get students to and from school is needed. Go to the school and ask what the needs are.

For some activities that you may want to do as a volunteer, your only limitation is your mind—and permission from the teacher.

Most elementary schools also offer volunteering through participation in the Parent Teacher Association (PTA) or Parent Teacher Organization (PTO). Both are organized with a governing board and committees that partner with the administrators and teachers of the schools to do things like raise money for special events or projects, or build new playgrounds. Schools, both public and private, are always in need of additional

Preschool, Kindergarten, Elementary School Levels

There may be restrictive requirements at any given school, and at any grade level. In many, any foodstuffs must be commercially prepackaged: they cannot be prepared in a home. Anything with nuts may be prohibited. There may be group birthday party celebrations by month or quarter, or birthday celebrations may not be allowed at all. Make sure you ask all the questions you need to understand the rules.

IMPORTANT!

funding to support cocurricular activities or special projects. So if you're looking at volunteer involvement at school, understand that at least some of your efforts will be directed to various fundraising activities.

Just as at the preschool level, start your quest for volunteering with a conversation with the teacher. Ask what is desired and see if any of the suggestions fit with your interest and schedule. Again, if you will be in direct contact with the students the individual school or school district may have an application procedure you will be required to complete. This varies quite a bit, so be sure to ask about it.

If you want to get involved with the PTA or PTO, by all means contact the current chair of the school's organization and ask how it is organized, when the meetings are, and what you can do to help. I guarantee they will be delighted to hear from you! The contact information is normally available in the school office.

Middle and High School Level

Volunteer participation at the middle and high school levels will change. At the middle and high school level, the position of a room parent or grandparent is an unlikely option. At the elementary level, students changed classrooms less frequently. In most middle and high schools, students are moving from classroom to classroom throughout the day based on the subject being taught. Students also are becoming more and more involved with cocurricular activities such as band, orchestra, choirs, theater, football, basketball, baseball, soccer, tennis, golf, dance, debate, Japanese club, and the list goes on and on. Also during this time, students are often involved with activities outside of school such as scouting or 4-H.

Schools at all levels still have volunteer clerical and phone answering needs in their administrative offices. The individual school PTAs or PTOs still need significant adult involvement and support on and with their boards and activities. Additionally, each separate cocurricular activity requires a lot of adult supervision, support, and oversight. You're going to be every bit as exhausted as your very engaged student.

If any of the performance, debate, or sports activities of the school include travel, chaperones are a must. Theater and show choir costumes must be made, sets need to be built. Marching bands need to move all of the instruments along with the students. And this is just the beginning. And again, you may be asked to help raise extra funding for these kinds of unfunded expenses.

While the school has its PTA/PTO board, each activity area can also have its own adult volunteer oversight board (athletics, performing arts, etc.). Each volunteer board will have committees, lists of what it needs from volunteers, and who to contact to get started.

There may be student special projects, many DIY. These might include collecting school supplies for children who are in need, or clothing for a nonprofit organization, or collecting blankets and teddy bears for children who are ill. While these projects are student driven, adult volunteer supervision is normally required. Again, contact the school office, the PTA/PTO board, or the student's homeroom teacher.

High School Level

I'm using my son as an example again. In high school he was involved in several extracurricular musical groups. His school had an adult board that supported the performing arts, called Patrons of the Performing Arts.

Annually, PPA held (and still holds) a show choir competition. This event had its own huge volunteer event committee. It took a year's planning and hundreds of volunteers to make it happen. My assigned area of the event was buying, preparing, and serving food to the attendees. During the years I participated, the volunteer team annually served over a thousand bodies in the two days of the event. You can see that some of these volunteer commitments can be substantial.

Example

The positive part of volunteering at the middle and high school level is that generally the only qualifying criteria for doing so is desire to do it and willingness to show up. Additionally, according to the National Education Association (*nea.org*), regardless of family income or background, students with involved parents are more likely to:

🔍 Earn higher grades and test scores, and enroll in higher-level programs

🔍 Be promoted, pass their classes, and earn credits

🖋 Attend school regularly

🖋 Have better social skills, show improved behavior, and adapt well to school

🖋 Graduate and go on to postsecondary education

College Level

Ah, college. Your student is becoming a self-sufficient adult. Are you looking at being an empty nester soon? At the college level your opportunities to volunteer are going to look very different.

As students go to college they are now in charge of their own lives. They make their decisions with significantly less input from you. They may be at a different address, likely living in a different state.

Your volunteer involvement, if any, with that college or university will likely stem from either you being an alumnus of the institution or you being invited to become involved in some way by your student. That is assuming you live in the same area where your student is attending college. It is also assuming that your student wants you involved. This may be your opportunity to take a step back and really focus on your individual volunteer interests going forward, rather than your child's.

However, if you think you would like some kind of collegiate involvement and/or if you're an alum of a college or university in your area, you may want to see how you can become involved there. Colleges and universities have boards of trustees, in addition to areas of special interest that offer volunteer options. A campus art gallery or theater or sports venue or dining room may involve volunteers. You may have been a member of a fraternity or sorority on campus. These organizations are often looking for volunteer support in their chapter housing, with events, or with fundraising. The website of the college or university will likely have a clear link to volunteering on their campus.

To Summarize...

- If a parent or grandparent, your direct involvement in your student's life through volunteering at their school will help ensure higher levels of life success.

- There are all types of volunteering that you can do in schools from direct student support to board service.

- Volunteering for early-learning through high school level educational institutions is deeply valued by schools; it makes a critical difference in the quality and quantity of excellent experiences for the students.

- Area colleges or universities often offer a higher level and often a wider range of volunteer options.

Chapter 12

Direct Programs for Nonprofit Organizations

In This Chapter...

- 💡 Human service
- 💡 Medical support
- 💡 Fine arts programs
- 💡 Long-term disaster relief

Volunteers often start their unpaid community involvement by becoming directly involved with programs, and clients, of their favorite charity. That might look like tutoring at a youth organization in an after-school program or acting as an aide for outings for seniors, or being a docent at a museum.

When most people initially think of volunteering, helping a real, live person in need comes to mind. You may visualize playing basketball at a YMCA with underprivileged kids. You may think of taking your elderly neighbor to the doctor. This means you will be in direct contact with people who need your help. This is the closest, most immediate, kind of volunteer work you can do. You will see the instant effect of your time and efforts. It will definitely touch your heart. Sometimes getting involved in this kind of volunteering is as easy as showing up. Sometimes it will mean advance planning and some pretty intense special training. Either way, you're investing a lot of your personal emotional being, so don't let it surprise you, positively or negatively, if you find it can be strenuous.

This chapter is organized into four major activity groups. I am not intending to include every single type of direct volunteer service available to you. I am listing only samples of activities and where you might go to sign up. Make this investigation your beginning. The doors will continue to open for you.

Human Service

After religion, human service needs receive the most attention from donors and volunteers. "Human service needs" means that life-safety or quality-of-life issues are primary concerns for the client. For an excellent list of human service nonprofit organizations in your area, your United Way (*unitedway.org*) is a good place to start. If you go to those sites, you will be able to find the correct partner organization closest to you.

Youth Services

Often we see in the news a report that shows a child or youth who has ended up in a bad situation. We see reports of neglect or abuse or abandonment. Traffic accidents can leave children orphans. If you live in an urban area, you may have experience with gangs. If you have volunteered in a school, you may have met a student who is not doing well because of a difficult home life. These young people are classified as youth at risk.

At a lesser-risk level, there are kids who may have less-than-adequate adult supervision after school, or who have a harder time than others managing school work. If you're willing to make the time for them, it could make a huge difference in their success as adults.

There are several youth-focused nonprofits just waiting for your help. Boys and Girls Clubs (*bgca.org*) provide after-school and summer activities, athletic leagues, and studying and mentoring support for youth. YMCAs (*ymca.net*) and YWCAs (*ywca.org*) have extensive athletic and activity programs for youth. Big Brothers Big Sisters (*bbbs.org*) pairs each volunteer with a youth needing some extra attention, mentoring, tutoring, or just plain friendship. Some BBBS groups even offer to pair volunteers with clients who may have cognitive challenges. The overall goal is to help the youth be as successful as possible.

Youth Program Direct Services

Look locally for great opportunities. For instance, in San Diego, the Eugene Bowman Economic Empowerment Center targets at-risk youths ages nine to seventeen by approaching the families holistically. Programming includes mentoring, tutoring, school-to-work transition services, entrepreneurship program, substance abuse prevention, violence prevention, after-school program, and victim services for women and children (*empoweringyouth.org*). Volunteers are critical to helping all of the kids who need help.

Example

BBBS, YWCA, BGCA, and YMCA will likely require references, an interview, and a background check. All of these places, and more, depend on volunteers to make their programs work.

In addition to the big name national groups, there may be youth residential or community facilities in your area that have kids who just need someone in their corner. Consider youth residential facilities, neighborhood centers with youth programs, or youth-focused after-school tutoring or athletic programs. Do an online search for youth programs in your city and see if there is a local nonprofit that will fit your needs.

Of course, not all youth are at risk. Many youth organizations offer enhanced learning and leadership training experiences. Some of these may be membership organizations, or educational organizations.

Examples of youth membership organizations are Boys Scouts of America (*bsa.org*) and Girl Scouts (*girlscouts.org*). These organizations depend on volunteers running nearly all of the programming. Both organizations require some training, an application, and background check. You are not required to have a youth in scouting to become involved. Both of these programs emphasize accomplishing leadership and work skills, camping, and community volunteerism by the individual scouts.

Elder Services

You may have heard the joke, "Who wants to be one hundred? Answer: Anyone who is ninety-nine." We are all going to get older. It is a simple function of the calendar. As the baby boomer generation is exploding the retirement-age population, the demand for services for older adults is increasing exponentially. Aging can bring with it increased medical, physical, emotional, and mental needs. Senior care is focused on helping our older population remain as independent and healthy as possible. Help for our older population can come in several forms, including food, transportation, mental health, safety, and secure affordable housing. In your area, it is likely there are one or more agencies that address these needs. It is also likely these agencies need volunteer support.

Most cities and counties have well-organized senior services programs. Look at the websites for your city or county. Use

Elder Services

One of the national programs that help seniors is Meals on Wheels (*mowaa.org*). It delivers meals to ill or frail elderly on a set schedule. One in six seniors in the United States is food insecure. Two and a half million seniors and half a million veterans receive home-delivered or congregate meals via Meals on Wheels programs. Volunteers deliver the meals—all of them. At the same time, a well-person check can be done to ensure the elder client is okay.

Example

keywords "senior services" or "aging services." If there is a senior-day-care center near you, maybe it needs volunteers to help with activities or events. Volunteers can provide tax preparation services, emergency services, home repair, or transportation. In Connecticut, for example, you can access aging services information at *ct.gov/agingservices*.

Also feel free to call or walk into an independent elder care residential facility in your area. Most will be delighted that you're willing to help with program activities, driving seniors to and from doctor appointments, taking residents shopping, or simply keeping them company.

To find the programs closest to you if you're a senior and want to volunteer, go to *usa.gov* and it will link you to volunteering after retirement, including Senior Service America (*seniorserviceamerica.org*). AARP, originally American Association of Retired Persons, is a wealth of information, including volunteer opportunities for older citizens (*aarp.org*). AARP also has a volunteer-access website for all ages of volunteers: *createthegood.org*. Another option as an older volunteer would be RSVP, Retired Senior Volunteer Program, which can be accessed through *nationalservice.gov*.

Shelters: Homeless and Abuse

The need for safe shelters is depressingly unfortunate as well as a firm reality in today's world. There are approximately 670,000 homeless people in the United States in any given year, due to poverty, joblessness, a lack of affordable housing, or need for safe emergency shelter. One of every thirty children are homeless, and around seventy thousand veterans are living on the streets at any given time.

Most towns and cities, or counties, of any size have a shelter of some kind. Some are for families, some for women and children, and some are for men only. Some may be limited to veterans and their families, or to youth only. Being emergency housing, they are twenty-four-hour programs; volunteers are critical to making sure the doors are open and services are available around the clock.

The National Coalition for the Homeless (*nationalhomeless.org*) gives you all of the current data regarding homeless and the connected issues of hunger and hate crimes against the homeless. Under the Volunteer tab is the quote, "Think globally and act locally." This is excellent advice. Check your local resources. Call your city or county governments and they can guide you to local shelters.

All of these organizations require some kind of application, training, and background check. Once you have finished specialized volunteer training in something like helping abused women and children, identifying and helping drug addicted clients, helping clients access other community services, there might be a higher expectation for your work. For instance, once I completed training in emergency counseling victims of domestic violence and sexual abuse, I became a mandatory reporter for child neglect, and abuse under the laws of my state. Make sure you understand what will be expected.

Homeless shelters often house, or are affiliated with, food banks. Foods are distributed through the food banks to homeless or in need, typically on a scheduled basis. Some shelters offer open kitchens serving meals daily. Food is donated by companies, restaurants, and individuals to both the food banks and the kitchens. Volunteers are needed to accept deliveries of foods as well as organizing and distributing foodstuffs at the food banks. Shelters (or other community sites) that offer free meals on a regular basis always need someone who can cook, serve, and clean up the dining area. Again, check with your local agencies or government to see where your help might be needed.

If you are volunteer staff at any kind of shelter, you will be very close to the everyday lives of the adults and children living there. Your kindness, understanding, and empathy will be important. Your tasks may include helping clients prepare for school, getting a job, finding affordable housing, or learning new skills as well as being a good listener. Your professionalism and ability to detach will be important in order to help them help themselves. It is a balance. You will no doubt become emotionally involved. Your feelings are important, and will be appreciated by the people you help. You will need to be careful of crossing the line of too much personal attachment. Make sure you understand yourself in relation to each situation. If you think that you will become so emotionally entangled that you're unable to be effective with the job assigned to you, you may want to consider an alternative role. On the other hand, it is inexpressibly satisfying to see a client get that job, or watch kids smile again, or see a family move out to a new home, and know that in some part you helped with that success.

Medical Support

If you have been ill or had a medical crisis and required hospitalization, I am guessing you did not ask the medical personnel helping you at the time if they were a volunteer. Chances are that at least one or two of the people you encountered in the hospital were volunteers. You might be surprised how many actually are giving their time in roles like these. Hospital or clinic volunteer programs offer great choices. In addition to hospitals and clinics, there are many other interesting medical volunteer possibilities.

Hospitals and Clinics

Volunteering in hospitals has progressed well beyond only delivering flowers or meals or mail, although all of those jobs are still important. Virtually all hospitals have well-developed volunteer programs in place. In a typical hospital, you can volunteer as young as fourteen years old, although at that age some duties will be restricted.

To volunteer in a hospital, you will need to verify that you are healthy. Regardless of age, and because you will be around ill patients, you will likely be required to complete an application and interview, prove you have been inoculated against measles, mumps, and rubella (MMR), do a two-part TB (tuberculosis) inoculation, and have a background check. Hospitals take the health and security of their patients very seriously.

You will also probably be required to sign a confidentiality agreement, again for the protection of the patients. Under the HIPAA (Health Insurance Portability and Accountability Act) laws, the confidentiality requirement is absolute. You will never be allowed to discuss any details of what you see or do if a patient is involved.

Hospitals will train you in their volunteer procedures. Your volunteer training will depend on what department or area in which you choose to serve. Most hospitals offer many areas. But no matter where you're assigned, as you work your volunteer shift, you will learn to love washing and disinfecting your hands constantly. Contact the volunteer coordinator in a hospital near you and find out what opportunities it has available.

Most medium and large size hospitals offer a well-developed volunteer program with multiple areas of interest. Mercy Medical Center in Cedar Rapids, Iowa offers volunteer options in all of the following areas (including knitting or crocheting at home for new babies or cancer patients). It is an amazing list of choices and experiences:

Admissions, Cancer Center, Cardiac/Pulmonary Rehabilitation, Dialysis, EAP Family Services, Emergency Department, Endoscopy, Flower Delivery, Gift Shop, Nursing Care Facility, Hospice, Human Resources, Information Desk, Intensive Care, Diabetes Center, Cardiovascular Center, Mail, Medical Library, Organizational Development, Pastoral Care, Physical Therapy, Pianists, Print Shop, Radiation, Substance Abuse Treatment Center, Surgery, Volunteer Services, Wheelchair Maintenance/Dispatch, and Women's Center. *MercyCare.org*

Smaller community medical clinics are another alternative. A clinic may be a satellite of a particular hospital or it may be an independent facility. It may be located in or near a hospital or by itself in a neighborhood or small town. Many of independent clinics are free or take patients on a sliding fee scale, so donated labor is both necessary and appreciated in delivering services. Volunteer work in a free community clinic can come in many forms, including doctors and nurses, administration and pharmacy support, or even maintenance. Again, you would have to complete an application, be up to date on the same inoculations, sign a confidentiality agreement, and possibly pass a background check. And like a hospital, medical personnel, volunteer or not, must abide by clear medical performance standards.

Example

Clinics

Community Health Free Clinic (CHFC) in Cedar Rapids, Iowa, is an example of an independent medical clinic that delivers all medical, dental, and vision services, plus other specialty clinics, free of charge. It also offers a prescription assistance program. This clinic has a fundraising program to pay for hard costs (cash and in-kind contributions) as well as some staff. However, since it never charges for services, volunteer doctors, nurses, administrators, pharmacists, ophthalmologists, and dentists are an absolute requirement to ensure delivery of services.

CHFC has over forty thousand unduplicated patient charts, with around eleven thousand patients active at a given time. The staff consists of approximately fourteen full time equivalent positions. The volunteer component is extraordinary. The clinic has approximately five hundred to six hundred active volunteers working each month. In this clinic, the position of volunteer coordinator is critical, and the volunteers are the reason the doors stay open. The recruitment and training program for these volunteers is comprehensive and effective. The retention rate of volunteers is better than 90 percent.

Specialty Training Options

There are several kinds of medically based volunteering that may interest you. Becoming a volunteer in special medical situations may take quite a bit of training and education to become certified, so if this is your area of interest, be prepared.

Earlier we talked about volunteer fire departments. Much of the country continues to depend on volunteer firefighters and the emergency medical technicians who are part of the departments. Being a volunteer firefighter, EMT, or paramedic takes significant initial training as well as continuing education, the same as a paid position would. Starting out as a volunteer for these kinds of jobs may be even be an avenue to a new profession. You may even want to volunteer for seasonally fighting wildfires with forestry services. The time demands can be high, so make sure that you can successfully blend your work and volunteer schedules. EMT volunteers may be able to work for an ambulance service or for special events such as concerts and festivals.

If you love to hike or climb mountains or sail in the ocean, or if you're already a pilot, you may want to train and volunteer for search and rescue teams (*nasar.org*). If you have a dog that would fit into this kind of situation, even better!

A more sedentary activity may be staffing a crisis hotline. Do you have a suicide or sexual assault crisis facility that provides immediate help via telephone to people who need someone to talk to? Again, this will take training, but you can make a huge difference to someone who feels like they have nowhere else to turn.

Emergency medical and crisis mitigation teams are often called upon to jump in after a damaging storm or other disaster. You can become a volunteer trained in crisis management including providing citizen safety, first aid, food, shelter, clothing, transportation, and counseling. If you volunteer at the site of a catastrophe, you could very well be providing support to both the victims and the other crisis personnel.

For any of these choices, contact your city or county emergency management agencies or human service nonprofits to get involved. Do this in advance so you can complete any training required. Then you will be ready to go when the need arises. To find links to an emergency management organization in your area, go to the Federal Emergency Management Agency at *fema.gov*.

Fine Arts Programs

When it comes to fine arts organizations, I have heard supporters of theaters, music, visual arts, performance arts, and museums refer to the arts as the "poor redheaded stepchild" of the nonprofit world. That may be true when it comes to receiving a high level of cash contributions. However, the fine arts area is a gold mine for volunteer involvement, and it is a lot of fun!

Performance Theaters

Both community theaters and professional theaters that offer all kinds of performances need lots of volunteers. If you like meeting people you may want to usher at play or musical or concert. Usually ushers are "paid" by being allowed to see the performance at no charge. If you have a community theater, audition for a play, or volunteer to build sets or sew costumes. Community theater volunteer involvement has highs and lows in terms of hours of commitment. The closer the opening night, the more hours you can expect to devote. Once the run is over, you may have no time scheduled until the next event.

Theaters have websites that post volunteer needs as well as audition schedules in advance. If you like to act or sing and dance, take a chance! If you are terrific with a staple gun and hammer, show up to build those flats! You should contact the theater person designated to manage volunteers. The email and phone is generally on the website as well. Also most theaters have a sales booth with logo products of the current show. As a volunteer sales person, you get to see most of the audience! You might need to learn how to use a cash register.

Museums and Galleries

Art museums, sculpture galleries, historic sites, or iconic churches may be of interest to you. Tourists flock to these kinds of sites daily, from The Alamo to Metropolitan Museum of Art, from the Smithsonian Institution (nineteen museums) to the National Railroad Museum in Green Bay, Wisconsin. All of them engage volunteer docents to guide visitors through the exhibits and properties, sharing the details of the history and the artifacts. Volunteers also staff the stores and the ticket sales stations.

Generally, there is an application process and a background check if you will be handling money. The exciting part for a volunteer is being able to learn so much about the exhibits and being able to share it with lots of people. If you like meeting new people, this may be a perfect fit for you.

Community Events

I am highlighting community events a little bit because I think they sometimes get overlooked as a volunteer option. Most cities and towns have some kind of celebratory days or events that are celebrated annually. It may be a holiday parade, or a Fourth of July picnic. or a summer music and food event. Most of these kinds of events take a large number of volunteers to make everything happen.

Community Events

If you live in the Chicago area, an example is the Taste of Chicago, considered Chicago's premiere outdoor food event. It is a massive event requiring hundreds of volunteers. The City of Chicago is the sponsor, and the website is *cityofchicago.org*. It is as simple as clicking on the volunteer link. While you are there, you can also investigate volunteering in other ways for the City of Chicago.

Example

Some events are sponsored by a city council, some are sponsored by a nonprofit or business, but, either way, the entire community is invited and engaged. You very likely know what they are in your town. If you know someone who has been involved with an event in the past, start your questions there. If not, go on the Chamber of Commerce or area economic-development websites.

Long-Term Disaster Relief

We have already discussed volunteering to help manage a natural disaster such as a flood, or tornado, hurricane. The immediate needs, of course, are safe interim housing, clothing, food, and transportation for victims. But what happens after the first week, or month?

If a lot of rebuilding is necessary, such as after Hurricane Katrina in New Orleans, it will take a lot of time and many, many hands.

Following larger natural disasters like the floods of 2008 in the upper Midwest, Hurricane Katrina, and Hurricane Sandy in New Jersey, teams of volunteers have traveled to the areas to help rebuild housing and infrastructure as well as clean up debris. These teams, or individuals, can be formed by churches, or human service nonprofit organizations, or a service club, or just about any entity that thinks it can bring volunteers together to help. You can even establish your own volunteer group from your neighborhood.

These volunteer groups generally commit for a matter of a few weeks or a month or two. Housing and food is generally provided to the volunteer workers, along with the supplies necessary to do the work. Sometimes the hosting organization will bring supplies as well as the volunteers.

This kind of work is very hands-on. It is tremendously satisfying because you can see what you have built. It can be challenging because you may discover muscles you never knew you had, and you may be afraid you will never be clean again.

Again, any of the nonprofits or groups mentioned above will have information on these kinds of volunteer choices. Other options to find places that welcome your help include *volunteermatch.org, relief.org,* or *volunteer.org.*

We have covered a lot in this chapter, and hopefully given you a lot to think about.

To Summarize...

- There are countless ways to volunteer working directly with clients of organizations.

- Places to get involved may include religious institutions, schools, fine arts programs, hospitals and clinics, and human service agencies.

- Be prepared to become trained in your chosen volunteer specialty.

- Some opportunities may include direct-service programs, medical support, fine arts and special event involvement, and community crisis management.

Chapter 13

Organizational Governance

In This Chapter...

- Board-level commitment
- Responsibilities of a board director
- Different kinds of boards to consider
- Fiduciary obligations as a board director

In this chapter we will take in-depth look at volunteer governance of nonprofit organizations, specifically through serving on a board.

If you're particularly interested in being involved with a nonprofit, but you have limited time or limited interest in direct service with clients on a weekly basis, you may want to look into governance opportunities—in other words, volunteering to serve on the board for your favorite charity. Your reasons may include adding to your résumé, representing your company in the greater community, or wanting to be more closely connected to others serving on a particular board. Or maybe you're just passionate about personally making sure the organization is successful. All of these are valid reasons to look at board service.

Nonprofit boards can vary quite a bit in size and function, as well as in the skill sets of the directors. There are legal obligations and risks in serving on boards, and you should have a true passion for the mission of the organization if you are serving at that level.

Board-Level Commitment

Serving on a board requires from you a higher level of commitment to the mission. Boards are responsible for the overall operation, strategic planning, financial health, and compliance of the charity. Board service takes time. It takes becoming well informed on all applicable issues. It means dealing with corporate problems. It means approving, then financially supporting, the programs of the organization. Board directors are usually long-term supporters, highly visible community leaders, and professionals with skills necessary on the board. A board is at the top of the nonprofit organization pyramid. The buck stops with the board. On some boards, the work can be at a level that you find yourself having a second, unpaid, job. It can be very rewarding to serve on a board. Be prepared to be amazed at what you will learn.

But before you begin, make sure you understand what you're taking on. Let's explore your responsibilities as a board member.

Responsibilities of a Board Director

If you have served on a board in the past, you may be aware that sometimes new board directors do not have a clear idea of their personal obligations or of the expectations of the charity. When thinking about serving on a board, talk with the staff and a board director or two in advance. Before you say *yes*, make sure you understand the details of the job.

There is a higher level of responsibilities that come with being a board director. The job of the board is oversight and governance of the nonprofit. It is not the job of the board to manage the day-to-day tasks of the organization. The CEO or executive director (they are the same thing) will manage the daily operations. Stay focused on the big picture and long-term planning.

Typically, you will find that the work you do as a board director falls into two basic formats. Most of the duties of a director are accomplished in a team or group environment. Some tasks are done as individuals.

As a team, the board manages the development of the mission statement, the case for support, and the core values through a strategic planning process. The board's long-range or strategic plan will include tasks, timelines, measurable objectives, and targeted outcomes to help guide the work of the organization. The board makes sure that the organization is in compliance with its legal duties and that each director completes and signs a conflict-of-interest policy on an annual basis. The board sets fiscal and organizational policies and monitors required compliance. The board approves the overall annual programming as presented by staff, and approves the annual budget. If the charity has an endowment or investment fund, the management of that falls to the board as well.

The team also assures the financial viability of the organization by establishing a fund development plan and fundraising initiatives, in addition to approving earned revenue programs. It hires and annually evaluates the executive director/CEO. The successful board also does an annual self-evaluation to make sure they are accomplishing their goals.

Duties you might complete as an individual include making fundraising calls, being a leader on the board, talking about your charity to friends and businesses in your community, or working as occasional unpaid staff. I should caution you to make sure that when you volunteer as staff, you should take off your board hat and answer to the head of staff just as a paid employee would. Always, it is your personal responsibility to attend meetings, after having read all materials in advance. Keep informed of all matters pertaining to the organization and board activities to make the best decisions.

The areas that a board does not generally manage include daily processes of programming or direct supervision of staff, hiring, termination, and evaluation of staff other than the executive director/ CEO, implementation of board policies and decisions in daily operations as well as statistical, donor, and program record keeping.

Having given you these lists, you should probably understand that there are some organizations that may, of necessity, find these lines sometimes a little flexible. But that happens customarily in start-up, grassroots nonprofits, or the occasional organization that is heavily staffed by volunteers.

Responsibilities of a Board Director

There exists a huge amount of information in the nonprofit world about board service and governance for volunteer directors. You can actually overwhelm yourself with information and advice on how to effectively serve on a nonprofit board. A few excellent resources that offer more in-depth information are:

🔍 BoardSource—*boardsource.org*

"BoardSource is dedicated to advancing the public good by building exceptional nonprofit boards and inspiring board service." BoardSource provides education (print and webinar), resource materials, training, and conferences.

🔍 Association of Fundraising Professionals—*afpnet.org*

AFP offers publications, training (live and webinar), mentoring resources. It is not necessary to be a professional to access the information.

Inspiration

Nonprofit Board Services for the GENIUS

My colleagues Susan Schaefer and Bob Wittig have written *Nonprofit Board Service for the GENIUS* just for those seeking to serve on nonprofit boards. The authors move sequentially through the stages of nomination, early candidacy, and more advanced topics. It's a fun, informative read that candidly highlights a board member's ups and downs, and I highly recommend it if you're considering volunteering to join a nonprofit board.

forthegenius.com

Different Kinds of Boards to Consider

There is an amazing array of different kinds of nonprofits in our world. Each has its own personality, culture, and ways of doing business that may be different from other organizations. At the same time, be sure that all of the boards you're considering use best practices in how they function as a governing body. What kind of a board are you considering?

Classic Board

What I am referring to as a classic board is the typical board that fulfills the duties as listed above. That would include monthly or bimonthly meetings, serving on board committees, participating in board planning sessions, aiding in fundraising initiatives, and representing the organization in the community. Generally, these board directors may have limited interaction with clients served by the organization, but more-detailed involvement with the monthly financial, legal, or policy matters. Boards can vary in size from three to thirty or more directors. I have been involved with one board that had sixty-one directors. The smallest I have served on numbered four directors.

The smaller the board, the more difficult it is to seat effective committees, assuring that the work falls to all of the directors all of the time. The larger boards can have the converse situation of sometimes not effectively engaging all of the directors in the business of the nonprofit because the number of directors is too high. On very large boards, directors can sometimes feel like they are lost in the sheer volume of people in the room. It is important that you investigate how the board is constructed. Is the size right for you? If you want to limit your hours to just the monthly meeting, look at a larger board. If you want to be more deeply involved, choose a smaller board. Either way, make sure you intend to be as active in supporting the organization as your life allows.

When you're being actively recruited, get a written list of expectations, a copy of the articles of incorporation and bylaws, an organizational chart, and a summary of the programs of the charity. Be informed before you say yes, because once you do, the charity will be depending on you to deliver. As a side note, as a director you will be expected to make financial gifts to support the charity. Some boards require a set annual amount, whereas some simply ask that you give a gift at a level high enough that you really care how the money is used.

Foundation Board or Board of Trustees

Here, names can get confusing, as they are sometimes used interchangeably. For some charities, a board of trustees and a board of directors are the same thing. In this case, the duties of the board would be the same: setting policy, financial oversight, approving programming and supervision of the executive director (the classic board). For other organizations, a board of directors and board of trustees have separate functions. In the latter case, the board of

WATCH OUT!

There Should Be a Bright Line Between Board and Staff Functions

It is often true that, due to limited financial resources, the directors of charities double as unpaid staff for the organization. Office support, special event management, direct client services, or transportation are among services that a board director might provide.

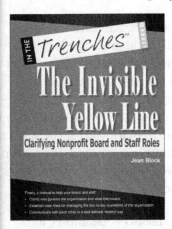

If you choose to become involved with this kind of "hands-on" board, be aware that you must adjust your thinking depending on what you are doing. In the board room, you're a director and you supervise the executive director, including hiring and terminating. If you are providing daily operating labor, you are working for the head of staff, and you have to remember to think as a (free) employee. As a volunteer employee, the executive director supervises you. This is the kind of situation where blurring of the line between these two roles can happen.

My colleague Jean Block wrote a book that you will find both entertaining and enlightening: *The Invisible Yellow Line: Clarifying Nonprofit Board and Staff Roles.* If you've watched a football game on TV, you'll be familiar with the yellow line that's visible to viewers but invisible to the players on the field. Using the "invisible yellow line" metaphor, Block guides you through clarifying roles in governance, management, finance, planning, human resources, resource development, and recruitment. *charitychannel.com* directors will fill the classic board duties and a board of trustees is typically tasked with a specialized role. Generally, this specialized role will be major fundraising or management of a directly held investment or endowment account. If an organization has both a board of directors and a board of trustees, both boards actively support the one charity.

Additionally, in many communities, there is a community foundation. A community foundation will have a volunteer board as well, normally populated by philanthropic and community leaders. A community foundation is a nonprofit entity, but it fulfills its duties a little differently than a single charity. The foundation will be looking at the needs of all of the nonprofits in its area, not just one. And it will be both raising funding from the community and distributing charitable funding to nonprofits.

Private foundations work in much the same way, except that they typically have one source of funding (a family, a corporation, etc.). Funds are commonly distributed to several nonprofits from each private foundation. Private foundations may have restrictions on who is eligible to serve on its board (family, employees, etc.).

Grassroots Board

There are approximately 1.5 million registered nonprofits today. Of all of those, 75 percent have expenses of $500,000 or less. This indicates that there are many start-up or grassroots charities. Typically, the boards for these smaller charities have smaller numbers of directors, and often board directors get involved in the daily operation of the organization due to limited staff and limited funding.

Fiduciary Obligations as a Board Director

Serving as a board director carries enhanced expectations of moral, ethical, and legal standards of behavior. These are typically referred to as fiduciary duties.

Historically, I have found that some people may interpret this in a flexible way. *Be careful of that.* You're charged with acting in a reasonable and prudent manner, and for the benefit of the organization. There are very clear definitions of fiduciary duty in most state laws. You may want to become familiar with the standards.

Many states have laws protecting board members from liability to third parties who sue the organization. These laws are designed to encourage citizens to serve on nonprofit boards. Even so, you might find yourself having to hire an attorney to defend yourself even if you didn't do anything wrong—at considerable expense, not to mention stress. For that reason, I strongly encourage you to avoid serving on any board that does not have a directors and officers liability policy in place.

A word of caution: State laws protecting board members from third-party liability as well as directors and officers liability insurance typically do not protect you from liability to the organization if *you* breach *your* fiduciary duties. Make sure that any board you are thinking of joining has adequate on-boarding training, including training on your duties. If it doesn't provide this training make sure you understand your specific duties some other way, such as by consulting with a local attorney competent in the law of tax-exempt organizations.

In the United States, board-member fiduciary duties are established at the state level, and can vary from state to state. I suggest that you check with your state's secretary of state's website for a description of your fiduciary duties. In **Chapter 26** we discuss volunteer fiduciary duties, as well.

Go on, Give It a Try!

Whether your choice in board service is a grassroots board, a classic nonprofit governance board, or a foundation or trustee board to oversee investments and endowment, make a determined commitment. Serve with interest, passion, and enthusiasm. Be open to being educated about issues the board has to face. Be accountable for your actions and a willing team player. You will find lifelong friends that you might not have otherwise met, you will have fun, you will learn a lot, and you will make a difference in your world.

To Summarize...

🔍 Serving on a board of directors requires a higher level of commitment and legal performance.

🔍 The responsibilities of a board director include organizational oversight and direction, programming approval, and financial health.

🔍 Choices of boards of directors include classic boards, foundation boards, boards of trustees, and grassroots boards.

🔍 All board directors are legally bound by the ethical and fiduciary duty of care, duty of loyalty, and duty of obedience.

Chapter 14

Special Events

Special events can be big and exciting. Or they can be smaller and intimate. Events can also take a lot of labor hours, so any amount of time you can give to one will certainly be appreciated. Additionally, special events offer a fun social life and an opportunity to meet people and get involved in activities that you might not otherwise consider.

In the business world, special event management is a significant profession. Here we are only going to explore volunteer participation in the world of charitable special events. The choices in variety and size of events can be overwhelming, so let's investigate and try to find the right fit for you. Once you do a few different events you may find that you have discovered a new career as an event manager!

There are many reasons a charity may host an event. An event will bring in new donors, may raise funding, may honor participants, and will publicize the work and value of the organization. Events can encourage board participation, build supporter contact lists, and bring together diverse groups of people. By attending, participants support the mission and goals of the organization.

There are also many reasons volunteers choose to be part of an event. Events tend to be social, you will meet a lot of people and maybe work with someone you want to know better, you will gain skills, and you may even get to meet a rock star who is playing the event. Whatever your personal motivation for wanting to get involved with a special event, you're benefiting both the nonprofit and yourself.

All events can take a significant amount of time to plan, execute, and clean up. The good part is that events have a clear beginning and end of the process, so you, as a volunteer, can plan your life accordingly. With most special events, you should also probably be prepared to get physically active to some extent.

Events can be initiated on a national level, regional level, or local level. If an event is new and fairly complex with a lot of sponsorships, plan on taking the better part of a year for the event committee to plan and execute the event. A repeat event or a smaller event will take less time.

Finding an Event Setting

Take a few minutes to stop and look around you and think about all of the special events you have attended right where you live. They come in all shapes and sizes and themes. Some have a national focus and some are much more localized. Some are quite mission focused, some are pure entertainment. The majority of them require volunteer support for success. In other words, you're surrounded by volunteer opportunities.

A committee for a successful, existing annual event (national, regional, or local) is generally formed and meeting eight to eleven months prior to the event date. For a new event, a committee may be formed twelve to eighteen months, or more, in advance. It depends on the scope of the event and the financial sponsorship level required for support of the event.

Nationally Sponsored Events

Nationally sponsored events are those that take place on the same date, in the same way, across the country. Consistency is the standard. The setting of these events is, however, local, and implemented by local volunteers.

Some of the funds raised by these events go to the local chapter area; some go to the national organization. All of the events require volunteers to plan, recruit other volunteers, publicize, and staff the event. If you're interested in a particular national charity and you don't have a personal connection with anyone who is involved, simply go online to find the local chapter or simply phone the chapter nearest you. You can look at who the charity serves, or what kind of event is available. Do whatever appeals to you. You can ring a bell for a red kettle, or recruit a team of walkers, or help the students at your child's school collect funds.

Some nationally sponsored events may be more than one day, with multiple smaller special events involved. An example is October Breast Cancer Awareness Month sponsored by American Cancer Society (*cancer.org*). This themed month may offer many smaller engagement events in your local area during the thirty days. A few other one-day event examples are National Wear Red Day for the American Heart Association (*heart.org*) or the National Day of Giving (*givingtuesday.org*), which encourages everyone to spend one day giving back.

Regional or Local Events

In your community there're likely nonprofits, churches, municipal, or regional governmental entities or other affinity groups or organizations that hold events. These events may or may not be solely charitable fundraising events. These events are more geared to local or regional areas, and are not nationally focused.

Local Event

A fun and colorful special event in Las Vegas is the annual Las Vegas Great Santa Run. In early December each year, approximately ten thousand participants put on Santa costumes (provided with paid registration) and run to benefit Opportunity Village, which serves people with disabilities. To maximize participation, participants are also encouraged to do two additional connected-but-smaller events, the Blitzen's Bar Crawl and the Slotzilla (a zip line ride on Fremont Street). It is huge fun, attracts thousands of participants and a big audience, and brings in significant financial support for the organization's programs. Hundreds of volunteers are needed to make these events run. *opportunityvillage.org*

Example

More Unique, Smaller Events

Smaller, sometimes unique, special events are more present in your life than you may realize. They also generally take less time and fewer volunteers to arrange. You may help with serving weekly dinners at your church to those struggling in your community. Planning, cooking, serving, and cleaning up constitute a small special event. Have you helped with the year-end banquet for a sports team? Prepared food? Called for volunteer help? That is a special event. Has your favorite charity asked you to hold a cocktail party or a dinner or a luncheon in your home for folks who have given a donation, or who are being asked for a donation? Again, this is a small special event.

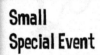

Small Special Event

One of my favorite creative ideas is a local bank staff that collected purses women no longer wanted or needed, held a wine-and-cheese-tasting special event to sell them, and gave the proceeds to a free health center. That was a fun, small, very successful, special event.

Pure Genius!

Where could you look to see what is available in your area?

- School bulletins or newsletters
- Local newspaper
- Friends
- Place of worship
- Chamber of Commerce
- Convention and Visitors Bureau
- Grocery store community board
- Local television newscasts
- Website search with community name and "event volunteer"

Choosing an Event Type

Take time to decide what kind of event appeals to you. There are large festival-type events, gala-type events, dinners, fairs, carnivals, telethons, fishing competitions, concerts, walks or runs, golf—the list is endless. How involved do you want to be? Are you more physical or cerebral? When you decide what you want to do, go for it.

If you can imagine an event, it can probably be planned and implemented. Some you could be thinking about are large-venue events (concerts, trade-shows, food festivals, etc.) that are profit-focused, or a mix of profit and nonprofit benefit. Generally, those have primarily paid staff, aided with a mix of volunteers. Here we are focusing on ideas used by nonprofit organizations to enhance community visibility and organizational mission, serve their clients, bring in new volunteers, and hopefully make money. Here we're going to take a short look at different kinds of nonprofit events. This list is not meant to be exhaustive, simply suggestive.

Annual National Trademark Events

Many national charities hold annual events. As we discussed before, they are implemented locally. Typically, volunteers are invited to participate on the event committee, with a chair or honorary chair who will attract attention and attendance. These larger national organizations often supply a step-by-step manual for the implementation of the event. Certainly there can often be local enhancements, but the organization generally requires consistency in timeline, marketing, branding, registration systems, printed materials, record keeping, volunteer training and staffing, as well as logo items and event day operations.

Since there are 1.5 million charities in the United States today, it is just not possible to list them all here. Examples of a few national organizations staging high-visibility annual trademark events locally or regionally include Special Olympics (*specialolympics.org*), March of Dimes (*marchforbabies.org* or *marchofdimes.org*), American Cancer Society (*cancer.org*), American Heart Association (*heart.org*), National Kidney Foundation (*kidney.org*), Boy Scouts (*bsa.org*), Girl Scouts (*girlscouts.org*), Big Brothers Big Sisters (*bbbs.org*), Boys & Girls Club (*bgc.org*), Variety

Choosing an Event

For some kinds of events, you may be faced with an opportunity to travel to work the event. Make sure you understand if the charity is going to cover any travel expenses for you, or if you're expected to pay for transportation, housing, and food. If you are going to be reimbursed, get the agreement in writing in advance.

WATCH OUT!

the Children's Charity (*usvariety.org*), UNICEF (*unicefusa.org*), and Junior Achievement (*juniorachievement.org*).

Large-Scale Regional or Local Events

Large local or regional special events in your area may be festivals, parades, or unique specialty events. With some exceptions, these kinds of events would not be typically connected to a national charity. Generally, these events take a large organizing committee and numerous volunteers. Using the methods of finding these events discussed above, ask the organization to join the planning, then working, of the event.

An example of a large scale event is the New Orleans Jazz & Heritage Festival and Foundation, Inc. Multiple music festivals and concerts are held during the year, all of which require volunteer support. The festivals include Jazz Fest, blues, R&B, Cajun & zydeco, Latin music, African drumming and dance, or down-home jazz. The Jazz Fest alone is a large-scale regional event, plus the other concerts, festivals, lectures, literary events, and gallery exhibits add to the volunteer choices. *jazzandheritage.org*

Smaller-Scale Events

These smaller events are not the ones that get TV or news coverage. They might be school related, church related, neighborhood related, or cohort-group related.

In schools, there are always occasions like sports events, musical or theater special events, field days, banquets, student trips, competitions, or festivals, plus more. These always need volunteers, both student and adult. Connect with the PTA or PTO, the principal's office, or faculty specific to the area in which you want to volunteer. The school may have a form and process you will have to complete.

Churches often have both regular and periodic events that wouldn't happen if it weren't for willing volunteers. Festivals for religious holidays, community meals, and wedding planning services may be some of the opportunities for event volunteering in your place of worship. Call your pastoral staff and see what is available.

Do you belong to a neighborhood association or neighborhood watch? In one place where I used to live, several square blocks of neighbors gathered for a picnic every summer. A dead-end street was closed to traffic, and there was food, music, and friendly fun. Volunteers put this together every year. It resulted in a strong sense of community and great relationships with neighbors.

Do you belong to a Rotary Club or Optimist Club or Lions or a professional cohort group that meets regularly? Does your group hold special events for socialization or to raise funds for nonprofits or education? This might be a terrific way to get to know the other club members and make a difference

WATCH OUT!

Choosing an Event

If you're ever intending to begin a new special event, remember that all special events have a limited useful life from year to year. It doesn't matter if it is a national event or a neighborhood event. It has a beginning and grows, but eventually it declines in attendance and financial proceeds, not to mention the number of volunteers willing to support it. Also, during the first year or two, as the event is becoming known, it probably won't make as much money as you would like. Have realistic expectations about the time limit of effectiveness. Visualize it as a curve that goes up, then comes down.

Before you initiate an event as a volunteer, be very clear about your expectations. Are you looking for fast funding? Are you providing a great time for clients? Are you trying to increase public awareness of the organization?

For every event, do a return-on-investment (ROI) analysis after each event is over, including all of the staff and volunteer hours at a definite dollar value. When all the costs are counted, did the event make money? With that assessment in mind, does a low financial return matter if more volunteers joined and community awareness was increased, or if the clients you serve had a wonderful experience? Only you and the organization can make those determinations.

Be honest. Do the assessment every time the event happens. Over the long term the trend should be clear. You will know. It will be really difficult, but when the event stops being successful in fulfilling expectations, change or stop the event and move on to something that works better for you and the organization.

at the same time. Ask someone on the governing board of the group for information. You can find out more about volunteering for different types of organizations by looking it up in other chapters of this book.

The Process in the Life of an Event

Even if you're *only* a volunteer, when it comes to events, plan the work and work the plan. Start in plenty of time, put the plan in writing, and develop a timeline. Then keep to the timeline. Here, I am going to give you an example of a new outdoor special event, with tasks you may have to complete. Every event looks a little different, but you'll get the idea.

Task	Start Date	Responsible	Expected Cost	Completed
Set event date	18 months in advance			
Set chair and committee	18 months			
Set site	17 months			
Permits and licenses	17 months			
Logo/artwork	17 months			
Sponsorships	14–11 months			
Media support	11–10 months			
Food	12–10 months			
Entertainment	12 months			
Guest list	8–6 months			
Printed materials	8–6 months			
Save-the-date card	4 months			
Mail invitation	6–8 weeks			
Logistics (traffic, parking, bathrooms, water, lights, security, tents, electricity/gas power, etc.	6–4 months			
Volunteer shifts	4 months			
Volunteer staffing	3 months			
RSVP returns	20 days			

Task	Start Date	Responsible	Expected Cost	Completed
Publicity	All forms from 3 months on			
Event	Event date			
Follow up committee meetings, ROI	1 month			

This plan format is assuming you are volunteering on the event committee. Make this kind of plan of work, or one similar to it, for your event. Make sure all tasks are assigned to someone to complete. You will be amazed at how much more manageable an event can be if everyone understands what is going to happen, when it's going to happen, and who is going to do it. It also helps build a more accurate budget. It's fair to warn you, if you don't already know this: there are always crises as events unfold. Some you may be able to anticipate, some not. Stay calm, use common sense, and focus on safety. It will generally work out.

What Is the Right Fit for You?

You know your interests and capabilities. If you love to be outdoors, you may want to look at more sports or athletic events. If you have students in school or who participate in community teams or other doings, you may want to focus on those activities. If you like more elegant, social events you may want to connect with wine tasting events or galas of some sort. You may make your decision based on your commitment to the charity, or based on the fun of the activity, or on friends and soon-to-be friends who are already involved. You may like bowling or fishing or golf. You also know your schedule and energy level.

Involvement in events may even lead you to a career. You can obtain a certificate of event management from various educational options, and become a professional in the events industry.

When getting involved in special events, take your time and look at several options. Understand how much time and effort you have to commit to the process. The challenging part is that special events can be very time demanding and physically exhausting while they are in process. However, there is an end date. It doesn't last forever, and the sheer entertainment you can enjoy, the skills you will learn, the people you will get to meet and work with, and the benefit to so many involved in the event makes the whole experience amazingly satisfying and rewarding. Most of all, have fun!

To Summarize...

- Special events can be amazingly varied and exciting.

- Special events benefit both the nonprofit and the individual volunteer.

- Events take planning and require significant volunteer hours for execution.

- Consider your personal situation and time availability, then choose an option—national, regional, and local—and get involved.

Chapter 15

Government and Politics

In This Chapter...

- Municipal or county participation
- State involvement
- Federal volunteering
- Political activism

Becoming a volunteer for your city, your county, or your state is somewhat different than approaching a charity. Your purpose as a volunteer will be focused on a specific governance topic rather than a charitable mission. Even more different is volunteering for your preferred political party or advocating for a public issue that is important to you.

Towns, cities, counties, and states welcome citizen involvement. Have you ever attended a city council meeting? Maybe there is a street you want paved, or maybe you would like a stop sign installed to control traffic flow at the nearby grade school. You go to the city to ask, right? But who are you supposed to ask? Do you have a county board of some kind? Or do you wish you could have some effect on how business is done in your county but you have neither the drive nor the money to run for office? What about your state government? At the state level, are you baffled about how decisions are made, or are you concerned about how business is done in a given department? Would you like to get better informed and more deeply involved with state-wide issues? Then getting involved in local, regional, or state government may be an option for you.

Municipal or County Participation

You might be surprised, or even shocked, at the number of boards and commissions your town or city government needs to staff with volunteers. You can go to the municipal website and find the link for volunteers, or "apply for boards and commissions," or whichever link looks like it has the information. Generally, in this situation, you will be asked to submit an application or interest form, add a résumé of some sort, and often a cover letter explaining why you would like to serve on this board or commission. If you don't want to look online, the typical place to find this information at your municipal building is the city clerk's office. I live in Las Vegas, and currently there are more

Pure Genius!

Municipal Involvement

While living in eastern Iowa, I was privileged to be able to serve several years on two municipal volunteer boards. The first was called the Grants and Programs Committee. This committee was charged with distribution of Community Development Block Grant funding and HOME Investments Partnership Program funding through a competitive grant process. It was a tremendous opportunity to learn in-depth the operations of the numerous area nonprofit organizations that applied for these funds. This funding is Department of Housing and Urban Development allocations that are distributed and administrated on a local level for affordable housing and similar needs in the community.

Additionally, I served as an airport commissioner for the Eastern Iowa Airport Commission. The duties of this commission are operational oversight of the airport, airport improvements, and oversight of compliance with aviation standards in addition to economic development through accessibility and use of the airport.

You can see how varied the options can be. Both of these positions were mayoral appointments, and very rewarding.

than thirty such boards and commissions. They vary from the Arts Commission to the Historic Preservation Commission to the Senior Citizens Advisory Board to the Traffic and Parking Commission. Generally, you must be a resident of the city or town to be eligible to serve. The city council typically reviews and approves placement of volunteers on these boards and commissions when a vacancy occurs. The appointments may be filled on a regular schedule, or they may be filled only occasionally.

Boards and commissions customarily have authority to make interim decisions or recommendations, but the final decisions are made by the governing body (city council or mayor, county commission or commissioners, state legislature or governor). If you serve on any of these boards or commissions, your term is generally at least a year, sometimes much longer. You can also expect to be reappointed unless you wish to resign. Be prepared to spend time doing in-depth learning about the workings of the boards, the applicable law, and how to do your job the most effective way. It will help if, once appointed, you can find a mentor or advisor already on the board or commission who can fill you in more quickly.

Most cities have a volunteer link on the city website. Download an application for the position you are applying for. Fill it out, add any additional information that is requested such as a résumé and a cover letter, and submit it. If the website says how long the process will take, wait that long. If you haven't received a response, call and ask. Your active interest will go a long way.

Counties have a lot of the same issues and boards as cities, with the addition of rural issues that a city might not have. According to the National Association of Counties (*naco.org*) there are 3,069 county governments in the United States today. The system of county government dates back to 1634 when the first county government was established in Virginia. Just like cities and towns, counties are generally governed by an elected board, commission, or council. You may have boards of county supervisors in your state. County boards do substantially the same work as a city council, simply on a county-wide basis.

The method to find information on volunteer boards, commissions, or committees for the counties is also much the same as for a city. Go online and look for citizen participation links, and you will find many ways to get involved. Again, you will likely be asked to complete an application, and maybe submit a résumé and a letter as well. The county board will review applications when a vacancy happens, and make a decision. Be patient. I have known of individuals who have applied repeatedly and waited a few years to be appointed because there were no vacancies on the boards for which they were applying. In the meantime, go to the county board or commission meetings. Get to know the county board members. Volunteer for short-term tasks for the county through individual departments. County commissioners or board members, like anyone else, tend to choose people they personally know and trust over someone they don't know. Let them get to know you.

In county government you can get involved in everything from agricultural zoning to weed abatement to public health to highway construction. It is a banquet of choices.

Not All Counties Are the Same

Counties are an important presence when it comes to engaging volunteers, but not all counties are exactly alike. In Louisiana, "counties" are called parishes. In Alaska, counties are called boroughs. United States territories (Puerto Rico, Guam, Northern Marianas, American Samoa, and American Virgin Islands) do not have counties. In a few states, counties do not have governing boards, so make sure to do your research. Each county in the country has its own unique system.

Observation

State Involvement

Applying for volunteer involvement at the state level can be a little bit more challenging. As you go up level to level (city to county to state), the varieties of volunteer involvement increase, and likely some volunteer jobs will require at least some travel, particularly if you don't live in the state's capital. The application process is also more competitive at the state level. Prior experience on city or county boards or commissions will be an advantage. Skill sets specific to the position you are applying for will be a plus.

There are more boards and commissions available at the state level. There are boards that focus on professions that require state licensing (dentists, opticians, cosmetologists, court reporters, massage therapists, attorneys, etc.). There are advisory boards for specialty interests (libraries, common-interest communities), cultural affairs, examining entities, taxing, transportation, veterans' affairs, education, agriculture, and the list goes on and on. Again, go to the state website and search for volunteer options. State volunteer websites are usually very informative.

Keep an open mind. Once you look over the list of state boards, you may find something you haven't considered. You will certainly have to complete an application. You may need a résumé or other specialized background information, and possibly letters of recommendation. These positions may be easier to secure if you have specific set of skills that is needed, or if your local, county, or state legislator recommends you. But even if you don't know a legislator, or if you don't have a huge list of background experience, apply anyway. You bring your own unique talents to the table. It is also good to be aware that sometimes volunteering at this level can lead to expanding opportunities for a new, paid, career for you.

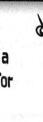

In Nevada, There Is Even a Commission for Volunteers

Nevada even has a commission dedicated to volunteerism: Nevada Volunteers. It serves as the state commission for state and community service. It is charged with administering AmeriCorps state programming and is dedicated to enhancing volunteer and service involvement. So in Nevada you can volunteer to serve on a board for recruiting and placing volunteers.

nevadavolunteers.org

Example

Federal Volunteering

At the federal level, you may want to work as a general volunteer for a federal agency or you may want that important position on the board or commission that oversees the agency. At the entry level, volunteers for federal agencies should expect to go through an application and interview process much like a regular job. Nationally, there are countless choices to become involved at the federal level. The place to start is *volunteer.gov* or *usa.gov*. You search for positions by state, agency, city, or your interests. This option is for general volunteering as well as a road to find positions on various federal boards or commissions. One example is serving as a volunteer board member for the Selective Service System. You are appointed on a federal level, but serve regionally or locally. Another example of either general or board involvement is NOAA or the National Oceanic and Atmospheric Administration. Again, you would be appointed federally, but may serve either on the oversight board or as a hands-on volunteer through NOAA's fishery service, ocean service, weather service, or sea grant program (*noaa.gov*). And remember, Peace Corps volunteers are approved on a federal level.

Example

Volunteering at a Federal Level

The experience of a student with a federal internship:

While a student at Luther College in Decorah, Iowa, I studied the fall semester of 1996 in Washington, DC via the Luther Institute. Luther Institute staff assisted me with my written White House internship application based on my expressed interest.

Approximately five weeks before I arrived in Washington, I learned of my placement in the Bill Clinton White House gift unit, which is responsible for the logging and tracking of all gifts to the First Family and senior White House staff in accordance with congressional statute. I worked full time September to December and took classes in the evenings.

Financing such an experience at first seemed daunting. I found the Luther Institute had an annual Daniel Frank Ruble Memorial Scholarship for which I applied and received. That scholarship was the difference between me eating ramen noodles all semester and buying real groceries in Washington.

What an honor for a student to experience the executive branch first hand and see via the gifts the esteem with which people hold the Presidency! The experience allowed me to live a small bit of history and develop early full time working skills.

Researching scholarship and other funding options is time well spent. Go create your own adventure based on your own passions—it's worth it!

Dawn Svenson Holland

Through the *volunteer.gov* or *usa.gov* websites, look for the link to the agency or board that interests you the most. Download its application and decide if you're prepared to work through the process. The White House (*whitehouse.gov*) as well as senators and representatives offer volunteer internships in their offices. Search the websites for the legislator of your choice. Go ahead and take a chance.

However, at the top federal level, applying for a position on a federal board or commission is an entirely different process. You would be required to have significant background in the board commission's area (such as the Federal Trade Commission, the Federal Election Commission, or the Securities and Exchange Commission), as well as an in-depth personal investigation

IMPORTANT!

Five Steps to a Presidential Appointment

1. Have a history of working full time (paid or volunteer) on the presidential election campaign. Also, having a history in volunteering on the local, regional, and state level helps.

2. Donate to the presidential election campaign at a significant level, or bring in donations from others.

3. Use your personal connections, particularly those you have cultivated in your prior volunteer involvement, and particularly if they are elected officials. According to Chris Matthews (*msnbc.com*), "It's not who you know, it's who you get to know."

4. Have outstanding credentials as an expert in your field that will benefit the appointed position.

5. Apply for the specific position you want, and continue to volunteer in the meantime. Make sure you're clear and specific about the position you applying for. Don't be subtle. If you don't ask for what you want, you won't get it.

Items 1 and 2 open the doors. If you haven't done them, apply anyway. A history of volunteering plus items 3, 4, and 5 are the most important. *govloop.com*

Good luck.

into your life. At the highest level, these positions must have congressional approval. Some are direct appointments by the President of the United States. Generally, you would need to be nominated by your United States senator or representative, an expert in the field, or by a high-ranking military individual. Presidential appointments, whether volunteer or paid, are very hard to attain. There are an estimated three thousand applicants for every position filled.

If you are appointed to a federal board or commission, you will likely have to travel to Washington, DC or wherever the agency is headquartered, so be prepared for that time and expense commitment. You will learn those details during the application process so that you can make a fully informed decision.

Political Volunteering

In this book, we are mostly talking about volunteering for nonprofit charities. However, I think we need to give a quick overview of political volunteerism. It is a big focus for the United States. Political campaigns are not charities, but they do accept donations and cannot survive without volunteer support.

Political volunteering becomes a top-of-the-mind awareness item every four years during national presidential elections. In addition to these national contests, there are periodic local and state elections that attract large numbers of committed and passionate volunteers. By volunteering for a political campaign, you are truly exercising your right and passion for civic involvement. It is a unique, time-limited way to volunteer.

Getting started in volunteering for political candidates or causes is simple. Contact the local office of the political party in which you are interested. It will be delighted to have your help. The staff provides training and assigns you to phone calling, door knocking, driving the candidate, social media management, or any of countless other jobs. Campaigns often recruit volunteers from a state with a high level of volunteer engagement to work in another state that might have a lower population and therefore fewer volunteers.

When involved in politics, remember that volunteering might be more emotionally charged than the typical nonprofit volunteer involvement. People can get quite passionate when talking about their candidate or

Political Volunteering

For the 2008 presidential election, busloads of volunteers were driven from California to Nevada to help with the GOTV (Get Out The Vote) process. They stayed in Nevada several months. The most impressive part of how effective the volunteers in Nevada were was on Election Day. Each voter identified as supporting this candidate had a door tag on their door by 6 a.m. Then at 9 a.m. the volunteers went back around to each door to knock and remind the voter to get out and vote. By 1 p.m., all voters had been called, offering transportation to the voting place. If the computers did not indicate the voter had voted by 5 p.m., they were called again with the offer of transportation. Volunteers called all day, and some drove all day to get voters to the polls by the poll closing time. It took hundreds of volunteers in my precinct, thousands in the state, to make what was a record turnout happen.

The campaign did help with the cost of housing and food in this situation, but did not pay the volunteers. In this kind of out-of-town initiative, you, as the volunteer, can stay the length of time your schedule allows. I have seen volunteers from Michigan travel to South Carolina to volunteer during an election year, and stay up to six months.

Starting as a political party volunteer on the local level can lead to deeper involvement, and possible paid staff positions, with the party at the state, regional, or national level.

advocating their candidate's positions. If you are working for a campaign, the hours can be intense and long, but they are finished when the votes are counted. Ethics and energy are very important in political volunteering.

Governmentally based volunteering is an important and sometimes somewhat hidden option. When you investigate your city's boards or your county's commissions, make sure you gather as much information as possible. Be sure you both want to get involved and that you are willing to fulfill the obligation for which you are applying. You may want to talk to someone currently involved, or a past board member. They can give you some insight that is likely not found in research. If it is important to you, do it. As a side benefit, it will also look great on your résumé.

To Summarize...

- Volunteering for municipal or county boards or commissions is focused on governance issues rather than charitable missions.

- State volunteer involvement may require a higher level of qualifications and may take longer for approval.

- Volunteer positions at the federal level are more competitive. Federal volunteer involvement can include roles as a general volunteer, as an intern, or as a board or commission director.

- Political volunteering is cyclic and partisan, and demands a significant commitment of time.

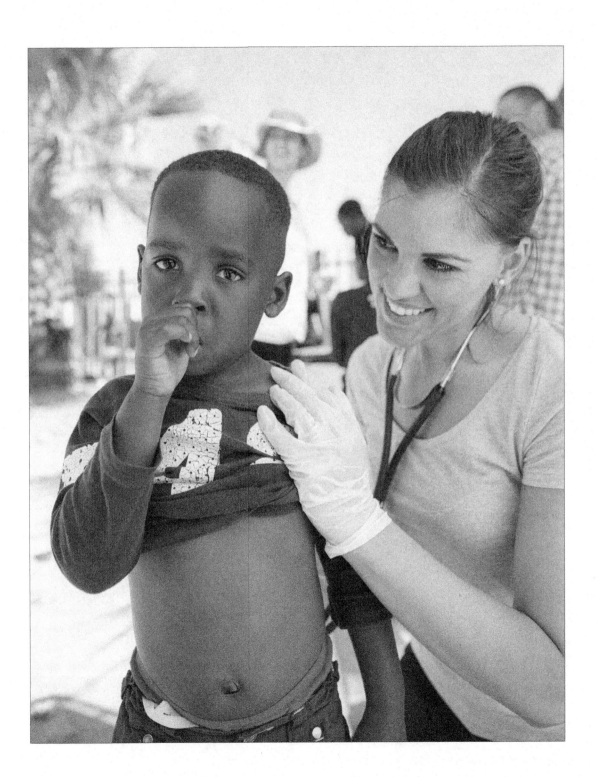

Part 4

Volunteering Abroad

There is a whole world waiting to be discovered! Volunteering abroad is a firm commitment in advance preparation, time, money, and finishing the job. Additionally, you have to take into consideration issues such as safety, health, documentation, travel, and possibly specialized training. Being informed and organized in advance ensures the best-possible experience. You will certainly have an extraordinary, once-in-a-lifetime adventure.

Chapter 16

Identifying the Right Opportunity

In This Chapter...

- Where do you want to go?
- What do you want to do?
- What do you need to know?
- How will you manage cost and length of stay?

It is a big decision to volunteer abroad. You will need to make sure you are choosing the right option and are fully informed and prepared before you go. Have you thought about where you might like to travel? What kind of job you might like to do?

You know what your personal strengths, skills, and challenges are. In considering the option of traveling beyond the border to volunteer, collect enough information to make the right choice for you. Be nosy and demand to know all of the details involved—good or potentially bad.

This is the time to do in-depth research. You will find that traveling abroad to volunteer takes time, money, dedication, and dependability. You want to thoroughly consider your personal needs, physical limitations, goals for your involvement, and budget. Before you commit, make sure that you're willing and able to complete your commitment to the program.

Where Do You Want to Go?

The biggest decision, of course, is deciding where to go. Let's get started!

Country

It is thrilling to think about getting on an airplane or a boat and journeying to a country with a totally different culture and language. However, if you haven't gone further in your thinking than you want to go to some as-yet unidentified country, get out a world map. Start with a list of countries that appeal to you (remember, successful people make lists). Do you have any language skills that you want to improve? Would you like to learn a new language? Do you mind long travel times or is being closer to your home country important? Do your preferences include cities, rural, hot climate, colder climate, desert, or oceans? Is there a particular country that either you have always wanted to see, or that offers a project for which you would like to work?

Now that you have your preliminary list, you will need to find out how manageable travel is to those countries, and if they

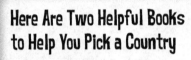

Here Are Two Helpful Books to Help You Pick a Country

Have you considered Europe? To help you pick a country in Europe, I recommend *European Travel for the GENIUS.* The authors give you a country-by-country description that is priceless in making your selection.

If you not only want to save money but discover how to tour a country away from the "touristy" areas, I recommend *Budget Travel for the GENIUS.*

forthegenius.com

Inspiration

might offer the volunteer programs you're looking for. To ensure as safe a destination as possible, check the website *travel.state.gov*. Learn to love this resource. You will find a lot of information there you will need as you get into this process. At this State Department site, you can find out if there are any government travel cautions, travel warnings, or travel alerts telling you to be careful of, or to completely avoid, travel in certain countries. The do-not-travel or cautionary warning alerts listed may reduce your list of preferred destination nations.

The State Department website *travel.state.gov* also gives you details about obtaining passports, visas, locating embassies and consulates, how to be a safe and successful traveler, inoculations, and a host of other information. We will be discussing much of this in more detail in later chapters.

WATCH OUT!

All About Travel Warnings for Countries

Governments issue warnings to let their citizens know about safety concerns that may affect travel to a particular country or region. In the United States, warnings are issued by the State Department.

Travel advisories are released for a variety of reasons, including terrorism, natural disasters, political unrest, wars, health emergencies, and outbreaks of crime. Warnings may also cover areas of the world where a government does not have the ability to respond to the problems of citizens traveling there—for example, if the government doesn't have an embassy in a particular country, or if the functioning of its embassy is threatened by local violence.

Many governments make a distinction between long- and short-term travel advisories. The US Department of State issues travel warnings for ongoing problems such as civil wars and unstable governments, while travel alerts cover temporary issues such as natural disasters or election-related demonstrations.

A travel advisory—no matter how strongly worded—cannot legally stop you from traveling to a particular place. After reading an advisory, it is up to you to decide whether to heed or ignore the advice. While your government will try to help you if you run into trouble abroad, you will always be traveling at your own risk.

Get Opinions

Go online. Talk to your friends, or friends of friends. Take a look at social media. Definitely delve into reviews and critiques of various programs as you go through this process. Each organization has testimonials posted online or on request by mail. Ask if you can have permission to speak with one or two past volunteers to get a more-detailed understanding of all of the written and unwritten adventures that might happen. Most are cooperative but prefer to take your contact information and give it to the past volunteer to have them contact you. In talking to people, it helps to have a list of questions in front of you so you don't forget to ask everything you want to ask. Write down their answers so you can compare and evaluate.

Do not skip the vetting process once you choose an option. Make sure your choice is a highly rated, positively reviewed program. You don't want to end up three thousand miles away stranded because the program is a scam. The website *ethicalvolutneering.org* can give you some insight into what questions to ask and what to look for when doing your research.

What Do You Want to Do?

By now, do you have a clearer idea of what kind of position you prefer? There are countless organizations and options just waiting to be discovered by you! There are some website resources that are a compiled list of, and link to, many other volunteer programs. Or you can do an online search with terms including "volunteer overseas," "volunteer abroad," or "volunteer vacations." While doing your research, be sure to look at all of the details of each program so you can make an accurate comparison.

Following are illustrations of different kinds of volunteer options in other

What Do You Want to Do?

There are several websites that offer volunteers one application that can be distributed to numerous volunteer program options at the same time. One example is *GoAbroad.com*. This site is a clearing house that will connect you with choices for volunteering abroad, interning abroad, teaching abroad, and studying abroad. It also offers TEFL (Teaching English as a Foreign Language) employment abroad. This site will directly connect you with specific organizations that can provide the experience you prefer.

Perspiration

countries. This is not meant to be comprehensive list, but simply a sample of what is available to you. Let your imagination fly! You can access information through a website that offers multiple links to different international volunteer organizations, or you can to go each individual organization's website. Of course, all of this information is available by surface mail, but it takes a very long time.

Direct Aid (Disaster Relief and Medical)

People are most aware of direct aid and disaster relief organizations, particularly right after a catastrophic event. Many of these relief organizations have high public visibility.

Natural disasters also seem to attract the highest number of volunteers because of the immediacy and the breadth of loss after it happens. Typically, volunteering overseas in a disaster area is available to you whether or not you have training in emergency skills, such as advanced first aid or CPR. However, these skills do help. Disaster volunteers fill the needs of victims in the form of temporary housing, transportation, food (prepared and supplies), media management, clothing, EMTs, first aid, and finding scattered family members as well as whatever else might be needed during a disaster recovery operation.

The best place to start is a local disaster relief organization chapter (if one is near) which will have the process to apply. Examples of direct disaster relief organizations include the American Red Cross (*redcross.org*) and Project

Direct Aid (Disaster Relief and Medical)

This is a sample list of international disaster relief organizations that use volunteer support- take the time and do the research:

◆ Child Fund International
childfund.org

◆ Catholic Relief Services: *crs.org*

◆ International Rescue Committee: *theirc.org*

◆ Lutheran World Federation: lutheranworld.org

◆ Oxfam International: *oxfam.org*

◆ Relief International: *ri.org*

◆ Save the Children: *savethechildren.org*

A list of more international disaster relief programs can be found at *appleseeds.org*.

Perspiration

Hope (*projecthope.org*). You can also go to the International Committee of the Red Cross (*icrc.org*) and ask to volunteer in an international project.

Another high-visibility international relief organization is Doctors without Borders (Médecins Sans Frontières). It does both disaster relief and long-term medical crisis projects. Much of the staff is paid, but there are also options for volunteers. The focus is the delivery of emergency medical care in areas of war, poverty, or wherever there is need. Currently, Doctors without Borders (*doctorswithoutborders.org*) has teams in more than sixty countries. Even if you're not medically trained, there are needs in the areas of logistics, transportation, food service, and child care. This application process may take a little longer and be a little more complicated. Make sure you're fully informed about all of the options.

Select-a-Program Organizations

"Select a program" is my name for organizations that either link you to many other named charities that offer international volunteer programs, or organizations that directly manage volunteer programs in several countries. Both are great places to look for choices because the information is all in the same place. Both of these resource options offer general volunteering, under-eighteen programs, internships, groups, and skilled volunteer opportunities.

The most famous volunteer abroad organization in the United States may be the Peace Corps (*peacecorps.gov*). It operates a little differently than many of the volunteer abroad programs, as participants receive a stipend and must commit to a longer term. Like the other organizations we have discussed, Peace Corps programs are offered in approximately sixty countries. The Peace Corps is, however, a government platform, not private. You will need to apply nine months to a year before you expect to serve, and you must be at least eighteen years old to apply. The Peace Corps time commitment is a full two years, unlike some other alternatives where you can pick the length of your time in-country. Within the Peace Corps, you can select the country or project that most appeals to you.

You may prefer to focus on volunteering in the arts, child care, the environment, or wildlife surveying. Pick a country, pick an interest area, and pick the specific kind of job you're looking for. Next, pick the amount of time you want to spend and the dates you want to participate, then sit back, read the websites, and find the best fit for you.

An example organization that offers multiple links and immediate application access is GoAbroad (*goabroad.com*). This site offers programs but will also connect you with International Volunteer Headquarters (*volunteer.org*) or GVI (*gvi.org*) for more alternatives. With GoAbroad, you would initially apply through the website but be matched with and coached through the final application process by the actual volunteer program you have chosen that fits your criteria. You may have to do a second, more-detailed application to the specific nonprofit for which you will be volunteering. If you find the cost of the program is an issue, GoAbroad can also make suggestions on how to find funding for your trip.

GVI USA (*gvi.org*) is an organization that puts you directly into a program you have chosen. The choices are done in the same way as mentioned above, but GVI partners with the in-country nonprofit and helps directly supervise your experience. Just as with GoAbroad, you can choose subjects such as marine conservation, sports, children, or working with elephants in Thailand.

Most of these programs offer individual, group, vacation, professional, as well as family volunteering. You pick both the time frame and the length of stay tailored to suit your life (except the Peace Corps). These are only a few of the possibilities that are there for you to explore—there are more. However, be careful to ensure the organization you choose is highly reputable and dependable.

Student Specific

Student age-specific programs can be either study exchange (with or without a volunteer component) programs or solely volunteer-focused programs.

Student-Specific Volunteering

Global Volunteers (*globalvolunteers.org*) offers student targeted programs (as well as adult individual and family) and intensive support and training, including language skills. Programs are located in Africa, Asia, the Caribbean, Europe, North America, South America, or the South Pacific.

GapYear.com (*gapyear.com*) specifically targets students who want to take a year off to volunteer. This website is a select-a-program website that will link you to your target interest area or country.

Example

Most of the above programs have student study options. If you're looking for course credit, look at targeted student-exchange programs through your high school or college or access several study programs through the International Student Exchange Programs (*isep.org*). Opportunities that offer study credit are typically focused on volunteer choices for students or student-age participants.

Virtually all of the programs mentioned above have student or student-age volunteer abroad options. Some have comprehensive gap-year opportunities specifically developed for college-age students. Many of the volunteer vacation options will work for students or students with their families.

Skill Requirements—What Do You Need to Know?

Next thing to think about is what skills you might need as a volunteer abroad. Once you determine the country and pick a program for which you're going to apply, you will understand what the charity will be expecting from you. You will have a good idea of the skills you will need to help them. You will also be able to identify any new skills you might need to learn for the job.

The charity or the destination program should let you know any unique proficiency needed by their participants. Some programs may prefer that participants have some advance expertise such as CPR training. Some have no prerequisites at all, and will fully train you in what you need to know. Some

A Banquet of Choices

Cross Cultural Solutions is one organization that offers multiple volunteer programs in Cartago, Costa Rica. Some of the options are the Aging with Dignity Project, the Child Development Project, and the Education and Literacy Project. None of these programs require specialized skills in volunteers. *crossculturalsolutions.org*

United Planet offers medical volunteer opportunities for trained doctors, nurses, dentists, dental students, nutritionists, and therapists, as well as nonprofessionals who are interested in medicine. Definitely, medical skills and education are required to fill these volunteer positions. Countries offered include Ghana, Ecuador, Romania, Peru, Tanzania, and Nepal. *unitedplanet.org*

Example

programs are focused on volunteer students or young adults, some offer family participation, and some are looking for more mature, experienced volunteers, singly or in couples. If the volunteer is older, the program or charity may be looking for a particular professional background such as engineers, medical professionals, teachers, urban developers, business entrepreneurs, farmers, or mechanical specialists.

Keep in mind your goals, expectations, and any skill sets you possess or you might need. You will be using this information when you complete your applications.

How Will You Manage Cost and Length of Stay?

Know in advance that volunteering abroad will cost money. How much depends on the program, if you're going alone or with others, and whether or not financial aid is possible. As you gather your information, you will find costs for each of the choices you're considering. Find out if the costs include travel. You may have to pay for travel all the way to the destination, or possibly to a US city where you will gather with other volunteers prior to being transported to the country. You can choose how much you are comfortable spending overall when you're viewing the websites. Most of these expenses will be required to be paid in advance.

When you are calculating the out-of-pocket costs, be sure to include the costs of your passport, appropriate clothes, any specialized equipment you might need, inoculations, and gifts you may want to take for people you will be meeting. Also, you will need cash for souvenirs and food along the way. Some programs offer limited financial support, so be sure to ask about that.

Don't get defeated when you're looking at the costs. There are several ways to fund your trip that will not include destroying your life savings. Your program officer can help you with this, but you can also apply for scholarships, do a crowdfunding campaign, hold fundraisers, and ask friends as well as friend's parents. There are also many volunteer opportunities that are free, so definitely look for those. The very rare volunteer opportunity may even pay a stipend under certain circumstances.

When deciding how long you wish to be abroad, take into consideration your job restrictions, travel time, and most essentially, recovery time after you return. Once you choose a country and project, find out if participation is on a preset schedule (you will have to meet calendar dates) or a rolling schedule (you can show up pretty much any time, with notice).

You may have to negotiate a little with your employer or school for your vacation dates. Build in the time to get there and get back home. Understand that simply because you have a schedule it does not mean that your method of transportation or weather will comply. Most importantly, give yourself at least three days on your return to get over jet lag, food readjustment, and laundry demands.

To Summarize...

- Start with a list of preferred countries, program topics, and jobs you're looking for.

- Do in-depth research through websites, reviews, and prior participants.

- Select a program and complete the application and budget, and carefully schedule the time you will be away.

- Be prepared for the cost of the program, or develop funding initiatives to pay for it.

Chapter 17

Requirements and Applications

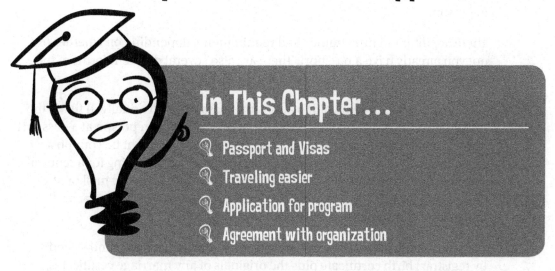

In This Chapter...

- Passport and Visas
- Traveling easier
- Application for program
- Agreement with organization

You have chosen your country, your travel time, and your program. This is the time for the details. Both the United States and the organization for which you will be volunteering have paperwork requirements. Some of this might seem boring but you need to get the red tape taken care of before you leave. Be sure to plan adequate time to get it all completed.

The first place to start is obtaining your passport. Once you're enrolled in a program you will also need visas for the country or countries you are visiting. There are some options for a higher level of personal protection for your trip that you may want to consider. Once you decide on a program, you will want to make sure you understand how the program works, what you can expect, what they can expect from you, and please, please get it all in writing. Make sure you have a signed agreement that covers all contingencies.

Passport

The strongest piece of advice I can give you is that you should apply for your passport as soon as you are even *thinking* about traveling abroad. It can take time. You may already have a passport, so check to make sure that your trip will be completed before the passport expires.

Start at *travel.state.gov.* This website has all the details on how to do what you need to do to get your passport. The first thing you need to know is how fast you need the passport, and is this a first-time application? The answers to those questions determine where you must apply and whether or not you must apply in person.

There are different time frames and requirements depending on whether or not you already have a passport. There are also several different forms of the application depending on for what you are applying.

You must be sixteen years old to apply for a passport individually. If this is the first time you're applying for a passport, you must apply in person at a passport agency, a passport application acceptance facility (this might be your post office branch), or a US Embassy or Consulate. If you're applying for a renewal and you live in the United States or Canada, you may do this by mail or at a passport agency. If you live abroad, you must renew your passport at a US Embassy or Consulate. Minors must always apply in person.

With new applications, be sure you have your certified (signed and sealed by registrar) birth certificate plus the originals of any marriage certificates, divorce decrees, or adoption orders. If not born in the United States, original naturalization certificates or certificate of citizenship are required. Copies will not be accepted. The originals must be shipped with your completed application forms when you submit them. (I honestly had a hard time with giving up my original documents, but they were all sent back to me with my passport, in good shape.) If applying for a minor, you must have proof of your parental relationship and a signed parental consent. There are more details for requirements on the *travel.state.gov* website, so definitely take a look.

Don't forget to have your color passport photo taken. It must be in the correct size, two inches by two inches overall, with the size of your face from top of hair to bottom of chin not more than one and three-eighths inches. Passport photos can be obtained in several places. US Post Office branches generally ask you to make an appointment. Or you can go to a Walmart or a fast-photo store to get what you need.

Fees vary, depending on the kind of passport and how fast you need it. Standard time for response is six weeks. You can pay to have the passport expedited and receive it in about three weeks. Expedited handling to eight business days requires yet a higher fee and proof of travel dates to justify issuing the passport that fast. Once you have submitted your application, you can check on the processing status on the *travel.state.gov* website.

Passport

The National Passport Information Center offers automated passport information 24/7. You can also make an appointment at a passport agency during certain hours.

NPIC@state.gov

Example

Both passports and passport cards are available. You can order only a passport, only a passport card, or both a passport and a passport card. A passport card can be used for travel to and from the United States and Canada, Mexico, and Puerto Rico.

Visas

Most countries require visas for entrance into the country. A visa is a right-to-travel permission issued by the country you are visiting. Once again, go to *travel.state.gov* to find the country to which you are traveling. It will give you the visa requirements along with the immunizations required for travel in that country as well as any alerts. A little later in this chapter we will discuss program specific requirements as well.

Depending on the country, visas are required for tourists, students, volunteers, interns, business travel, just about reason you can develop. Some of the international programs will apply for visas for the whole group of volunteers traveling, so make sure you know what you need to do either way. You will need your passport in hand before you apply for your visas.

Some countries may require written confirmation of where you will be staying, what you will be doing, and a copy of your return itinerary and reservations to leave the country before they allow you to enter. Your volunteer program can help with the best way to make sure your documentation is in order. Visas have additional fees (for instance, $30 for Venezuela, which is good for a year but limited to a total of ninety days in-country). Contact the embassy for the country you are entering via website or telephone. As always, you can use a letter of request through surface mail, but add sixty days to processing time.

The visa requirements for each country are different, so be sure to check on your country.

However, continuing to use the country of Venezuela as an example, you must also provide:

- Verification of employment or student status signed by employer, institution, or the volunteer program, with contact information, or proof of retirement.

- Original US passport with at least six-month validity, plus extra copies of the personal information pages.

- Two color photographs, the same as your passport photo.

- Copy of most recent personal bank statement showing enough cash to support you (the traveler) while in-country.

- Proof of housing while in-country.

- Copy of flight itinerary, showing exit date from Venezuela; or the same exit information if you are traveling by sea (date, ship).

- Proof of residency if not US citizen.

- Personal interview and criminal-background check is at the option of the Venezuelan embassy.

- Prepaid return addressed USPS Priority Express envelope with tracking number to send completed visa to you.

Visas

Remember, the visa is issued by the country you're traveling to, not the United States. These countries work on their own timelines, so make sure you apply early enough. Think in terms of a minimum of ninety days. Your selected organization will help you apply for and obtain visas for its programs.

WATCH OUT!

Applicants must personally appear at the Venezuelan embassy or a Venezuelan consulate to apply. Sometimes it can get a little complicated.

Although this is both passport and travel advice, it is worth stating here that you may have entry and exit fees charged by the airline or the country. Make sure you have enough money with you to cover those. Also, some countries require a full page in your passport to stamp, so make sure you have some blank pages. The fifty-two-page passports are no longer issued, so if your passport is full but not expired, you may have to renew your passport before the expiration date to get the clean pages. Once you have your visa in hand, put it inside or attach it to your passport. Keep them together, and keep all of it with you.

While traveling, take several color copies of your passport and visa with you and keep them in separate places (purse, luggage, with a friend, in your e-reader, etc.). Don't let your passport and visa out of your control if at all possible. If they are lost or stolen, contact the nearest embassy or consulate immediately, and get them one of the color copies of your documents so they can be replaced quickly. Otherwise, you could be stranded abroad with no way to leave the country or to reenter the United States.

Traveling Easier

There are some "trusted-traveler" programs that may ease your way going into and out of different countries in addition to a program that registers your location and itinerary in case of problems while you are abroad.

There are four programs suggested by the Department of Homeland Security. One is the Transportation Security Administration program (*tsa.gov*); three are under the US Customs and Border Protection umbrella (*cpb.gov*). Additionally, there is the CLEAR (*clearme.com*) program as well as the STEP registration program under the US Department of State (*travel.state.gov*).

Transportation Security Administration—TSA

The TSA offers Pre✓ to help you skip the long lines waiting to move through the security lines at the airport. You may enroll online at *tsa.gov*, but you must also visit an enrollment center to provide your fingerprints and identification. Currently the fee is $85 for a five-year membership. This will speed you through the security check lines, and you may not have to remove your shoes and coat, or laptop from its case.

US Customs and Border Protection

There are three trusted-traveler programs available to you, depending on where you are traveling. For expedited entry processing at land and airport borders, you can choose Global Entry (passport or lawful permanent US resident card required), NEXUS (no passport required, must be US or Canadian citizen or lawful permanent residents of either country, generally used for US/Canadian travel), or SENTRI (requires proof of citizenship and admissibility documentation). Each of these includes TSA Pre✓ benefits. NEXUS and SENTRI also include the Global Entry benefits. Currently, the Global Entry fee is $100 for five years, NEXUS is $50 for five years, and SENTRI (often used at the US-Mexico border) is $122.25 for five years. All can be applied for online, but all require a personal visit to an enrollment center (usually at an airport) to be interviewed, fingerprinted, and photographed. The card will be sent to you in the mail after you are cleared through Homeland Security. When I applied, this took several weeks.

CLEAR

The CLEAR program (*clearme.com*) is for-profit and is not governmental, but provides the same benefits that TSA Pre✓ does in the skipping of the long security check lines. It is similar to the Global Entry Pass program. Clear Pass moves you through the security lines on the way *out* of the airport, while Global Entry helps you when *reentering* the country. Again, apply online (*clearme.com*), then go to your nearest airport with the Clear Pass kiosk with your ID and your assigned member number, have your iris (yes, your eye) scanned, and you're set. Currently, this cost is $179 per year, with additional family members priced at $50. CLEAR is not in every airport yet, so be sure to check to confirm that you are near a CLEAR airport before you spend money on this. CLEAR also works in tandem with TSA Pre✓, so if you have one of these programs, you can generally access the service of the other.

STEP

STEP is not an entry or exit system. It is a way to keep track of you as you travel. It is a system that will find you and warn you if you end up in an unexpected situation while traveling. STEP stands for Smart Traveler Enrollment Program. It is a service of the Bureau of Consular Affairs, Department of State (*step.state. gov*). This is a free service. It allows you to enroll your trip including travel details with the nearest US Embassy or Consulate. The Embassy or Consulate will keep you informed of any safety issues in the country where you are traveling. It also makes it possible, and easier, to find you or notify you if there is a family emergency at home, civil unrest in the country, or impending natural disaster near you, so you can make informed decisions about your personal security. Conversely, it can help your family members locate you if they feel you're in danger.

You can register with STEP at any time, and you will receive any travel alerts and warnings about the country to which you are traveling well in advance of the time you leave.

Application for Program

Once you have identified the program for and country in which you want to volunteer, the program will ask you to complete an application. If you apply through an umbrella organization, you may be asked to complete an intake application. With this, the organization can assess how to best place you, or if there may be some concerns about what you have chosen to do. You will have to answer questions about why you chose this particular program, do you bring any previous experience to the placement, and are you good working with people that have very different life experiences than yours? In my case, I'm in my sixties and get along great with almost everyone, but I am not qualified to do deep-sea diving. So doing marine conservation in Mexico for advanced divers may not be a good choice for me!

If you apply directly to a specific project, you will also have to do an application for it. However, be sure to do in-depth research on the quality and safety of any single program in another country before you commit. I recommend using the umbrella organizations, as they have done this research and qualified the programs as well-organized and safe, and as the kind of experience for which their applicants are looking.

Once you have passed that first application, you will likely be asked to complete a second, more-detailed application specifically for the program you have chosen. At the same time, the program officer assigned to your particular project will let you know of any additional requirements. Some programs fill up quickly or may be hard to get in to. You should plan to apply to more than one, so you can be sure to find a placement.

Agreement with Organization

Again, each program and each organization has its own specific requirements. Be sure to get a complete list from your program officer so you don't miss anything.

One example is a program of GVIWorld (*gviworld.com*). GVIWorld offers a volunteer option of teaching children in Fiji. This program provides education and support for a better quality of life as well as to help this targeted community become more self-sustainable. GVI works in partnership with the Fiji Ministry of Education.

A sample of additional requirements and notices from Fiji and the program are:

◆ Be prepared for primarily vegetarian cuisine, cooked by volunteers.

◆ Primary method of transportation is walking; site is located forty miles from a medical center but buses or taxis can be available.

◆ Women and men are required to wear long skirts/sarongs and shirts with at least short sleeves, no bare shoulders, while volunteering. If doing construction, long pants are acceptable. When off duty or traveling, shorts are acceptable.

◆ Participants must have a limited authority-to-work visa in advance ($190FD, about $90 USD) and short-term work permit will be issued upon arrival ($669FD, about $315 USD). Cash is required for payment.

◆ Participants must have a written criminal-background check (in English) to get a visa, and a hard copy of this when entering the country.

◆ Participants must have extra passport photos.

◆ Participants must have traveler's insurance.

◆ Participants must complete a medical form.

◆ Participants must present an itinerary showing your return to your country of origin when entering Fiji.

◆ Understand that fresh water at the volunteer site comes from rainwater.

You may or may not want to agree with some of these but please follow them for the best experience for all concerned. If you don't comply, you may not be allowed to participate.

The programs have a set price to cover housing, food, training, field trips, and wages for the in-country staff. Check with your program specialist to find out. If you're going to a remote area, you may want to confirm if any of the costs include evacuation or medical costs.

Agreement with Organization

Your program of choice has accepted you. Congratulations! At this point, you will be asked to contractually commit to what you say you intend to do. In this agreement should be what the umbrella organization is expecting from you, what the program or project is expecting from you, and what you will receive in return from each of them. Read it carefully. If it is the Peace Corps, for instance, you are agreeing to two years of your life. Many will have standards of performance or behavior in addition to strict travel, pretrip training, or many other options. Before you go into another country in these times of international conflict, make sure you have a clear way out. Try to make sure that the program has a solid and implementable plan to get you out of the country quickly if the need arises.

Cautionary note: make sure there is complete understanding by all parties. If it is not in writing, there is no agreement.

Now, you're almost ready. Do you have all of your inoculations? Do you have other items you need to take? Are you prepared for the unexpected? Have you done your cultural research? No? Then read the following chapters.

To Summarize...

- Volunteering abroad requires extensive advance paper work. Plan enough time to complete these.

- You will need a US passport, visas from the destination country, and any additional paperwork required by the country or the program.

- There are several traveling programs to make your travel safer and easier.

- Make sure you have the complete agreement with your volunteer program in writing, signed by all parties, before you leave.

Chapter 18

What to Expect: Be Prepared

In This Chapter...

- 💡 Learn before you go
- 💡 What's under your personal control while traveling
- 💡 What's not under your personal control while traveling
- 💡 Surprises while in-country

Unexpected challenges while traveling abroad can range from the merely inconvenient to the dangerous and frightening. Just getting to your initial destination can be an adventure all by itself. Understanding the culture and customs of the country to which you are traveling *before you go* will deeply enhance your experience.

Try to plan for any eventuality. Decide in advance to travel with sensitivity and patience. Be open to all experiences without negative prejudgment. Conversely, you also are ultimately responsible for your own personal safety. Cautions are not meant to be alarmist; they are simply meant to inform. The best advice is to use common sense, be situationally aware, and follow your gut instincts.

It may seem as if I am writing you a travelogue here. The information is important if you have not traveled abroad yet, and it is good basic information that you will need. You're certainly welcome to investigate in more detail, and a few resources are provided for that.

Learn Before You Go

You could be headed to Myanmar, or France, or South Africa, or Central America—any of a hundred other places. What language will be spoken around you? What kind of local culture and traditions exist among the students you will be teaching or in the village where you will be helping to dig wells? While you're waiting for your passport and visas to get through the processing steps, take the time to learn as much as possible.

> **Perspiration**
>
> ## Learn Before You Go—Example of Learning Language
>
> If you are going to a Spanish-speaking country, you might want to start by memorizing the following phrases:
>
> | Spanish Phrase | English Translation |
> | --- | --- |
> | *Buenos días* (bway nos dee ahs) | Good morning |
> | *Buenas tardes* (bway nahs tar days) | Good afternoon |
> | *Buenas noches* (bway nahs noh chayss) | Good evening |
> | *Hola* (oh lah) | "Hi" with people you know |
> | *¿Cómo está?* (coh moh es tah) | "How are you?" if you don't know someone |
> | *¿Cómo estás?* (coh moh es tahs) | "How are you?" if you do know them |
> | *Bien, gracias* (bee ayn, grah cee ahs) | Fine, thank you |
> | *Por favor* (por fah vohr) | Please |
> | *Gracias* (grah cee ahs) | Thank you |
> | *Mucho gusto* (moo choh goos toh) | Nice to meet you |
> | *¿Habla inglés?* (ahblah een glays?) | Do you speak English? |

Your program should have a country manager or project expert assigned to it. This person will be able to give you a lot of information regarding dress, local customs, the housing to which you will be assigned, and how your volunteer engagement will take place. Be sure to read it all and ask questions. Often, T-shirts or polo shirts will be supplied by the organization for volunteers to wear while working on the volunteer project, so take that into consideration regarding clothing choices. You may want to purchase an extra shirt, depending on how long you will be there.

If you get a chance, try to learn at least a few words or phrases of the local language that could come in handy. It will help in reading street signs, talking to taxi drivers, or asking the location of the nearest bathroom. Again, your project expert can help you with that.

Be hyperaware that people where you're visiting may not have the same standards of behavior, clothing expectations, economic means, or view of the world you might be used to in the United States. They also may not have the freedom to express personal opinions in the same way US citizens enjoy. Respect these differences. Try to respond and act in a way that will not make you or them uncomfortable. It is usually best to remain neutral on any subject that may be controversial in any way. Decline to express strong opinions in casual conversation, as you may be offending someone unknowingly. Never share personal information or opinions with strangers in bars, at hotels, or on the street.

Many programs and organizations offer a reading list or online webinars for more in-depth study. Be sure to take advantage of these ways to learn. Go the library or search online for more information. There are history books, current event resources, and travel guides. Read them all. *You can never have too much information.*

Would you like to see where you are going? You can download Google Earth (*earth.google.com* or *googlemaps.com*) or another global-mapping search program. The basic version of Google Earth is free. Once you put the address or area you're headed to in the address line, it will take you to a bird's eye photographic view of where you are headed. This will help you get oriented before you arrive, which, if nothing else, will give you knowledge of travel routes to help avoid being taken for a too-long drive by a taxi driver. In more remote areas, you will also be able to see any highlights such as nearby rivers or mountains that you may want to explore.

You will likely have time to do general sightseeing while you are in-country. Even though you may be tired from working on the project, don't let any opportunities pass. Plan on what you want to see before you go. Be flexible once you get there, as you may discover something else you want to experience as well. Find out in advance about methods, costs, timing, and location of transportation to and from tourist sites. Try to make sure not to go alone on these side trips. Take enough cash with you. We'll talk about how to store it later.

Under Your Personal Control While Traveling

There are things you will be able to control during your adventure, and things you will not be able to control.

Let's look at what you *can* control. First and foremost, be on time. I know it sounds simple, but having personally missed flights, it is better to be two hours early than two minutes late.

Plan Ahead

Plan ahead for sight-seeing. For instance, if you're going to be anywhere in Europe, you may want to purchase train ticket packages for travel during your off time. Purchase these before you leave the United States. There are many online options.

If you want to see a popular museum in your travels, purchase tickets before you go. For example, if you intend to see the Louvre Museum, figure out the day you will be there and buy your ticket. Otherwise, you will be spending your whole day in line just to get in the door. You may want to try *getyourguide.com* for available tours and tickets available in many major cities throughout the world—from Dubai to San Francisco.

IMPORTANT!

When arriving at the airport, remember you are traveling internationally, so give yourself enough time to arrive, get checked in, go through security where you are likely to be searched at least minimally, and get to the gate—all without running. Be sure you have your passport and visas easily accessible at all times, but be careful not to leave them or lose them somewhere. The airline agent at the gate will need to see the passport once you arrive there.

On a totally domestic flight destination, all you need is the boarding pass at the gate. It is not the same if you're headed out of the country. Even if the flight you are first boarding will connect with another within the United States, you will be required to show your passport at the initial boarding gate.

You will likely be flying into your project country a day or more before your volunteer experience begins, and staying the night before in a hotel recommended by the organization. Be sure to allow enough time when you make flight reservations to take into consideration weather cancellations or delays, mechanical problems, interim hotel reservation issues, or jet lag. All of these can, and do, happen. Also please stay in a hotel recommended by the organization. Don't look for a "deal" or second-guess the experts. They are recommending the hotels for good reasons: security, accessibility, affordability, and ambience. Trust them; they do this all the time. Generally, the organization will provide transport from the hotels to the volunteer site and often will offer day-before or evening-before training to the volunteers.

Under Your Control When Traveling

There are several comprehensive resources that offer detailed advice on how to travel successfully. Check out *transitionsabroad.com, travelzoo. com, worldtravelguide.net, fodors. com* or, if you're going to Europe, one of Rick Steve's travel guides for your destination country. Also check out *Budget Travel for the GENIUS* and *European Travel for the GENIUS*, both mentioned in a sidebar in **Chapter 16**. Try *lifehacker. com* for advice on credit cards and currency management.

Perspiration

If you will be traveling through several time zones, do yourself a favor. To minimize jet lag, for several days before you leave, try to adjust your sleep patterns to the new time zone. Hydrate before you go, not just as you're leaving. Drink a lot of water and skip the caffeine and soda. Try to exercise as much as possible both before and during the flight. While traveling, walk the hallways of the airport or the aisles of the aircraft. You will have more energy, you will adjust more quickly when you reach your destination, and you will avoid medical problems that can happen when flying long distances.

If you have prescription medications, take them on the airplane with you in the original bottles, and have an original prescription signed by your doctor with you.

Pack light and leave your expensive jewelry at home. Buy an affordable wristwatch for the trip that you won't care about losing. You may want to dress a certain way for enplaning and deplaning, but bring a change of very comfortable clothing for the flight itself. Take a bottle of water and a few energy bars just in case. Do not drink out of fountains and drink only from new bottles of water that have never been opened. Learn to love antibacterial gel for your hands, as soap and water may not be readily available.

Not Under Your Control While Traveling

My sister Mary would disagree with the lost luggage being only 2 percent. She has "lost" twenty-nine suitcases while traveling, and five were never recovered. For her, the loss is a little over 17 percent, but she still laughs about it. (This is why you always carry valuables and prescriptions with you in the passenger cabin.)

Mary's philosophy is to buy basic, affordable luggage (not designer), and to avoid packing her most expensive shoes bags, suits, etc. She avoids putting anything in checked baggage that would devastate her were she to lose it.

As a protest, Mary wears a T-shirt that shows lost luggage circulating as one of the rings around the planet Saturn.

Pure Genius!

Not Under Your Personal Control While Traveling

If your flight is delayed or canceled, the first thing to avoid is panicking. A hint here is if your flight has a connecting flight, reserve the flights that have a good amount of time in between so if the first one is delayed, you still may have time to make the connection. Otherwise, go to the gate agent and make reservations the best way you can to get to your destination. This is why you travel the day before, or even two days before, depending on how far you are traveling. It's important to note that if you are bumped from a flight by the airline because of overbooking, you should receive vouchers for food and possibly a hotel—though weather or mechanical delays may not get the same perks from the airline. If you're renting a car at your destination, make sure the reservation includes your flight number and landing time; if you don't show up when expected, it can see that your flight is delayed and, hopefully, hold your car for you.

You have the option of purchasing trip-loss or theft-and-trip cancellation/interruption coverage in advance. This kind of policy can be just for these items, or can be combined with a trip medical insurance policy.

Though lost luggage is a nightmare, it's solvable most of the time. The statistics say only 2 percent of baggage is never found. Generally, luggage is found within a day or two. The airlines are typically cooperative about bringing the lost luggage to you. If your location is in a more remote area of your destination country, or if you're at sea, that may be a little more problematic. Your program staff can help with the solution. In case you don't know, the Unclaimed Baggage Center in the United States is in Scottsboro, Alabama. Unclaimed luggage is eventually auctioned off.

While no one wants to think that you, the volunteer who is doing so much good, is in danger while traveling, it can happen. By using good sense, you can lessen your risk. This section is not mean to frighten you, just to help you be aware. The chances of serious problems are very low. However, in our world today, I think it is foolish not to be as prepared as possible.

When choosing an airline or other way to travel, avoid carriers that are high risk or that are too relaxed about security. Choose flights that have the least number of connections, minimizing the opportunity of running into a crisis of some sort in the interim stop airport. As is blasted over the speakers in every airport, do not leave your luggage alone, do not agree to watch anyone else's luggage, and do not *ever* carry any item onto or off of the aircraft (or in or out of the airport) for anyone else.

When choosing your seat, try to sit in or near an exit row. If

Not Under Your Control While Traveling

The Ackerman Group LLC (*ackermangroup.com*) publishes an excellent treatise on the dangers of international travel, "Managing Travel Risks—Tips on International Business Travel." This publication focuses on executive business travelers, particularly in unstable or hostile countries. However, there is a significant level of detailed information that can be applied in all kinds of situations. It is worth a read.

The Ackerman Group also offers security awareness training for travelers.

IMPORTANT!

something with an unruly passenger happens in flight, it is better to have a window seat which will help protect you by keeping you out of the line of direct action. Think about not wearing flashy jewelry. Dress conservatively, and avoid obviously using reading or entertainment materials that may be considered offensive by another culture. If you have country stamps in your current passport that may be considered a problem in your destination country, you may want to get a replacement passport before you leave so the pages are blank.

Surprises While In-Country

Everyone who travels runs into problems eventually. The goal is to simply figure out how to best manage them. Decide in advance to stay calm and show patience, both verbally and nonverbally. Use common sense and listen to your instincts. Above all, pay attention—be situationally aware.

Transportation and Hotel

It is not common in the United States, but in most non-US major airports in the world you will see armed soldiers in the airport when you land. Don't worry, it is standard. However, if they appear tense and are moving fast, stay out of their way. I remember being shocked in 1976 when I first landed in Athens, and saw all the guns. It was very much beyond what my reality had ever been. On that trip, it was the same in Cairo, Amman, and Tel Aviv. As you can

How I Saved My Own Life

Take only logo-branded taxis. If you have to walk a few blocks to a hotel or public place to find one, make the effort to do it. Avoid a driver, anywhere, who comes up to you and wants to give you a "deal." You may pay a little more, but you will be safer. I didn't take that advice while traveling in Montego Bay, Jamaica. I ended up in the middle of a muddy sugar cane field with the driver stepping out of the car and three of his friends walking out of the high sugar cane. Every alarm in my head went off, so I got behind the wheel and drove off, leaving the driver. I took the car back to the hotel and called the police. Their opinion was that I probably saved my own life.

WATCH OUT!

imagine, it is much more intense now with the current tragic events and threat status in the world. A word to the wise is if you hear something that sounds like firecrackers, find a safe place and stay there.

When going from the airport to the hotel, take the taxi from the approved airport taxi stand. Try to avoid the person hustling you in or around the airport to take the person's personal car. Note the driver's name and taxi number. Be sure that you have all of your belongings when you get out of the taxi.

Stay in reputable hotels on main thoroughfares as much as possible. Keep your hotel key on your person or turn it into the hotel desk when you go out so you don't lose it. Ask the hotel for the best routes to your destination, if not supplied by your program officer.

Currency and Money

With the advice of your program staff, take enough money with you for what you will need and some for what you will want. You can usually exchange US dollars for the currency for your country before you go. It does cost a fee to exchange money. Most countries have ATMs, at least in the cities. However, try to use the ATMs in the banks or hotels, not on the street. Your bank or designated American Express offices can exchange currency for you. If you're in-country, use only approved exchange places—don't buy currency on the street. Some countries (e.g., Cuba) prefer tipping in American dollars, so ask your program staff to let you know about tipping practices.

Tourism and Socializing

If you have the time and energy to do some sightseeing before you need to report for you job, that's great. However, stay in the populated areas, and ask the hotel to arrange transportation to and from the sights you want to see. You may have time at the end of your trip or during a break to do the tourist thing as well. With the program officer, plan ahead what you want to see and do, so you are prepared with your schedule, transportation solutions, and enough money.

You are going to meet a lot of wonderful people. You may be staying with a local family. You will socialize, maybe sometimes going to restaurants or hotels or bars or clubs. You're going to want to talk to everyone you can and find out as much as you can about the country and culture you are visiting. This is all wonderful. However, be careful about sharing too much personal information with strangers. Keep your phone on your person, along with any money or papers. Buy your own drinks, preferably in unopened bottles. Don't leave them alone on a table. Just use the same common sense you would if you were out partying hardy at home.

Program Problems

No matter how much planning by the program staff, sometimes adjustments have to be made. Transportation can break down, volunteers can become ill and not be able to participate, natural disasters or local unrest can happen. Have a thorough conversation with your program officer about what has happened in the past, how it was managed, and what might go wrong in the future. Make sure you understand and agree with how a crisis or challenge will be handled, so you will know what to expect.

International volunteer programs have centralized or area offices in the countries they serve, and sometimes that office may offer the only communication system available to you for the outside world. Make sure you have all of the contact information for any in-country personnel for the organization you are representing and how to contact them in an emergency. The organization should have a system in place to extricate its volunteers from the country if there is an extreme or life-threatening situation.

Keep the old adage, "plan for the worst, and hope for the best," in mind. This adventure will be one of the most important times of your life, so make sure you stay safe and healthy. Planning well in advance, plus being situationally aware throughout the trip, will make all the difference.

To Summarize...

- Prepare yourself in advance for travel, starting with passports and visas.

- Study the culture and at least some language phrases to use.

- Proactively manage your travel with common sense and situational awareness, including using the established, respected hotels, transportation, communication systems, and access to money.

- If problems arise, work proactively with the program director to resolve them or, if necessary and as a last resort, leave the country.

Chapter 19

Travel and Medical

In This Chapter...

- Before you go
- While you're in transit
- While you're fulfilling your volunteer work
- While you're sightseeing

If you prepare in advance to be healthy, you are in generally good shape. Not all countries have the level of sanitation or clean water that the United States does. There may not be a drug store down the street where you're going. And as we have been saying all along, excellent preparation results in a much better experience.

Once you know where you are going and when, make an appointment to see your doctor. Take a written list of the requirements of your program with you. First, make sure you are in good health and able to fulfill your assignment. Second, you need to make sure you are up to date on your standard inoculations. In my experience, most adults don't even remember when they last got a tetanus booster, and you will need to be current on that inoculation as well as those for measles, mumps. and rubella, and maybe pneumonia, flu, and even the Zika virus.

Before You Go

Your program may require completion of a physical examination form and/ or your doctor's approval for participating. Additionally, you may need any of a wide variety of specialized preventative inoculations if you are traveling to an area where risky diseases are prevalent. These might include yellow fever, malaria, typhoid, or several even more frightening options. Your program will also have a list of suggested or required shots that you can share with your physician of choice. In larger cities, there are travel clinics that specialize in getting you ready and they will know what you will need. Schedule these inoculations well in advance. It can take quite some time to order and receive the vaccines, and sometimes there are vaccine shortages.

Make sure you have any medications (with duplicate original written prescriptions) you might require from your doctor, including treatment for diarrhea. It isn't a glamorous subject, but 60 percent of travelers internationally suffer from Traveler's Diarrhea. It is a very real problem, and thinking you can tough it out may end up causing you both severe discomfort and awkward embarrassment. You also may want to take a brief written medical history with you, including any medications you take on a regular basis. If you end up needing medical attention at some point, this may save time in getting you the correct treatment.

Jet lag is also a very real issue. Some people have no problem with changing time zones, and others may be challenged by a time change of only an hour or two. Until you acclimate to the new time zone, it might be a challenge resetting your internal clock to be able to sleep. Sleeping pills can be very tough to shake off, so be careful with those. I suggest you try melatonin for jet lag instead, which is a naturally occurring hormone in the body which helps regulate sleep cycles. Melatonin can

Before You Go

There are several websites that can help you with information about preventative medicine when traveling internationally. Check these for information on warnings and outbreaks:

◆ United States for travel vaccines: *vaccines.gov*

◆ Center for Disease Control: *nc.cdc.gov*

◆ World Health Organization: *who.int*

IMPORTANT!

be found in drug stores, health food stores, and grocery stores. It comes in tablets, gummies, and quick-dissolve pills. There are also many other natural jet-lag remedies available from health food stores or online. Try them before you travel to make sure they work and that they don't have unpleasant side effects for you.

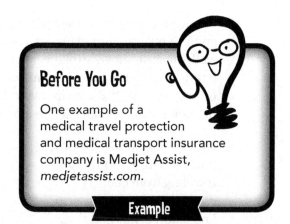

Before You Go

One example of a medical travel protection and medical transport insurance company is Medjet Assist, *medjetassist.com.*

Example

Check with your program about the exact extent of the medical insurance coverage it provides. Then check with your medical insurance carrier to determine whether or not you will be covered abroad. If between these policies you're not fully covered, you can purchase a supplemental medical insurance policy for the term of the trip only. In addition to trip cancellation or trip interruption and baggage loss or damage, medical travel insurance policies offer coverage for emergency medical or dental needs and emergency medical evacuation. Hopefully, it will never be needed. But if it is needed, it may help you obtain higher quality and more immediate medical treatment, or medical transport back the United States if necessary. There are many insurance companies that offer this coverage. It is generally affordable, as the coverage is short term, for the duration of your travel only. An online search will give you numerous options to investigate.

While You're in Transit

We talked a little about this earlier. The two basics when traveling anywhere is to exercise when you can and to keep hydrated. Hydrating means drinking water. Alcohol, carbonation, and caffeine will simply dehydrate you. However, in drinking water, drink only bottled water from a known source that has not yet been opened. If that is not available, use water purification tablets. These can be found at any camping equipment store, online, or through your pharmacy. Carry them with you in your backpack. Make sure that they are strong enough to manage the water no matter what microorganisms are present.

Exercise is as simple as walking. Try not to sit too long, including on an airplane. If you're waiting, just take a stroll. This will keep your circulation moving, reduce swelling in your ankles and feet, give you more energy and alertness, and help you sleep when the time is right. Isometric exercises are good if you're confined in a seated position too long and are not allowed to walk the aisles in an airplane. Mini-stretch and flex your shoulders, arms, hands, and feet as much as you can while seated to help keep your muscles from cramping. It also helps avoid blood clots in your extremities, which can happen if you are crammed in a pressurized cabin too long.

I know it sounds unhealthy, but avoid fresh food while traveling from country to country. There is no way to know how it was handled. Other countries may not have the same sanitation standards as does the United States, and you have no idea how the fresh food was prepared. Eat only what packaged food you brought with you or purchase only prepackaged, sealed, commercially prepared food on your journey. This is not the time to experiment! You don't want to become food-ill flying over the Pacific Ocean. While it may not be gourmet, airline food is generally safe.

If a new acquaintance along the way offers you food or beverage, let the person know how much you appreciate the offer, but decline. There is plenty of time to experience new cuisine once you arrive. Use common sense and be safe. If you're staying in interim accommodations after arrival and before you are posted to you volunteer duties,

While in Transit or While Doing Your Volunteer Work

The rule about only drinking from bottles that have unbroken seals applies even in restaurants. Be sure the server opens the bottle at your table. While in Egypt, I watched restaurant staff take water bottles out the back door and refill them with a hose in the alley. It was very disturbing. Due to city water infrastructure in Cairo being iffy at the time, the tap water could have had things like typhoid and diphtheria in it.

Even being what I thought was careful, on two trips several years apart I became very ill from parasites from beverages in both Rome and Cairo. Both times it took a lot of antibiotics and several days to recover. If I had paid better attention, this could have been avoided.

WATCH OUT!

limit yourself to your hotel dining room or to a restaurant recommended by the hotel. If you order a drink, drink beer or wine that is newly opened in front of you. Never drink anything with ice in it. Freezing bad water does not take the germs out of it. Brush your teeth with bottled water. If you are in the shower, don't allow the water to get in your mouth. You don't want to start out your adventure in a clinic or hospital.

While You're Fulfilling Your Volunteer Work

You have arrived at your volunteer project! Your on-site program liaison will get you into your housing arrangement. This could be a tent or dorms or with a local family or in a variety of local housing. The system for preparing and eating meals, the daily schedule, systems of transportation to and from where you need to go, as well as any special details will be given to you. Make sure you ask about anything that doesn't make sense to you. Flexibility is the key.

When it comes to local food and drink, take it slow. These may be new foods to you, and you may want to eat small portions until you know how your body is going to tolerate the new items. Keep to bottled water. If that is not possible, use your water purification tablets. Typically, one tablet does one liter of water so make sure to bring enough. Try to avoid anything with alcohol. You may be in a country that does not serve it. But if you are offered a drink, declining is a good idea until you're acclimated.

Find out from your program liaison how emergencies are handled, including medical emergencies. Determine how communications, both with the program people and your family, are managed. Make sure the program is very thorough about how to leave the project or area if there are local civil or weather disaster problems. If you are housed with a local family, make sure you ask about what they need from you while you are living in their home. If you have anything like a food allergy, tell them. Remember that wide varieties of foods and meats are not available to many areas of the world where you might be volunteering.

If strolling around the town or city in a remote area, do not buy food from a street vendor unless you're with a host and the host vouches for the vendor's food safety. In some areas, a pub is fine for both food and beverage. In others, you will need to keep to well-known restaurants and hotels. Use common sense to figure it out depending on where you are. If your instincts make you feel, or smell, like something is off, listen. Don't eat it or drink it.

If you will be doing heavier physical labor, consider bringing muscle-relaxing ointments. If you will be in hot sun, bring a high-SPF-rated sunscreen. Bring a hat and extra eyeglasses and sunglasses. If in a hot and humid country, bring strong insect repellent with you, but check to see if the ingredient DEET is allowed. It may or may not be in your preferred repellent. Some countries ban DEET, as it is considered a carcinogen. Know before you go.

Bring over-the-counter anti-inflammatory remedies or pain reducers, as you don't know if they will be available. Antibiotic ointment and bandages are important. Get enough sleep, eat cautiously, and if you become ill, contact your program staff immediately.

While You're Sightseeing

You will have breaks in your volunteer work. During these breaks, be sure to see as much of your destination country as you possibly can. Sightseeing is an important part of your experience. Your program may provide transportation, or your local family might be able to help you travel, or you might be looking at taking buses, trains, and taxis. As much as possible, map out your recreational sightseeing before you leave. If you will need them, make hotel and tour reservations in advance and carry printed copies of the itinerary and reservations with you.

Identify places of safety along the way, just in case. File these sightseeing plans with your STEP program as well as your volunteer program, and then follow them. If you decide to change your plans at the last minute, let someone else know exactly what those changed plans are.

Medically speaking, you simply need to follow all the precautions we've already talked about in this chapter. In addition, wear flat-soled shoes that cover your feet but won't give you blisters in case you have to walk a long way while touring. Remember that it is safer to sightsee in numbers, not alone. If possible, have a charged cell phone with international capabilities and activate the GPS in the phone. Take one or two external batteries to recharge your phone.

If you become ill or injured, you should already have a way to contact your program liaison for help. Use it. If you are near a US Embassy or Consulate and are able, try to get there. Since you know you should always keep your passport, visa, and the Embassy or Consulate addresses and phone numbers with you at all times, you should be able to find assistance fairly quickly. Any of these sources can find you the medical aid if you need it. In the most extreme medical situation, you may have emergency evacuation coverage if you purchased a travel medical insurance plan. Be aware that if you're covered by Medicare or Social Security, these programs do not provide any kind of coverage outside of the United States.

Be aware that local law enforcement, depending on which country you are in, may or may not be able to offer you the level of response you need. Language barriers, traditions, and resources available will affect if and how they can help you.

Medical problems can happen when you travel. Take the personal precautions we've discussed to minimize any problems. Be aware of where your aid providers are and how to find them in an emergency. Think common sense, safety, and caution, and you will be fine.

To Summarize...

- Make sure you're medically prepared before you leave, including purchasing supplemental medical travel insurance coverage.

- Take precautions to stay healthy during your trip.

- Plan to safely see as much of your destination country as you can.

- Have a plan about what to do in case of emergency or medical problems.

Chapter 20

Practical Considerations

In This Chapter...

- Wear it
- Carry it
- Use it
- Don't forget it

Now is the time to get even more organized. Practical considerations for me are *What do I take? How do I carry it? For what kinds of contingencies do I need to plan? What can I live without and what is essential—really critical—that I need to take with me?*

The answers are going to be different, depending on who you are, where you're going, and what you'll be doing. You will be traveling long distances. You will likely have to personally carry everything you are taking with you more than once. At the same time, you will need to take important items with you since there may be limited places to buy what you discover you need when you get there. It can be a little bit challenging to figure out all these logistics. I would suggest making lists, revising them, and asking your program officer for suggestions to manage this process. Try not to do your packing at the last minute. Find an area in your home where you can collect and arrange (stage) everything you plan on taking, so you can see it all at the same time, and make final decisions.

Wear It

Deciding what clothing to take or not to take can be amazingly challenging. Your program people will give you a list of recommended clothing. Please believe them. It is likely you will be purchasing some specialized items that you will need. When shopping, focus on camping stores or stores that specialize in clothing and other essentials for travel. These stores sell clothing that is light, packs well, wears well, and washes easily in a variety of water situations. Buy materials that don't need ironing. Please remember that denim jeans are much heavier than other materials, so limit the jeans you take.

You're not doing a fashion show. Clean and neat is the order of the day. In some countries, make sure you are wearing clothing that is considered acceptable in their society. Unless you're swimming quite a bit, don't consider short shorts. Leave your barely-there bikini swim suits (women) and Speedos (men) at home. Try to buy in a basic color theme, adding brighter colors with a scarf, soft hat, or light jacket or belt. If you will be in a very cold climate, make sure you take the appropriate outerwear, hat, gloves, thermal underwear, and socks.

Find out what kind of shoes you will need every day. Make sure that the shoes are comfortable and broken in before you leave. Limit yourself to two pairs (athletic shoes and well-made sandals, for instance) plus one pair of flip flops for showering. If you will be doing heavy hiking, then hiking boots may be in order. Women, think carefully about high heels, and take the advice of your program liaison.

Leave your valuable jewelry at home. Buy an inexpensive watch that you don't care if you lose. If you will be heartbroken if you lost a personal item, don't take it. Ladies, if your ears are pierced, use simple, inexpensive, studs.

How much clothing you take will be based on how long your volunteer project lasts and how long you will be traveling or sightseeing in addition to the project time. Choose what to pack understanding that you will be doing laundry along the way, maybe in a machine, maybe by hand. Plan for both. Once you have everything you want to take, or think you can't live without, laid out on your bed, cut it in half. As long as what's left includes what your program tells you to take, you are probably fine. For instance, if you need to take an outfit for a dressy occasion, take one, not two. Forget taking something "in case" you might need it.

Carry It

For luggage, think black suitcase plus any-color daypack or backpack. Make sure they are sturdy, but made of lightweight materials. I prefer a four-wheel roller bag for ease of use. Mark the bag with distinctive tape around the handle. A red or yellow or bright green bag is fine for domestic travel, but brightly colored bags can sometimes attract increased attention in transit that you may not want. It is frustrating to arrive at a destination and have no suitcase and no clothes.

Your daypack or knapsack should be wearable with two shoulder straps. Padded straps are better than nonpadded straps. This day pack (smaller version) or knapsack will hold your cell phone, chargers, tablets, travel documents, etc., so try to find one that is RFID rated to keep your information secure. If you can't find one like that, and as we mentioned before, purchase RFID blocking holders for your credit cards and passport. TSA locks are available for all types of luggage, and are

Carry It

Luggage security is a serious problem in international travel. Your program officer should have special attention on the group's luggage, but ask before you go if there are any extra precautions they recommend.

When traveling to Cuba, I observed Cuban families going to Cuba take their luggage to a special carousel where it was wrapped completely in plastic (after going through security and customs) to make sure no one was able to open the luggage while it was in transit. Some of these wrapped items were huge. American goods were so valuable at the time that theft from the luggage was nearly a 100 percent probability. These United States to Cuba family trips were rare and hard to schedule, and this was the only way that families from the United States could get items like household goods to other family members in Cuba, where such goods were either unavailable or not affordable. The street value of these goods, if stolen, was fairly high.

WATCH OUT!

definitely advisable for international travel. You really want your luggage locked as it goes through the back areas of any airport. Don't put anything important in your checked luggage. Clothes can be replaced. Try to keep to these two luggage items. The more you have to carry, the more you have to keep track of and the more items you can lose. When walking, put the backpack or the daypack on both your shoulders, leaving your hands free and making it harder to take the pack from you. If you want to take a small purse or fanny pack to use at certain times, make sure it is soft and will pack easily in your luggage while you're traveling. The smaller purse should also have a messenger-bag-type strap (over the head and across the body) for security. Fanny packs should fit around your waist comfortably and have a sturdy clip. All bags should be zipped closed at all times.

Use It

Laundry is important. We all like clean clothes, but we don't like washing them, right? Camping stores and travel stores sell both liquid and leaf (thin, paper-like sheets) laundry soap. You can use them in a machine or wash by hand. Warning: If using the leaf soap (very light, great for travel) it takes about five leaves to wash your clothes, so buy enough.

Take a first-aid kit. They come in all sizes. Camping stores seem to have the better selection in what the kits hold for the size and weight. You can also check out your nearest Red Cross office. Take additional antibiotic ointment and adhesive bandages, as there never seem to be enough of those. Make sure your kit has a splinter-pulling tweezer. You can put your water purification tablets in this kit as well as in your backpack.

Think about a small sewing kit. It will be enough to take one or two of the tiny ones you can get from a hotel. Add safety pins however. Also try to find a self-contained shower and toiletries zipper kit or bag. That way you can travel to and from any remote showering or bathroom facility without juggling shampoo, toothpaste, razor, soap, etc. It is all together, and you can just grab and go. You may want to include a washcloth and camping towel if you will be in a remote area or if they will not be provided where you are staying.

Decide to take only one or two credit cards with you and buy a RFID secure holder for them. Call your credit card companies in advance and tell them when and where you're traveling, and when you'll return. Otherwise, if you try to use them in a remote corner of the world, I can nearly guarantee the charge won't be honored. Do the same advance notification to your bank about your ATM card. If your bank is surprised by a withdrawal in another country, it may freeze your account. ATM machines are available worldwide. If using an ATM machine, make sure you don't use one on the street. Go into a hotel or bank to use one. The fee may be higher, but the risk will be a lot lower.

Call your cell phone company in advance. Make sure that, first, it has coverage in the country to which you are traveling, and, second, you order country-specific international coverage on your account before you leave the United States—international coverage is not automatic. The cellular company can add the coverage limited to the time frame of your trip, so costs will be contained. Taking your cell phone is important, and you will likely have coverage in major cities. But you need to understand that if you are in a remote area, there may be no coverage. Your volunteer program will also have telephone communication from its office or on your site, but you may have to make an appointment to make a call. Keep the phone charged, dry, and with you. If all else fails, you may be able to purchase a long-distance phone card to use from a phone in your destination country. It is best to purchase that card after you arrive in-country to make sure it will work. If your carrier doesn't have coverage in a particular country, ask your program director for the best option of a temporary or prepaid cell phone that will work in your destination country.

External batteries or chargers are essential in my life. I never travel without two completely charged external batteries for my cell phone and tablet in my carry-on pack. I use them all the time. They are available online or in many stores, but I do recommend strong ones (20000mAh) that will recharge your phone for days without having to recharge the external battery. Make sure you have the proper outlet connectors (USB to connector to AC or other wall outlet) as most

Electrical Adapter Kits

They're essential if you plan on using electricity to recharge your tablet or cell phone or razor. Find out from your program liaison which adapter kit you will need. Electrical systems in other countries can vary a lot in how they work. Some adapter kits have multiple connection options included. Be sure you have the correct set of charger connections.

IMPORTANT!

batteries do not come with those. Also, make sure you have a charger/converter cord to use for your cell phone that came with it. Otherwise, it may not charge properly. iPhone products have different cord connections than Android, so make sure you have the correct cords. Check with your cell phone carrier and see what it suggests.

Don't Forget It

There are two categories of items that are not required, but are strongly recommended. The first is, take a journal and camera, or make sure your phone can take a lot of photos. By a lot, I mean hundreds if not thousands. You will want an extemporaneous record of this trip in real time. If you don't like to write, use a recorder with enough recording space, or extra tapes or discs, to record. Make sure you can download your photos to an external drive or the Cloud (if you can access Wi-Fi) so they are secured for you in the future. Today's electronics make keeping these records so much easier than it has ever been. Take advantage of it.

Second, but maybe most important, take small, meaningful gifts for your host family or for people you meet along the way. They don't have to be huge (heavy) or expensive. They should mean something to you, should represent who you are or where you come from, or what is special and unique to you about the United States. Decide what to take after discussing this with your program liaison. These gifts are very precious to the receiver, so be thoughtful when deciding what to take.

Hopefully, you now know more about how to travel and volunteer abroad than you did before. You will certainly receive good training from your chosen program or project on the specifics of your tasks. You know from the last few chapters how to pay attention, how to take care of

Don't Forget It— Host Gifts

When traveling to a smaller country several years ago, the small gifts our local hosts wanted were bandages, antibiotic ointment, gauze bandages, adhesive tape, toothbrushes, toothpaste, and hydrogen peroxide. Also, children's books in either Spanish or English were requested. None of these items were easily available in the rural areas or in the less-affluent areas of the cities. I remember thinking how easy it is for US residents to take the accessibility of simple items like these for granted.

Example

yourself, and how to ensure you are safe and healthy. Just remember to always be situationally aware, use common sense, and be open to new experiences. No book or video can replace the excitement of hearing, touching, seeing, smelling, and tasting new places in person. While traveling and volunteering, don't make assumptions. Ask all the questions you need to of your program officer or on-site supervisor. The only bad question is the one you *don't* ask.

To Summarize...

- Plan to take clothing and essentials for traveling light and for easier care while making sure your choice of clothing is culturally acceptable.

- Leave valuables at home and limit luggage to a suitcase and a two-shoulder-strap backpack, with RFID protection.

- Take a camera and a cell phone. Add international service to your cellular account.

- Take gifts for your program host family.

Expectations When Volunteering

This section is about how to work the most effectively with your organization in a volunteer environment. Successful volunteering is a win-win relationship. As an engaged volunteer, you help the organization get energized support in all sorts of ways, and you get to learn new skills, find new friends, and just plain feel wonderful about doing good well.

Chapter 21

What You Can Expect from the Organization

In This Chapter...

- What you can expect your charity to offer you
- Clarification of the role of the organization
- Written volunteer agreement
- Intangible return to you as the volunteer

It is not only okay; it is *imperative* that you understand what you can expect from the organization to which you intend to give your time. You're encouraged to ask for what you need to do your job well, and to do it in a way that satisfies you. Don't be too hasty—take the time to talk with the organization representatives, and try to get your volunteer agreement with it in writing. The more you clarify processes and expectations in advance, the more successful the volunteer relationship will be for all parties. Remember, volunteers volunteer *in*, and they can volunteer *out*. You, as the volunteer, control the process.

Don't think that you are being self-centered if you have expectations for the experience. You are not. The organization will also have clear expectations of you. The key for success is full and interactive communication. Ask questions, ask for help when you need it, make it a priority to complete promised tasks, and, most of all, have fun!

Specific Goals in the Role of the Organization

Specific goals you can expect from charities as their volunteer are equally applicable across all varieties of volunteering. Most well-organized volunteer programs have written agreements, particularly those that provide direct service to clients. Ask to review the volunteer agreement in advance. There are several items you will need to be aware of, but they will all come together as a cohesive unit once you begin your adventure. If in fact your organization does not have a standard written volunteer agreement, ask them to develop one. This may be an opportunity for them to enhance their process.

Organizational Readiness

The first and most basic status you can expect to see when being recruited by a charity to become a volunteer is that the charity is structured and prepared to incorporate volunteers into the operation. It sounds simple, but more often than you might think, a charity asks for volunteers but has no work ready for them when they show up.

When you are talking to a charity about volunteering, ask to see its volunteers at work. Ask representatives where they need your help. Ask them to be specific about your duties and schedule. Ask if you can meet the person who will be supervising you. If the charity is not able to clearly tell you this information, it may not be ready for volunteer help. You may need to suggest that a representative call you when there is a better idea of what is needed.

Your Background Information

Does your charity know about you and what you are bringing to the table in skills? Has a representative interviewed you to find out what you're interested in doing? Were volunteering options explained to you? It is important that it understand who you are and what your skills and interests are, as well as the time you have available is so it can find the best fit. You may be an accountant, and the charity may be looking for that skill set.

However, if your volunteer intent is to work directly with youth, both you and the charity need to understand that. It is the obligation of the charity to find the most suitable occupation for your intent within the organizational volunteer opportunities.

Learning background also applies to you being given information about the charity, its mission, its programs, the kinds of clients served, and its goals for the community. Does this charity fit what you're looking for when you're thinking about investing your time and talent?

Job Description

Your charity needs to be very clear what performance it expects from you, in what it is asking you to do, and how it is asking you to do it. This avoids unintended misunderstandings and mistakes. Is there a written job description? Did you have the opportunity to read the job description or task summary of the position the charity is asking you to fill? Does it make sense to you and are you willing and able to meet the demands of the job? Make sure to ask any questions, and know that it is absolutely acceptable to decline any task for which you feel you are unsuited or which you are unwilling to do.

Training

Every task expected of a volunteer must include training of some kind. Regardless of how simple or how complicated the job is, the organization owes you instruction on how, when, and where to do it, how long it will take to complete the job, and what it expects the result to be when you're finished. Some training could take minutes; more complicated training

Training

In preparing to work with victims of domestic violence and sexual assault for a local charity, I was required to complete twenty hours of training at an Iowa Crime Victim Center (under Iowa Code Chapter 236A). Upon completion, this course of study ensured that I was trained to provide the best information and support to the clients and was well educated in the issues surrounding domestic violence and sexual assault. It was only after this training that I was allowed to interact individually with the clients.

Example

can take weeks or months. An emergency medical technician or a volunteer firefighter will certainly need more intense training and certifications. Helping with a special event or a mass mailing will take less training, and no specialized certifications. Working with youth or at-risk populations might require specialized learning by volunteers.

Many charities also require background checks of volunteers if the assigned work involves direct contact with clients served. You may be asked to sign a confidentiality agreement, or if you are a board director, you will likely be asked sign a conflict-of-interest form annually. All of these expectations should be clearly communicated to you before you agree to go forward.

Effective Use of Your Time

You're making a big effort to invest time and labor for your charity. It has a responsibility to ensure that your time is valued and spent productively. When you show up to work, there should be enough of a job for you to do and enough volunteers to do the job required.

Understand how much time you are committing to on a weekly, monthly, or annual basis. Will this work with your standard schedule? Will any required training be available around your work hours? What is the process if you have to be absent from a tutoring session or a board meeting or a committee meeting? For instance, I have served on several boards that had an annual attendance requirement. Don't assume that everyone understands the facts the same way. If it isn't in writing, or discussed thoroughly, misunderstandings can become a source of conflict.

Team Approach

Expect to be treated as part of the team. Being regarded as an important part of a passionate, engaged unit will make all the difference in whether or not you stay committed to and working for your charity. The charity can assure this by taking the time to listen and value your suggestions and feedback. It can include you in activities or meetings that apply to your duties. The organization can offer you extra training or opportunities, if you're interested. Get to know the staff and other volunteers with whom you are working. You will all feel that you are important to each other, and your lives will be richer with more wonderful people in it. Both you and the charity will welcome your full engagement.

Recognition

This is simple, but sometimes not offered as much as it might be. Expect to be thanked, frequently. This doesn't necessarily mean flashing lights and huge trophies all the time. A simple "thank you" from the charity goes a long way in saying "we appreciate your work, we value you as an individual, and we couldn't do it without you." From time to time, you should be able to see your name in the annual report or in a newsletter being recognized for your volunteer contributions. You should also expect a written letter of appreciation from the executive director or CEO.

Communication

Excellent, effective communication is a daily requirement for being positive and successful. This means if you see something that needs to be addressed, say something. Expect the charity to keep you up to date on any information you need to do your job well. If either you or your organization makes promises, it is important to make sure they are kept. Talk to each other, constantly. You should expect that the charity has a written communications process as well, in case of major issues that occur. Ask to have a copy of that process and be sure to follow it.

Intangible Expectations

The intangibles you will be taking away are very different for each volunteer, and are more difficult to define or quantify. However, the intangibles can be the intense color and personal return that keeps you, as the volunteer, passionately engaged. This is the personal return you are getting for the job.

Emotional Return

The real "pay" you will receive from volunteering, regardless of how or where, is the deep emotional satisfaction you will feel by doing something for someone else while having no expectation of payment. You're making a direct difference in someone's life. You may or may not ever meet these folks. If you are working for a cause instead of a client, you will know in your heart that, one person at a time, you and your cohorts are changing the world. These are some pretty big feelings. You will smile as you go to sleep at night.

Social Engagement

Without a doubt, your personal world will expand as you volunteer. You will be meeting all sorts of people who never would have touched your life if you had chosen to remain on your couch. You can become involved with an organization or cause that will offer the opportunity to meet the famous (or infamous) whom you have admired. There may be a community leader or iconic person of the community that you want to get to know. Rolling up your sleeves and working together on a project will give you that opportunity. Overall, you will be making new friends and engaging in new adventures with them. No one can have too many friends. Conversely, when you work with others as a volunteer, it raises your credibility with them as well. You have expanded your sphere of professional influence.

Skills Enhancement

Volunteering is the best way I know of to learn new skills or improve already existing talents. You don't have to pay tuition and spend years in continuing education courses to increase your expertise in whatever your choice of task might be. You don't have to pass tests, or prove anything to an educational review group. You simply need to show up and learn! Then you can carry these new competencies with you when you choose to move on. How exciting is that?

You understand now what you can expect from a charity for which you're considering volunteering. The next chapter will discuss what it can expect from you. Keep remembering that this is a synergistic relationship where all parties win.

To Summarize...

- What you can expect from your volunteer involvement with a charity is both tangible and intangible.
- Expect the charity you're volunteering for to value and respect your time and efforts.
- Ask for a signed volunteer agreement and expect adequate training and resources to do the job.
- Expect your social and professional spheres of influence to expand, your skills to increase, and to feel that you're making a difference to the lives of others.

Chapter 22

What the Organization Can Expect from You

In This Chapter...

- Organizational understanding and preparation
- Commitment and follow through
- Willing attitude and work ethic
- Leadership and loyalty

We've talked about what you can expect from your charity. It is also essential to understand and agree to what your organization is expecting of you, the volunteer. You're serving as staff, albeit unpaid. Be aware that you are important in the success of the charity. Again, clear and comprehensive communication—in advance—is critical for an effective partnership.

The organization expects you to have made a considered and intentional decision to not only volunteer your time, but to volunteer it for the charity's particular mission with passion and dedication. This applies whether you're doing direct service with clients, are on a special event committee, or are serving as a board director.

Make sure you do your due diligence in becoming informed about the charity. Research is important to avoid getting into a situation that may not fit what you're looking for. Also talking directly with someone at the charity is important before you make a decision. While you want to work with your best friends where they volunteer, don't agree solely because they asked you. If you do, you run the risk of becoming frustrated, unhappy, and burned out quickly. At that point, both you and the charity lose.

It may be obvious, but first and foremost, do you clearly understand what the charity does? Do you know what programs the charity offers? Who it serves? How it serves its clients? Do you care deeply and believe strongly in what the charity gives to those it serves, as well the greater community? Does your heart expand and does your mind get excited about being a part making a difference through the work of the charity? If yes, then terrific—keep going! If not, move on to the next opportunity. Making sure the emotional and philosophical fit is right for you and for the charity is the place you must begin. If the fit is not good, be honest—no harm, no foul. Neither the volunteer nor the charity wishes for an unhappy relationship.

Organizational Understanding and Preparation

The organization will expect you to understand its structure, what your volunteer role will be, and what you will need to do to be prepared to fill your tasks. As we discussed before, you should have a written understanding, even if it is simple or informal.

Kind of Organization

You need to understand what kind of an organization you're looking for so you can be sure that you will find the right fit for you. Not all charities are organized for the same kind of purpose, although there are certainly similarities in structure. Human service charities tend to be focused on direct services to clients. Some nonprofits are dedicated to raising money for a specific cause. Some are pass-through charities raising funds for other organizations. Some nonprofits provide entertainment, historic, or artistic experiences. Some are focused on youth athletic involvement. As a volunteer, you get to choose from this banquet. It is your responsibility to understand how your choice of charity is structured. Your best sources for this information are the executive director, the board chair, the charity website, or the director of development.

Kind of Organization—Your Choice of Board

Virtually all nonprofits have boards of directors, and some may also have boards of trustees that could have a slightly different function. If you're interested in board service, investigate how to submit your name and background for consideration. Some board recruitment techniques are simple, some are quite sophisticated, but the organization will let you know the process when you ask.

IMPORTANT!

If you want to work directly with clients, picking a charity that has that option is, of course, essential. Many nonprofits offer direct service with clients, such as Boys and Girls Club, Boy Scouts, Girl Scouts, Salvation Army, community homeless shelters or domestic violence shelters, senior living facilities, Special Olympics, Little League, or schools, to name a few. What programs are you interested in that work directly with clients? When you're talking to the nonprofit, you will need to be specific about the kind of volunteering you want to do. The organization will expect you to fully understand the job for which you're applying, and be willing to do it.

Many organizations offer volunteer positions in special events, fundraising, or a wide variety of other participative activities in addition to direct service.

Some nonprofits are highly focused on special events, either for a specific cause or for funding to a variety of other charities. An example is Variety the Children's Charity, which does primarily special events to fund an array of programs for kids with needs. Fraternal or service organizations often hold events to raise funds for multiple causes selected by the group. Examples include Rotary International, Optimists, Masons, or Knights of Columbus. Events could include golf tournaments, 5K runs, Halloween Scary Houses, road rallies, or basketball tournaments.

The American Cancer Society, the March of Dimes, and the Make-A-Wish Foundation are examples of charities that hold events to support their organization's mission. You may choose to serve on an event committee for any of these nonprofits, or you may want to participate in the event as well.

When thinking about an arts and entertainment nonprofit, you may want to volunteer as clerical staff, a docent, an actor, a stage hand, or a teacher of young students, or you may even provide transportation to a youth performing group. Find out in advance what each charity has available for volunteer involvement. Then make an informed decision before you go through the door to offer your time.

Role as Volunteer

Your role as a volunteer is to work for the nonprofit as you agree to when you become involved. You have done your research and you know what the nonprofit you chose has available for volunteers. The charity expects that you will have freely and enthusiastically made a decision about what you want to do. The charity will do its best to make that assignment work for you. If what you want is not immediately available, you will need to have a flexible view. In the long term, the organization will make its best effort to place you where you want to be.

As a working volunteer, you can look forward to helping with undertakings that might include:

- Teaching
- Counseling
- Board of directors
- Event committee
- Fundraising
- Clerical
- Performance support
- Coaching
- Public relations and marketing
- Training
- Specialized services (e.g., physician, attorney, dentist, chef, etc.)
- And more

If any of the tasks assigned require specific training on your part before being accepted as a volunteer, make sure you're honest with the organization about whether or not you have that training.

The nonprofit expects you to follow its training and instructions about how to do what you are assigned to do. You will generally get simple instructions verbally and more complicated instructions in writing. Please believe and follow them. Nonprofits have invested a lot of time and thought into the design of the volunteer program and the management of you, the volunteer.

Most nonprofit organizations require you to sign and abide by documents that may include a confidentiality agreement, a conflict-of-interest policy. If serving on a board, the charity may ask for an agreement for a certain level of annual financial support. Your organization may have other requirements, as well. For instance, Boy Scouts require a background check for all completed volunteer applications. These applications and online Youth Safety Training must be completed annually by volunteers. These training requirements may sometimes seem overdone, but it is for the protection of both you and the charity. Additionally, you can add to that skill set you're building! When it comes to any financial commitment, try to aim for giving at a level that works for you.

"I Can Do It Better"

As much as you occasionally may want to, as a volunteer it is not your option to impulsively confront the nonprofit that it is not doing its job correctly, or to try to change things quickly and unilaterally. In the course of performing your tasks, you will no doubt see how some things can be done better. Follow the organizational chart (e.g., the pecking order) and have a chat with your immediate supervisor. The organization generally has a process to listen to and act on good observations by volunteers. Give the process time to work. Try to understand the working system in place, then approach your proposed changes politely and carefully. The one exception is if the situation is an immediate life-safety issue for a client. Then get help soon as you can.

WATCH OUT!

Commitment and Follow-Through

You have said yes. You have done your research, talked to people involved, and chosen the charity that is special to you. You know what you will be expected to do. You have done all of your training. The charity is expecting you to be deeply committed to what you are doing. Now it is time for you to show up. Do what you say you're going to do. The organization, and the people it serves, is depending on you.

Willing Attitude and Work Ethic

Fulfill your commitment to the best of your ability, with a smile, and a positive attitude. Keep a spirit of cooperation among your covolunteers. Be totally engaged and positive about what you're doing. The nonprofit will both expect and appreciate your stellar work!

Leadership and Loyalty

Your charity will expect you to be loyal. It will expect you to completely support its mission as well as keep confidential information confidential. Avoid the temptation to talk about the charity's internal workings. Any concerns should be kept within the organization's walls.

As a volunteer, you also have the opportunity to act as a leader both within the organization and in the greater community. Boards offer positions as officers. Serving clients directly offers supervisory positions. Special events always need event chairs, or committee chairs, or activity managers. You may have talents as a leader you haven't discovered yet!

To Summarize...

🖰 Understand and look for the kind of organization that you want to give your time and efforts to. There are countless choices.

🖰 Make sure you clearly understand what the charity is expecting from you.

🖰 Complete any training necessary.

🖰 With deliberate and positive intent, enthusiastically, passionately, and loyally support your charity to the best of your ability.

🖰 Take the opportunity to become a leader.

Chapter 23

Working with Covolunteers

In This Chapter...

- General work manners
- Understanding personal styles—yours and theirs
- Enhancing professional skills
- Expanded social contact

Y ou will meet and make friends with people whom you would never know if not for volunteering. Volunteering is also a professional relationship while you're working for the organization. Working with covolunteers really isn't much different than working with the coworkers in your place of business. In a nonprofit setting, however, volunteers are driven by commitment to and passion for the mission, not a paycheck. Volunteers also tend to develop a strong sense of ownership for the organization.

This chapter focuses on how to successfully work with all sorts of personalities that you will find in your volunteer journey. Most of us have held jobs of one kind or another, so it's likely that most of what I am saying here you already know. However, it bears repeating, as good manners and excellent work habits in any workplace are important, whether the staff is paid or not.

General Work Manners

It's likely you have worked for an employer before. Excellent office deportment is fairly universal. Volunteering isn't much different. Show up on time and be prepared to work or to begin your meeting. You may need to arrive a few minutes early to put personal items away and get settled. If it is a meeting, make sure you have all of your materials (that you have reviewed in advance), and an agenda. If you are doing direct service or administrative tasks, be ready to start. Finish that last cup of coffee. If you are consistently late, you annoy your covolunteers or organization's staff, and can very well hold up the work that they expected to finish that day. If you know you will be unavoidably detained, call in advance and let them know. Reschedule your shift, meeting, or duties if necessary. Everyone's time is equally valuable.

Be friendly. Take the time to look people in the eye and say hello, even if you're late or preoccupied. Making the effort to be pleasant goes a long way. If you ignore folks or are abrupt, you run the risk of unintentionally offending someone whose help you made need in the future. Everyone, including you, wants to be acknowledged, not ignored. It's unlikely you will become best friends with everyone you meet, but you will want to be friendly acquaintances. Make the effort to build good relationships.

As a caution, don't allow yourself to be sucked into the gossip machine that exists in every organization. This is doubly true concerning clients with whom you're working. Gossip is dangerous and destructive, usually inaccurate, and can significantly lower volunteer and staff morale. If someone around you starts this kind of conversation, ignore it. Simply

General Work Manners

There are numerous reference books on office etiquette if you're interested in more in-depth investigation. A few are:

◆ *The Essentials of Business Etiquette.* Barbara Pachter. McGraw Hill Publishers, 2013.

◆ *The Essential Guide to Business Etiquette.* Lillian Chaney and Jeanette Martin. Greenwood Publishing Group, 2007.

◆ *100 Things You Need to Know: Business Etiquette for Students and New Professionals.* Mary Crane and Associates, 2014.

Inspiration

smile and walk away. Tell them you have an appointment to have your shoelaces ironed.

Effective communication is critical for the success of any endeavor. Communicate honestly, clearly, and effectively. Internally, stick to facts and avoid personal judgment or opinion unless it's specifically requested by whoever is supervising your assignment.

Communication includes both written and oral. You might be asked to do emails or letters. In emails, avoid copying everyone you can think of; keep the list to people from whom you need answers or actions. Make sure all letters are approved for content before being sent. Keep copies or meeting notes of all communications so you have a good record of activities. Externally, remember confidentiality. If you love social media, post only general happy news about the nonprofit, never details of clients or intraorganization work. Private internal workings of a nonprofit are not available for outside social conversation, either.

If you're having problems with another volunteer, a program, a client, or an event, ask the staff person in charge for a private meeting. Be clear and business-like about your concerns and offer what you think is a good resolution. It isn't enough to just complain—you need to be part of the solution.

Mistakes happen. When it is your fault, apologize, figure out how to fix it, ask for help if necessary, and let it go. We've all goofed. The sun will still come up in the morning. If someone else erred, and you're asked what happened, don't throw the person who actually made the mistake under the bus. You can suggest that the supervisor solicit the person's version of what happened to help clarify the situation.

Clean up after yourself or the clients you're working with. If you're working on a project, or simply having a lunch meeting,

Accountability

We all hope we're perfect, but reality tells us this is a fantasy. If you make a mistake, own it, apologize, fix it, and move on. Try to do it with true contrition and a smile.

IMPORTANT!

don't leave food and other items on the table for someone else to take care of. Act like you are in your own house. Pick it up, put it away, or throw it away.

If you are involved in a special event, cleaning up is even more important. At the end of the event, you will be exhausted and not want to clean up anything, but take a deep breath and push through to the end. Event cleanup is as important as set up. Remember that all the other volunteers are as tired as you're. Try to have a special crew that comes in at the end just for the cleanup process. It really helps.

It all boils down to respect. Respect the work, the workplace, and everyone who is giving time and effort, in as objective a way as possible. Follow up when you make a promise. Do what you say you will do, when you say you will do it. Others are depending on you. Afterwards check to make sure what you delivered is working.

Understanding Personal Styles—Yours and Theirs

In working as a volunteer, you will undoubtedly run into a surplus of different kinds of personalities. The added layer with volunteers is that they often give themselves permission to be quite emotional about their work for the charity. Sometimes you feel like you and a covolunteer are speaking different languages. You feel like you either don't understand the attitude of another volunteer or you can't figure out how to help them understand what you're saying. It happens, and conflict can follow.

I have found that the answer for me is being aware of how different personality styles are defined, what different types of temperaments look like, and how to communicate with approaches different than yours in a way the other person can hear and understand you. You will become an effective communicator to covolunteers, staff, or donors to your charity, once you learn how to adapt to different behavioral traits.

However, the most important thing you need to do is to intentionally decide to accept each person, exactly as is, without judgment. Appreciate your covolunteers' commitment, and enjoy what they bring to the experience.

Try to look at your covolunteers and see how they approach the world. Try to think like they think. For instance, are they happier with pages of numbers than with talking about their family? Do they get upset with conflict? Are they "bottom-line" kind of people? Try to temporarily adapt your individual character traits to match theirs when you approach them. If they are distressed by conflict, talk quietly and ask how you can help. If they are more assertive, get to your point quickly and let them know clearly and concisely what you need from them. Try and fill their needs, if possible.

Feel free to do more research. Read a variety of authors on this subject for different ways to understand your personality and those of others. For those of you who are volunteering in directly fundraising for your charity, this information is amazingly valuable.

A few sources for defining different personality styles and how to work with them include (some sources are dated, but the information is still very effective):

My Style

My personal style is fairly assertive. I tend to focus on the goal and drive through the process until it is attained. I have learned the hard way that not everyone appreciates my personal style. While my intent is sincere, for a shy person or someone who prefers highly social conversations, I can seem pushy or insensitive. It's important to recognize that we have to slow down, pay attention, and be sensitive. We all teach each other, and it takes more than one person to get the work done.

I have learned to take the time to sincerely connect better with others, and truly appreciate each covolunteer individually. We are all working together for a common good, and every person involved in the work brings something important to the table.

Example

🔖 *The Social Styles Handbook.* Wilson Learning, Larry Wilson. Nova Vista Publishing, 2011.

🔖 *Adapt Your Styles to Win Trust.* Tom Kramlinger, PhD; Michael Leimbach, PhD; Ed Tittle, BA, MA; David Yesford. Wilson Learning Corporation; Nova Vista Publishing 2014.

🔖 *Seven Faces of Philanthropy.* Russ Alan Prince, Karen Maru File. Wiley Nonprofit and Public Management Series, rev 2001.

🔍 *The Ask.* Laura Fredricks, JD. Jossey-Bass, 2006.

🔍 *Asking Styles, Second Edition.* Linda Lysakowski. CharityChannel Press, 2017.

All these books are different in approach but all have valuable information you can use.

Enhancing Professional Skills

One of the best values about volunteering is that you will have the opportunity to learn new skills that you don't have to go to school to learn, and that you can put in your professional tool belt and take with you. Opportunities to learn something new is sort of like a hidden gift to you. Be sure to watch, ask questions, participate, and learn. And "do good" for others at the same time.

Think about food service, which rates typically high volunteer involvement. Have you cooked dinner for one hundred or five hundred? You might face this in a kitchen in a homeless shelter. What would you need to prepare and serve that many, other than bigger pans? There is a whole science about how to purchase food in quantity and how to cook it. Once you learn how to feed many, think of the wonderful dinner parties you can hold!

If you are volunteering in an office setting, learn all you can about computer software and hardware. Add the knowledge to your résumé and use it in future work. The logistics of staging a major regional special event will teach you more than you may want to know about how to manage food, shelter, city permits, sanitary facilities, crowd management, fireworks, and entertainment for ten— or twenty—thousand of your closest friends. Once you have this knowledge, you are a huge asset to anyone or any organization that may need your skills. For some, this may even lead to a career in special event management. It is a highly sought talent, particularly in metropolitan areas.

If you're volunteering for wildlife or marine life management programs, you may learn scuba diving along with the science, and discover a new professional calling. Your new skills may be as small as learning a new card game with a young child, or learning to ride a horse or paddle a canoe as a camp counselor. All of your new competences are important to both the charity you serve and to in your personal life. Higher self-esteem and increased professional marketability will happen for you.

The training your organization requires will increase your skills. Learning on the job will increase your proficiencies. Participating in new activities of any kind will increase your abilities. The list can be endless, so don't avoid learning new stuff. Take advantage of every scrap of new information you can learn as you never know when you will be able to use it. However, don't take on a job until you are trained and know how to do it. You will have to let the person in charge know if you are not trained and ready.

Expanded Social Contact

A certainty about volunteering is that once you become involved, you will unavoidably end up knowing more people than you did before you began. In fact, one of your goals in volunteering may be to get to know an individual who is already involved in the charity. Nothing builds good long-term relationships like rolling up your sleeves and working together.

Take the opportunity to expand your circle of friends. Make the effort to get to know your covolunteers (or charity staff) on a personal level. Meet after your volunteer work—for lunch, for a cocktail, to take in a movie. Of course, you won't become best friends forever with every person you meet, but you will be enriched by inviting those with whom you connect into your living room and into your life.

To Summarize...

- Working with covolunteers requires sensitivity, flexibility, and a friendly attitude.

- Be respectful of covolunteers' and staff time; show up on time and ready to work.

- Value learning and using new skills. Value what each covolunteer brings to the experience.

- By learning to adapt to other's personal styles, your increased social contacts and work relationships will be more effective.

Chapter 24

Interaction with Clients Served (Direct Service)

In This Chapter...

- Client needs in direct service
- Organization's needs for direct service
- Your personal needs in direct service
- Your rights as a volunteer in direct service

There is nothing more satisfying than working hands-on with clients and the work of the organization. You're directly delivering the mission up close. The clients—the mission—are the reason you're there. You're making a difference in lives or in how an organization operates, in a way that may not be obvious to you but means everything to them. Whether you're providing direct help to a new entrepreneur starting a business, counseling a battered spouse, shelving books in the library, caring for elderly shut-ins, or delivering Meals on Wheels, there are some things to think about in advance.

This chapter is primarily about you working one-on-one with individual clients, or doing the direct work of the organization. In essence it is about "getting your hands dirty." As a hands-on volunteer, you will be building close personal relationships with clients, staff, and other volunteers. Building a helpful and successful relationship is based on trust between you and the client, as well as you and the organization. Traits that individual clients and organizations are looking for from volunteers are trust, dependability, follow-through, and honesty. The lives of individual clients may be already in some kind of crisis or upheaval. As the volunteer in the client's life, you're the quiet oasis, the friend, the advisor, the coach.

What Clients and Organizations Need from Volunteers

Let's look at what clients and organizations need from you, the volunteer:

Training

In talking about direct service with individual clients, your client—child, youth, or adult—deserves to trust that you have been fully and appropriately trained to help. It is your job to make sure that you have received the proper training and that you understand and can implement the training. If you didn't, go back to the organization and ask.

You may be working with a child at risk or a senior in need. Your heart will be touched. Your emotions will be engaged. You may be tempted to over-promise what you can realistically deliver. Individual clients are emotionally and possibly physically vulnerable. They have a high level of need or they wouldn't be where they are. As a caring human being, you will want to fix what is broken. Of course, it is fine to do that, but avoid making excessive assurances about your capabilities or the resources of the organization. *Don't make a promise you can't keep.* Fall back on how you were

Training— Special Attention

In some situations, you may have had the training that makes you a mandatory reporter for abuse (child, adult, senior, even animal). If you are a mandatory reporter and you see a situation where abuse is taking place, the organization likely has a clear process for reporting it. Use the correct method for making the report, as the law requires certain steps be taken to enforce any charges as well as to ensure the safety of the person, or animal, at risk.

WATCH OUT!

trained for the job. The organization has a plan for how it delivers services. It understands its clients. The charity needs to depend on you doing your job the way the charity has found is most effective. If you do end up making a promise you can't keep, you can make things worse instead of better, or even cause liability issues.

The same standards apply if your service is to an organization (such as a library, a food bank, a kitchen facility, etc.) and not an individual. They need to trust that you will accurately and dependably follow your training, and that you work in a positive and reliable way. If you feel additional actions are needed, or something needs to be changed, go to the volunteer coordinator and the organization and talk about it. It is true that you are not being paid, but the charity is still depending on you to complete your tasks.

Whether with an individual client or doing technical or managerial services for an organization, don't take unilateral action unless there is an immediate life-safety issue. Check in with your volunteer coordinator or supervisor. If there is a life-safety problem, follow the organization's formal procedures for that kind of situation.

Confidentiality

You will be helping individual persons. Each has a living story, each has serious needs, and each has an expectation of absolute privacy when it comes to the details of their lives. It cannot be overstated how critical it is that you maintain utter confidentiality.

You're probably going to get to know these folks. You will talk about different matters and you will see many incidents, some of which may be tough on you emotionally. Plan on finding a way to stay emotionally detached enough to do your job well. At the same time, you need to keep all of your interaction with them confidential. You have likely already signed a confidentiality agreement with the charity. That was a piece of paper. It becomes very real when you have a person in front of you pouring out all of the person's problems and grief. The client is depending on you for help. The client is also depending on you to keep what they say confidential within the organization. Put yourself in the shoes of the client. Would you like to have the privacy of your problems discussed by strangers?

If you're working with the charity in a more managerial capacity, the rules are the same. This can include things like service on a board, shelving books in a library, answering phones at a school, or guiding tours at a museum. Typically, not much you see or hear can leave the organization, nor can you casually discuss proprietary client or charity information with covolunteers not directly involved in the same way you are. It means you cannot discuss what you see, hear, and experience with your significant other, your friends, or your banker (the last you can talk to if you have written permission of the organization). Put yourself in the place of the organization. Would your organization's good name recover if it is trying to correct problems and you damage it with careless conversation? Avoid the possibilities altogether. Keep information to yourself.

Example

Confidentiality

There are long and short forms of volunteer confidentiality agreements. *4good.org* offers a sample agreement.

A confidentiality agreement might include these provisions:

◆ Definition of confidential information: defines what is meant by confidential information, organizational records, etc.

◆ Definition of confidentiality: defines what constitutes disclosure of confidential information and what is not considered confidential information.

◆ Maintaining confidentiality: spells out what constitutes disclosure and what actions are expected of the volunteer.

◆ Use of confidential information: describes where the volunteer may use and not use confidential information in the performance of duties.

◆ Disclosure of confidential information: outlines restrictions on volunteer's disclosure of confidential information and as well as the penalties for an inappropriate disclosure.

◆ Termination of confidentiality and confidential information: outlines the terms for termination of a volunteer who violates the agreement as well as requiring the return of any confidential information by the volunteer.

◆ Plus the standard legal provisions including governing law and remedies; severability; waiver; entire agreement; general provisions; and, of course, appropriate signatures.

Dependability

We've talked about showing up on time. We've talked about ensuring you are properly trained and are following the training. There is more to being trustworthy. When working directly with clients or charities, they need to be able to depend on your openness and your honesty, and that you will deliver what you say you will deliver. Be consistent and dependable, even when you are telling them something they don't want to hear. Consistently do your best work. Be there when you promise to be. Listen thoroughly and empathetically to what someone has to say. Follow through on what you promise to do. Never lie. If you don't have the correct answer, say so, then go find out what that answer is and report back. If you're put in the position of taking care of any materials or assets of the charity, be sure you keep them safe.

Your Personal Needs and Rights as a Volunteer

In working in direct service, you as a volunteer have needs and rights as well. You're emotionally and intellectually invested in those you are helping, not to mention you are investing lots of time and physical effort. You want to keep doing it. Remember that you're part of the balance, the equation, which makes your work important. Sometimes it is easy to lose sight of your personal importance.

Be aware that you're not only investing time, you are investing yourself into what you're doing. Spend yourself wisely. The side effect of volunteering is that you may become deeply personally devoted. Sometimes it can be not only difficult, but emotionally devastating to detach from a client or a

Your Personal Needs

First and foremost, as a volunteer, *take care of yourself.* Get enough sleep, proper nutrition, and exercise. If you are not healthy, devoting a lot of time and labor to a nonprofit can be challenging. Not only will these life skills help you, you will be modeling this excellent approach to the people you are helping. It sounds simple, but you would be surprised how often volunteers need to be reminded to go home and get some sleep.

WATCH OUT!

particular situation. Be cautious about becoming too close, as the day will come that you will move on. Be sympathetic, empathetic, and enthusiastic, but be careful about having too much emotional ownership of what you do.

You are no good to yourself or the charity if you burn out or get defeated. Have realistic expectations of yourself, your work with the organization, and what can and cannot be accomplished. Set yourself up for success, not failure. Make any goals, short term or long term, attainable. If you exceed them, great! If you set expectations too high to start with, you're building in potential failure. Make sure you and the organization are in agreement in goals set and accomplishments made. Everyone wins.

To Summarize...

- In working directly with clients of charities, the clients have a right to expect that you're appropriately trained and that you're dependable in doing your job.

- Confidentiality is a priority at all times.

- You should keep your personal investment balanced when working with clients. Do not over-promise results.

- It is critical to you personally as well as the charity that you take care of yourself, physically and emotionally.

Chapter 25

Public Advocacy for the Organization

This chapter is all about the communications aspect of encouraging support of your charity in your community, or how to talk to others about what you do. Volunteers are in the unique position to be the best advocates for the organization, whether in a formal or casual setting. You represent the organization in your neighborhood, with your friends and acquaintances, at your church, and to virtually any people with whom you come in contact. Your passion and enthusiasm will encourage others to support the mission of your organization, and you do it with no personal benefit.

Most volunteers are deeply engaged in helping their charity of choice. You're excited, challenged, learning all the time, and you want to share that with others. You want to tell the world what a terrific job your organization does, how many people it helps, and what a terrific difference it is making to your world. You also want to let folks know how gratifying the work is for you personally. What do you do to spread the good word? How can you be effective in bringing new friends to your charity?

Be a Public Advocate

Advocating for a charity or cause is an outward-facing activity. You will be connecting with the general public to talk about the mission and needs of the organization. You will be asking for support for the programs and sharing how needed these programs are.

Your goal is to effectively convey what your charity accomplishes and the positive effect of that work, not only for the clients directly served but for the greater community. By doing this, you will be encouraging both immediate and future financial and volunteer support for the organization. You will be raising visibility for the charity as well as increasing knowledge and understanding of its core mission. Part of what you talk about will be educational and part will be asking for help and involvement.

When you talk to someone about your volunteer involvement, make sure you are focused on sharing positive news, exciting events, and heroic actions. Your organization very likely has certain terms or phrases that it likes to use about its programs in its public relations efforts. Become familiar with any brochures, advertising, initiatives, or activities of the group, department, or area about which you are speaking. Before you do it, ask the staff how they want a program or event or initiative presented. Occasionally, if there is a sensitive issue in the public arena

You Are the Best Advocate

Actor Christopher Reed was famous for being Superman in the movies. However, following a riding accident that resulted in paralysis, he became the leading advocate for those with spinal cord injuries. He was amazingly effective in raising awareness and support for a cure because he lived his cause.

Your personal experiences and passionate involvement will have more of an effect than anything else in bringing people into the circle of influence of the nonprofit. You love what you do. You love why you do it. You love where you do it. You love how it makes you feel. All you have to do is to share. You will be shocked at the scope of response you will receive.

Pure Genius!

about the charity, only a designated staff member is allowed to speak publicly about those details—so be sure to ask.

Where and How to Talk

Where and how do you approach folks? Figuring that out can be overwhelming. The answer is that there is no single easy answer to that question. It depends on your ultimate goal. Are you looking to fill an immediate need for volunteers? Are you asking for financial support? Are you educating an audience about the charity's mission or a particular program?

Informal Advocacy

Always the most effective is your personal touch. People respond best to individuals they know and trust. If you can look someone in the eye in an informal setting while you speak with passion and commitment, it is the most effective.

Stop and think about the times during the day that you run into someone you know. Conversations at church, school, the water cooler at the office, the coffee shop, the grocery store, the gas station... you get the idea. Just think about ways you can insert a comment here, an invitation there, and before long you will have your friends and acquaintances interested and involved. Parties, picnics, school events, playing golf, camping with scouts, or traveling on airplanes, trains, or buses all

Informal Advocacy

I used to live in a smaller city, where it was easy to know many of my neighbors and residents. I found that I did more volunteer recruitment, fundraising, and special event planning while going to the grocery store than any other single approach to folks. It seemed that everyone was there, in one aisle or another, and I never let an opportunity pass to talk about a nonprofit with which I was involved. In the grocery store, people were more relaxed, open, and receptive to just chatting about "this and that." I just made sure the "this and that" included their agreement to help with an event or project or gift campaign.

I must admit my trips to the grocery store made my son nuts. What should have taken fifteen minutes often took two hours due to stopping to talk.

Pure Genius!

offer chances to share and engage positive attention. Be passionate about the mission. Try to put requests for participation in terms of how much they are needed, how much fun they will have, and how good they are going to feel. Best of all, they can be working with you!

Informally, you also have the option of social media. Post invitations to events on your Facebook page. Talk about the charity and your involvement on your LinkedIn page. Celebrate the charity's accomplishments. You could do a video of an event (no faces, please, except yours, without written releases) on YouTube or Instagram. If you're raising dollars for a charity's special event, you can do it through your Facebook page. If it is a big catastrophe for which you are looking for financial support, you can even set up something like a special Facebook page or a crowdfunding page. Most charities have a donation option and a volunteer sign-up link on their webpages. Simply direct interested people to the webpages. Also don't forget to include a call to action—a demand for an immediate response. Most people will answer your request. Once people make the commitment, they generally follow through. The rate of response can be amazing.

Structured Advocacy

There are more structured ways to try to engage public support for your charity. Most of these have less of a personal touch but can reach more people at once.

Many nonprofits actively seek opportunities to present speeches about their work. Speeches to community groups, congregations, fraternal organizations, government groups, service organizations, or just about any group you can think of are all options for educating the general public about your charity and the positive work it does. If you plan on delivering a speech, you will need the consent of the nonprofit.

Giving a speech is not for everyone. But if you're willing to do a speech as a volunteer, your presentation will carry a lot of weight with the audience. Remember that the more you can include your personal anecdotes, the more effective the speech will be. The anecdotes are your personal touch to the folks in the audience you haven't yet met.

Another option is writing a letter, or several, to the editor of the local paper. Highlight the good that is being done by the charity. Ask for wide community support. Again, do this with the consent and input of the nonprofit, so you are putting your case in terms that blend with their public relations program. This can be very effective as the newspaper is likely delivering its information both in print and online.

Advocacy through volunteer lobbying or testifying before legislative bodies is a more intense method of cultivating support for the mission and the nonprofit organization, and highly effective. This takes time and often takes travel on the part of the volunteer. It also can take courage to be willing to face a panel of questioning legislators, or individual legislators in their offices.

If you're interested in this role, you first have to let the charity know. Lobbying or testifying can be intimidating if you are not experienced with it. As a volunteer, you will need to thoroughly prepare with the nonprofit and its public relations staff. Typically, you will go to the capital with a group, and will meet with legislators either in a group or at least with one or two other members from your entourage. If you will be publicly testifying, you will be prepared in advance by staff and advisors. If you do not choose to testify or make a statement, but attend the session in support, your presence will be noted by the legislators. Be assured anything you do will make a difference.

What Is and Isn't Appropriate

When you are speaking about and for your charity or mission of your choice, it is always appropriate to be honest, ethical, and positive. Negative or dishonest statements will definitely hurt the charity and very likely reflect poorly on you personally. Make sure you are delivering the message in the way the nonprofit has defined. Being honest does not include sharing details that would in any way violate privacy or fiduciary duty.

Always check your facts. Don't make up your own facts. Don't make statements that aren't or can't be substantiated. Gossip, secret-telling, and behind-the-scenes communications will never be appropriate or a good idea. Be emphatically supportive of the organization, and refuse to acknowledge those that would be hypercritical or destructive.

It's best to speak in more sweeping than detailed terms, if possible. You want to paint a colorful picture of the wonderful work your charity accomplishes. You want to impart the high value of your volunteer experience. Your goal is to make current and future friends and cultivate ongoing support for the nonprofit.

To Summarize...

- Advocacy for a charity or cause means connecting to the public to tell your story.

- Work with the charity to prepare how your advocacy will be presented.

- Connecting with supporters can be done informally, generally on an individual level.

- Formal advocacy would include speeches, legislative testimony, or meeting with community leaders to promote the mission of the organization.

Ethics and Other Considerations

The remainder of this book is going to talk about ethics and legal considerations. There are realities you may or may not ever have to consider. However, it is best to be prepared for unexpected problems.

Chapter 26

What Does Being Ethical Mean?

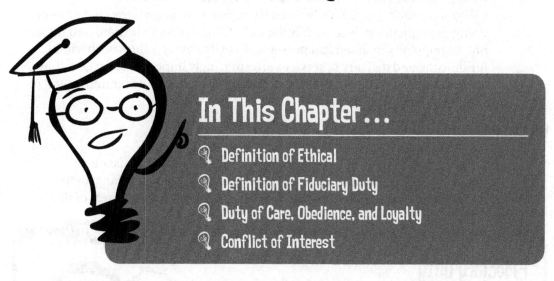

In This Chapter...

- Definition of Ethical
- Definition of Fiduciary Duty
- Duty of Care, Obedience, and Loyalty
- Conflict of Interest

When all is said and done, working as a volunteer does carry ethical standards and has fiduciary obligations, particularly if you're serving as a board member. "Fiduciary duty" and "ethics" are short phrases with a lot of meaning.

Fiduciary duty has legal definitions. In the United States, it is primarily based on the law of the state where the nonprofit organization is situated, though the US federal Tax Code can also be a source.

Ethics really boils down to basic morality—right vs. wrong. It sounds simple and clear-cut, but sometimes following ethical standards and fiduciary duties are not easy. There are subtle differences between the two, but typically someone who fulfills their fiduciary obligations is behaving ethically. The more aware you are and better informed you are about accepted legal and ethical standards, as well as how to protect yourself and manage negative situations, the more successful your volunteer experience will be. Remember, you have the same obligations and rights as a paid employee; you simply don't take home a paycheck.

Definition of Ethical

Ethics are basically the moral principles by which we live our lives. To say it another way, ethics consists acting in a morally correct way, or choosing right over wrong in taking actions. Ethics, or ethical behavior, seems to have a more universal understanding than the term fiduciary duty. An ethical professional (lawyer, doctor, etc.) will not add false charges to a bill. An ethical professor will grade your paper honestly, even if you two have argued over it. Sometimes doing the right thing because it is the right thing to do can be hard and make one unpopular. But an ethical person will do it anyway. Ethics in charitable fundraising and delivery of services are amazingly important, and how they are viewed by any charity should be thoroughly discussed and communicated to staff, board, and volunteers.

Definition of Fiduciary Duty

Fiduciary duty is defined as delivering the highest standard of care and behavior. People are placing their trust in you to do the right thing, in the right way, for the right reasons, at the right time, and in the interest of the

WATCH OUT!

Fiduciary Duty

Over the years, I have learned that each individual has a unique definition of "ethical" or "fiduciary duty." If you're acting in the best interests of the organization and client, honoring confidentiality, are making decisions ethically and in a prudent and business-like way, and acting in good faith, you are fine. As a general policy in nonprofit volunteering, it is best to completely avoid receiving, or appearing to receive, anything in return for the work that you do for the charity. This includes monetary and nonmonetary considerations. If you are uncertain about what decision to make in a given situation, consult with the chief executive officer or an attorney. Experience has taught me to err on the side of caution. The organization's needs come first. If something feels wrong (or "icky"), don't do it.

charity. Bankers, investment managers, and insurance agents are examples of professions that demand a strict adherence to fiduciary duty. Fiduciary duty is typically applied to executing specific duties.

Acting unethically or violating your fiduciary duty can be a serious legal matter, so it is good to understand the expectations as exactly as possible. Not everyone understands fiduciary duty in the same way. Some like to use the phrase as a threat or a weapon. If you have served on a board of directors, at some point you may have been accused of violating your fiduciary duty when in reality your accuser simply has an opposing opinion. Learn to understand exactly what fiduciary duty means so you can avoid feeling bullied by someone with a different agenda, but also so that you don't inadvertently make a mistake you'll regret.

Duty of Care, Obedience, and Loyalty

Each state has its own definition of fiduciary duty, which by inference includes ethical behavior. Simply stated, fiduciary duty breaks down into three areas:

- *Duty of care.* The requirement to act in an ethical, reasonable, and prudent manner, with intelligent consideration and in good faith.

- *Duty of obedience (or duty to act).* The requirement to be fully informed and ensure that all laws, regulations, financial standards, and

Fiduciary Duty

The best version of fiduciary duties I have found is in the *Iowa Principles and Practices for Charitable Nonprofit Excellence* (Rev. 2016). This book was developed by the Iowa Governor's Nonprofit Task Force in conjunction with the Larned A. Waterman Iowa Nonprofit Resource Center at the University of Iowa.

The book includes best practices, with matching principles, in the organization, planning, and operation of a nonprofit organization. It is focused on governance, which of course is accomplished primarily by volunteers (boards and committees).

This book can be downloaded free from *inrc.law.uiowa.edu*.

Inspiration

appropriate policies and procedures are followed, including not exceeding the scope of authority of your position; adherence to the mission of the organization.

Duty of loyalty. The requirement to put the interests and good of the organization before your own personal interests. Self-dealing is not allowed. Appropriately managing conflicts of interest would be a duty of loyalty.

Conflict of Interest

Avoiding conflicts of interest, or even perceived conflicts of interest, is a priority. At some point in your volunteer life you may face a conflict of interest. Conflicts of interest happen, but care must be taken that any conflict does not interfere with your duty of loyalty to the charity. Sometimes they are obvious, sometimes a little subtler. A conflict of interest would happen if a board director used the position on the board to vote for the director's own firm in awarding a work contract. This board director should instead be recused from any discussion or decision.

Conflicts of interest are not always black and white situations. But they can be managed. It is not possible to avoid them completely, so there should be policies in place to address how they are managed. All board members should be required to complete a conflict-of-interest statement annually. Having a formalized conflict-of-interest policy is a requirement under the IRS form 990 which every US nonprofit files yearly. Volunteers who are not board directors may or may not be asked to complete an annual conflict-of-interest statement.

An annual conflict-of-interest statement, including the individual's disclosure (if any), should include the policy adopted by the board of directors plus a space to report either that there is no potential conflict of interest, or that there may be a possible conflict and the nature of the conflict.

This intense attention to conflicts of interest may feel like there is an automatic assumption that you, the volunteer, are less than honest. That is not the case. When a potential conflict of interest is involved, you want to be hypercareful about how the process may appear. Perception is reality. Neither you nor the nonprofit want any chance of misperception that you are somehow personally benefiting (profiting) from the business of the nonprofit.

Again, your organization should have both a conflict-of-interest policy, explaining what a conflict of interest is for your organization and how any conflicts are to be managed, plus a form that allows your board members to disclose any potential or actual conflicts of interest. This form should be completed and signed by all board members annually.

Genuinely ethical choices, integrity, and good fiduciary practices when volunteering can be ensured simply by taking honest, positive action always in the best interests of the organization, while putting personal benefit aside. If you keep the mission and the service to the clients uppermost in your mind, you will make the best decisions.

Perspiration

When a Conflict of Interest Arises

Suppose you're serving on a board for a nonprofit that is going to build a building. You own a construction firm. You would like to have your firm bid for the work. What to do?

Start by disclosing your conflict to the board in advance of any project activity beginning. Decline to have any further involvement as a director in the request-for-proposal or contract discussions. The board will discuss whether or not it is in the best interests of the organization to invite your firm to bid. To enable board members to have this discussion free of your influence, leave the room. If the board then agrees that your wonderful company should be included in the requests for proposal, great. Again, during the RFP and bid-return process, you cannot participate in any discussion of the proposal, the bidding process, or any decision about which vendor is ultimately chosen.

Additionally, don't have any friendly side discussions with your fellow board members about the project while the bids are pending. Depending on the internal structure of your company, you may want to remove yourself as much as possible from the development of the proposal. The bids will be opened in a board meeting. They will be reviewed by designated specialists and a recommendation will be made to the board for final decision. It bears repeating: during all of these processes and when the final decision is discussed and made, you need to remove yourself from the room to avoid any possible appearance of self-dealing.

It goes without saying that seeking the guidance of an attorney competent in the law of tax-exempt organizations is a best practice in such situations.

Conflict of Interest

Sample Conflict of Interest Statement:
Community Health Free Clinic, Cedar Rapids, Iowa

Conflict-of-Interest Disclosure Statement

Name: _____

Check one or more:

❑ Board member

❑ Board committee member

❑ Officer

Check one:

❑ I hereby certify that I have (neither directly, nor through my relative(s) or via my relationship with another entity) no conflict of interest* with CHFC.

❑ I hereby certify that I have or may have (either directly, through my relative(s) or via my relationship with another entity) a conflict of interest* with CHFC, as follows:

Name of Person/Entity	Position Held	Nature of Conflict

*"Conflict of interest" includes (i) a relationship with an entity that competes with CHFC; (ii) a relationship with an entity that is involved, or is likely to become involved, in an adversarial proceeding with CHFC; (iii) a present or potential ownership, investment interest or compensation arrangement with an entity in which CHFC has or may have a transaction or arrangement; or (iv) a compensation arrangement directly with CHFC.

I hereby certify that the above information is true, correct and complete to the best of my knowledge, information and belief. I acknowledge receipt of the CHFC Conflict-of-Interest Policy, have read and understand the Policy and agree to comply with the Policy.

_____   _____

Signature   Date

To Summarize...

🔍 Ethics are basically the moral principles by which volunteers perform their duties.

🔍 Fiduciary duty is defined as delivering work with the highest standard of care and behavior. Fiduciary duties include duty of care, duty of loyalty, and duty of obedience.

🔍 Clear, written conflict-of-interest policies and procedures are critical to ensure appropriate and transparent work process.

🔍 Failure to comply with fiduciary duty can bring legal consequences.

Chapter 27

Internal Organizational Issues

In This Chapter...

- Board Director
- Program volunteer
- Periodic volunteer
- Volunteer fundraiser

Some volunteers may consider knowing how the organization operates internally (policies, procedures, processes) the boring part of volunteering. It may be dry, but it is important that you thoroughly understand as much background as possible about both the organization and about the clients for which you're volunteering.

For your personal protection as well as that of the charity, you should expect that excellent policies, procedures, and processes, as well as adherence to laws and regulations, are a part of the organization's operational structure. Your detailed knowledge of these items will directly affect your volunteer involvement. Examples of different policies include a conflict-of-interest policy, a policy about speaking to news organizations about crisis issues, or a policy about how to handle a parent being late to pick up a child in a day care program.

Policies, procedures, and processes come from well-organized planning and development of internal working standards which ensures the charity stays in legal compliance and delivers its best work. Some policies are fairly standard, such as confidentiality agreements and the conflict-of-interest policies. Procedures and processes will vary greatly from charity to charity and program to program. They are simply lists of how to do what you are being asked to do in the way the charity wants it done.

By having solid written standards, policies, and procedures in place, unwanted outcomes and getting distracted from the core mission can be stopped before they start. All staff and volunteers should know what to expect and how the programs will be delivered, or how the board will function. Depending on the size of the organization, these guides may be divided into administrative and program-oriented documents, or the charity may have just one version. If the documents you need to do your work are not shared with you during your orientation, by all means, ask for them.

Board Director

If you're recruited to serve as a board director, you should expect to receive information to prepare you, and you should receive a formal in-person orientation. Often, that initial information is in the form of a board book. There are several items that should receive, or that should be in the board book that is handed to you at your live board orientation.

As a director, you have a higher obligation of knowing and understanding what is going on within the organization. You will be making important decisions, so be sure they are well informed. Ask lots of questions. As you learn, try to make sure the information you receive verbally is factual, not emotional. Then give yourself enough time to absorb the factual information, plus assess the inevitable internal, unwritten culture that exists for every board and organization. You will grasp more as you go along, but you will need the better part of a year to become as productive as you would like to be. Expect most of the following, and if you don't see them during your orientation, ask about them:

- Articles of incorporation, with amendments (background)
- Bylaws, with amendments (background)
- Any other governing documents (background)

- Conflict-of-interest policy (personal conduct)

- Confidentiality agreement (personal conduct)

- Board volunteer contract (personal conduct)

- Annual personal giving agreement (organizational stability)

- Strategic (long-range) Plan, with any updates (the heart of delivery of the programs—action steps with timelines, outcomes, and assigned responsibilities)

- Organizational chart (organizational work flow)

- List of programs with descriptors of each (core work to deliver mission)

- Dates of meetings for the year (fiduciary duty to appear)

- Board committee list, with dates of committee meetings (organizational communications)

- Staff list with contact information (internal communications)

- Full board list with contact information (organizational communications)

- Minutes of the last three to four board meetings with accompanying materials (support for delivery of programs, financial oversight, and fiduciary duty)

- Any information that is unique to the organization and is necessary for the board director to read and understand, e.g., pertinent laws, regulations, public health requirements, geographic information, legislative information, etc. (fiduciary duty)

- Signature cards if checks are to be signed (fiduciary duty)

- Declarations page of directors and officers insurance policy (fiduciary duty)

- Any procedures in place for doing business, e.g., how to schedule committee meetings, how to order printing, who to contact with questions (organizational effectiveness)

- Summaries of issues currently in front of the board, with the agenda of the next meeting, if possible (fiduciary duty)

Confidentiality Policy

Example of a Short, Simple Confidentiality Agreement

[Name of Nonprofit] Confidentiality Policy

In the course of your work with [Name of Nonprofit], you will have access to confidential information about [Name of Nonprofit], our clients, customers, board members, fellow employees, fellow volunteers and donors. This confidential information is entrusted to your care and you are responsible for safeguarding any confidential information obtained during the course of your work with [Name of Nonprofit]. Preserving this trust is of the utmost value to [Name of Nonprofit]. To facilitate this value, you must recognize that you have access to confidential information and that this information shall not be shared or distributed to anyone or entity except as necessary to perform your duties.

You must further understand that your duty to protect confidentiality shall continue after your work with [Name of Nonprofit] has ended.

I agree to accept this trust.

_____   _____
Signature   Date

Courtesy of Clearly Compliant Inc.

Program Volunteer

A program volunteer is someone who works directly with clients on a recurring basis. A "program" is defined as a specific service that is provided directly to the clients served by the nonprofit. This might include tutoring for Boys and Girls Club, being a Scoutmaster for a Boy Scout troop, teaching classes on painting in a senior center, or providing religious teaching in a church. As a program volunteer, your three major focuses are to understand and be willing to do exactly what you are expected to do; to be thoroughly trained in your tasks, and any other requirements that will help you work with your clients; and to understand the overall organization of the charity. There are processes you will be required to follow to ensure you are qualified and prepared to do your job. As you join the other volunteers, documentation you should look for includes:

🔍 Schedule for training, and what you're expected to attain in the training

🔍 Copy of any laws or regulations you will need to know to do your job

🔍 Health testing requirements, if any

🔍 Investigative requirements, if any

🔍 Compliance testing, if any

🔍 Name and contact information of your direct supervisor on staff

🔍 Clear job description, with outcomes goals

🔍 Calendar of assigned volunteer times, with contact information and system for changing schedule

🔍 Materials necessary to do tasks

🔍 Organizational chart for staff managing your program, with contact information

🔍 Confidentiality agreement

🔍 Conflict-of-interest policy, if required by the board

🔍 Volunteer handbook, if any (will include policies and procedures)

🔍 Volunteer contract, if any, including expectations between volunteer and charity

🔍 Uniform clothing, if required

🔍 List of senior management and board of directors

🔍 Goals and objectives of program staff, as generated by strategic plan, if it affects how you perform your tasks

🔍 A summary case for support for the charity, so you as a volunteer can keep in mind the overall mission of the organization

Periodic Volunteer

A periodic volunteer would include someone who works on a specific project or is involved with a special event for a charity. For a certain period of time, the volunteer may spend a lot of hours working very hard, but once the project or event is complete, the volunteer's tasks are finished. When you and your covolunteers are ready to launch a project or special event, you should expect the following:

- Summary of the project or event, including date, time and location, theme, or reason

- Committee or covolunteer list with contact information

- Staff liaison contact information

- Expected process for completion

- Event or project timeline tasks and financial goals

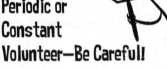

Periodic or Constant Volunteer—Be Careful!

Whether or not you volunteer every day or only occasionally, it is crucial that you abide by confidentiality standards always. Keep the charity's proprietary information and knowledge about clients private. This is true whether or not you sign any confidentiality agreement.

WATCH OUT!

- Sources for support of project or event

- Hard materials (print, swag, etc.) required to complete project or event

- Summary case for support of charity, client testimonials

As a periodic volunteer, you may not be working consistently with clients so you may not have had to complete all training requirements. However, you certainly are representing the organization in the community, and the work you're doing will bring in current and future support for the clients who are being served, so keep that in mind.

The lists of information may or may not be all available from the charity you have chosen. That's fine. If you feel you need at least some level of detail on some of the items, ask for it. In discussing this with the organization, you may give it a new awareness. It may be an opportunity to enhance the internal structure and help it work more effectively. You may want to volunteer your help in systematizing the information and documents.

The more you understand the internal organization and working standards of your organization, the easier it will be for you to accomplish what you want to as a volunteer. Without this information, volunteering can be come confusing and frustrating. You can end up feeling like you're not making a difference, and choose to quit. No one wants to see that outcome.

Volunteer Fundraiser

It is a universal truth that most volunteers who are asked to fundraise for a charity break into a cold sweat. Being afraid of asking for support is not necessary. While good personal relationships with donors are essential for success, fundraising is fundamentally a system of building relationships and keeping excellent records. Go about the task in a systematic way. Don't worry, the organization will prepare you, train you, and accompany you on any visits if you wish. Good preparation will take away your nerves. In the end, you're asking the donor, who you already know, to partner with you, the volunteer, in helping the charity fulfill its mission.

Fundraising campaigns can be for annual programs, for capital needs, for endowment, or for legacy giving. Materials you can expect are all of the printed materials including a case for support and any specific case statements, donor background and contact information, intensive team and individual training, follow up, and excellent administrative support.

The organization should also have clear written procedures for managing receipt of gifts or pledges as well as donor appreciation and acknowledgment. Make sure you understand and follow any requisites.

To Summarize...

🔍 Expect excellent organizational information and support when working as a volunteer board director, regularly scheduled program volunteer, a periodic volunteer, or as a fundraising volunteer.

🔍 Understand the policies and procedures that apply to your specific work.

🔍 Ask for intensive training as appropriate.

🔍 As a fundraising volunteer, take comfort in the fact that asking for support is a systematic technique.

Chapter 28

How to Identify and Resolve Conflicts

In This Chapter...

- Founder's syndrome or mission ownership
- Abrasive personality or bullies
- Dishonesty, ethical, or fiduciary violations
- Lack of dependability

Let's face it. Sometimes things simply do not go the way you want them to. Problems come up. No matter how well intentioned, occasionally there are conflicts or concerns you will run into as a volunteer. How do you identify them before they get out of hand? How do you manage them once they appear?

Conflict in the workplace is basically the same in a volunteer situation as it is in a standard paid work situation. Even though you are not paid, you still have the right to work in an environment without conflict or hostility.

As a volunteer in a nonprofit culture, however, you may need to assess how to react and manage a little more cautiously. The authority you have to manage conflict will be defined on an initial one-on-one basis by your personal approach; then, if the situation grows bigger, whatever the organizational processes are in place for conflict resolution. It is unlikely that as a volunteer you will be autonomous in dealing with larger internal volunteer staffing problems. If you are unable to resolve an issue on your own, remember that you're part of a team, and sometimes it takes the team working together to solve problems.

Identify Conflict

Clearly identify the precise problem you believe must be addressed before you refer it to someone else for resolution. It should be one that directly affects your volunteer efforts, or is a clear violation of law or standing regulations (which you witnessed), or an issue that will adversely affect the operation or reputation of the nonprofit.

If your issue is with one individual, go to that person. Ask to speak in private. Then calmly review your concerns and offer a solution that you think will work for both parties. If that solution is acceptable to both parties, implement it. If not, ask this person for another solution. If one cannot be agreed to, go to the volunteer supervisor and proceed with the organization's conflict resolution process.

If the problem is with a group, or if the problem concerns a

Identify Conflict Through Assessment

Conflicts can be either personal to you or they can, in your opinion, seriously affect the operation or reputation of the charity.

Take some time and do an assessment. Is the problem more incidental or is it fairly consistent? Does it directly affect you or how you're able to do your job? Does it affect the work of a department or the reputation of the nonprofit? Would you consider the issue a major issue (all violations of law are major), or not quite so significant? Is it something you personally observed or experienced or simply something that you were told? In a perfect world, what is the outcome that you think would be best? While doing this assessment, be sure to not base your assessment on unsubstantiated gossip. Write it all down, think about it, refine the information, and then take action if you think it appropriate. Taking no action is also a choice.

Perspiration

possible violation of law, ask to meet with the staff person who has immediate supervisory authority over that area. Again, accurately and calmly relay your concerns and offer a possible solution. Give the supervisor time to investigate, have further meetings, and develop a resolution.

There are times when tempers flare. Walk away until all parties have a chance to calm down. If the argument happens during a board meeting, recess the meeting until calm prevails. Never attack an individual personally. Keep your opinions and requests focused solely on the issue. Personal attacks will reflect negatively on you. In extreme cases, there could even be legal repercussions.

While the conflict resolution process is unfolding, maintain a positive attitude. Sustain open communications. You will get better results. Be sure that you actively listen to the other party's version of the conflict. Again, if your solution is not acceptable to the person, ask the person to suggest another. Remember, it takes two to disagree. Be honest about your role in the conflict. In the end, if it is just a difference of opinion, it is perfectly acceptable to agree to disagree.

If no resolution is acceptable to all parties, there may be further choices. Some nonprofits have a formal mediation process. Some do not. If you think a professional mediation service will work in your particular situation, by all means suggest it. Often an unresolved volunteer personnel problem is referred to the board executive committee as a human resources issue. The organization's personnel or human resources policies would then govern the outcome.

Too many times passionate folks threaten litigation to push their personal agenda. The only winners at that point are the attorneys, so try to get the issues settled before it gets to the level of legal proceedings.

It's not possible to talk about every kind of situation, but the following are the kinds of challenging situations with other volunteers, or sometimes staff, that I have found to be the most common:

Founder's Syndrome or Mission Ownership

In my experience, having a full-blown sense of individual ownership of the organization and all of its operations is by far the most repeated situation in the nonprofit world. This is often called founder's syndrome, as it happens often when individuals who were instrumental in founding or developing a charity act as the ultimate authority on all matters, regardless of the established organizational structure. Typically, those exhibiting founder's syndrome make and enforce decisions based on personal preferences and from a sense of entitlement, with little or no input from other volunteers or staff.

This attitude can also be present among long-standing volunteers who believe they have a right to override others because of their longevity with the charity or their belief that they have a higher level of passionate commitment to the mission. These volunteers tend to assume superior authority in making decisions, taking action, and managing other volunteers or staff. Unilateral conduct, often without adequate communication, is standard with founder's/mission owner's syndrome.

A situation of founder's syndrome can be very difficult to manage. Mission owners historically have given a lot to the charity and are often quite essential to the success of the organization. They are often the public face for the mission of the charity. Their contributions cannot be overstated. However, over time, as the charity progresses, the founder/mission owners often become mired in "the way it's always been." It can be difficult for them to evolve with the times, and there tends to be a lack of understanding of the benefit of working as a team player. It can be tough for mission owners to acknowledge that other volunteers have the same level of performance as do they.

How you manage it as a volunteer depends on your direct involvement with the mission owner. It may be something you simply observe. If that is the case, leave it alone and walk away. It will only become an issue if you in fact observe that laws or regulations are being violated, or if the reputation of the charity is at risk. Then follow the private report process to the immediate supervisor. While going through the process of getting a problem solved, understand that you will not change the personalities of the mission owners. Show them that you value their history and appreciate their contributions. Then just smile and move on with your own work. In receiving recognition from the organization, mission owners get the emotional reassurance and public credit that they seem to need.

If you're serving as a board director, there may be a larger issue if the mission owner is in constant conflict with the board. Again, to ensure this does not become a personality problem, establish written policies (impersonal) that limit authority, such as having limited board terms, or volunteer rotation systems, or volunteer/staff organizational charts and job descriptions. Be careful to honor the value these founders/mission owners have brought to the charity, and be kind about limiting their authority—but limit it nonetheless, to protect the organization.

In extreme cases, it may take a board executive committee directive to make any enforcement authoritative. If the mission owner continuously keeps the board in conflict and stops the work of the organization, your board may have to take more extreme steps. To honor the mission owner and at the same time limit the micromanagement problems, the board could establish a new advisory group. The advisory group could be a vehicle to give a higher level of recognition for past support, but it would be removed from management authority or responsibilities. Your governing board could hold a celebratory event to recognize the volunteer and promote him or her to this new, exciting level. Then, with the person's name in lights, the troublesome individual is removed from the opportunity of over-managing.

Abrasive Personality or Bullies

Encountering abrasive personalities or bullies is common to virtually everyone's life experience, whether as a volunteer or not. It is nothing new. However, how you handle them in a volunteer setting may be a little different than you might otherwise. Nose punching is not recommended!

In understanding the bullying or abrasive personality, it is important to remember that they are involved primarily based on their own ego and their own perceived agendas. Typically, I have found that a bully is not as committed to the mission of the charity as others might be. The bully is often using the philanthropic format as a vehicle to attain control or notoriety or some other self-goal. Let me just state again that you will not change personalities, so don't frustrate yourself by trying. Bullies are not interested in anyone else's point of view but their own. If you're confronted by a bully, ask the person to please stop. Put your hand up with the palm toward them as a visual stop sign. Then stop speaking and walk away.

If you determine that the issue is important enough for follow up, and if you think it will be productive, follow the process for an individual meeting with the other person. If you think that would be a waste of time, or if the other party is not willing to meet, go to the next step of reporting the confrontation to the supervisor and ask for your preferred solution. This may be a face-to-

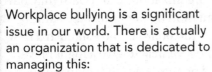

Abrasive Personalities or Bullies

Workplace bullying is a significant issue in our world. There is actually an organization that is dedicated to managing this:

Workplace Bullying Institute, *workplacebullying.org*

Observation

face meeting or something else, but it should be after the heat of the moment has died down. Generally, the issue will drop at this point (after the supervisor speaks with the bully) unless there is a significant reason to carry it further. If it goes further, follow the process to a reasonable end. Then keep on with keeping on, and don't carry a grudge. Try very hard to detach personally, and stay focused on systems, policies, and procedures. Avoid the bully and continue enjoying doing your work for the nonprofit. If nothing else works for you in getting this resolved, you always have the option of discontinuing your volunteer participation or asking to be moved to another area.

If the bullying continues and becomes intolerable, go to the organization's volunteer coordinator, the human resources director, or the chief executive officer. Then follow the established written processes of the charity. As always, keep your focus on the issues and not on the personality, if at all possible.

Dishonesty, Ethical, or Fiduciary Violations

A covolunteer or staff member who appears to be dishonest is a serious matter. Significant and repetitive obfuscation resulting in damage to programs or personnel as well as theft would fall under this category. Ethical or fiduciary breaches such as violating confidentiality, hiding a conflict of interest, or self-dealing are equally concerning.

If you directly experience or observe any of these happening, you should report the situation immediately to the CEO or the volunteer coordinator. Make sure you have factual and provable information. If you're alleging a fiduciary violation, make sure it really is a fiduciary duty violation, and not just a difference of opinion. Someone simply disagreeing with someone else does not necessarily constitute violating fiduciary duty. The organization will have written processes in place to address these kinds of situations, and, once reported, you will have to allow the process to work.

Be aware that any report of this kind falls under an expectation of confidentiality, on your part and on the part of the staff receiving the report. Because it is about a person, actions the staff may take will not be shareable with you because it would violate the accused's privacy. Additionally, you cannot discuss it with anyone else for the same reason.

Lack of Dependability

People don't show up when they say they will. People don't follow through on promises they make. People don't do their work in the way they were trained. And to make it worse, they don't call and let anyone know they can't follow through. It is frustrating and aggravating. You and your covolunteers are depending on them and they are AWOL. What do you do?

Again try to stay focused on a system or written procedure, not an individual person. Volunteers who feel attacked and criticized (even if you think it is justified) won't be volunteers very long. It is important to remember that nonprofits need volunteers to accomplish the work, so making every effort to work out a negative situation is usually the preferred track.

Set up a system for success. Call volunteers in advance to remind them of their schedule. Send reminder emails to covolunteers about what they agreed to do. Have an easy way for volunteers to contact the volunteer supervisor or staff in charge in case of problems. If they are not doing the job correctly, have a private meeting with the volunteer coordinator.

As a volunteer, your management authority is usually more limited than that of staff. In circumstances with conflict, use the least confrontational methods first to work out

One of My Covolunteers Is Way Wrong about Politics!

People who you don't understand or who do not understand you can seem abrasive. Make your best effort to be open to people who think and act differently than you do. Conflict will be avoided. Friends will be retained.

One of my best friends I met as a covolunteer. We have hugely differing opinions on politics, which can always lead to arguments. However, working together on our common cause, with respect and consideration, we have become close lifetime friends. We simply agree to disagree about presidential elections and change the subject.

Pure Genius!

a solution. Follow the charity's internal process for resolving more complicated problems. Keep focused on the issue, not the individual.

Your goal as a volunteer is to act as a team member to do the best job you can for the nonprofit. Some jobs can be huge in scope, so encourage your covolunteers to share the work as part of the team, unless you expect to do all of the work all by yourself. It helps if there is a spirit of cooperation. Don't expect to love every personality on the team, but remember, you are *all* there to make a difference in the world. In stressful situations, be highly aware of using kindness and respect in working with all of the folks with whom you're engaged. You will realize much more positive results. Celebrate the differences in personal styles, and keep your focus on the good you are doing.

To Summarize...

- Conflicts in the workplace should be managed as productively as possible.

- Develop an assessment, including identification of the conflict with proposed resolutions.

- It's best to base conflict resolutions on impartial policies and procedures, not on personal confrontations.

- Volunteers with founder's syndrome should be honored for their service and encouraged to move to an advisor capacity.

Chapter 29

Your Personal Protection

In This Chapter...

- Personal physical risk
- Personal liability for direct service
- General personal liability for volunteer work
- Liability insurance options

Unfortunately, we live in an age of litigation. If folks are unhappy, there is always the possibility they might threaten to sue. Most volunteering opportunities will go smoothly. Sometimes, however, you may want to be aware of being a little more careful when it comes to various kinds of risk. There can be personal physical risks or risks in your work with clients, or various kinds of personal liability exposure in your work as a volunteer.

As a board director, it will be your obligation to oversee the liability coverage of the entire organization. It is best to be as informed as possible, and to make sure *you* are protected as much as possible.

Be certain to ascertain potential risks in advance, and affirm that the proper protections have been put in place by the charity and by you. The good part is that as long as you are acting with good intent and within the parameters of your training, you're generally fine.

Personal Physical Risk

The danger of you sustaining an injury is more likely if you are working directly with clients in a physical activity. You may be playing basketball with teenage kids, ice skating with a group of seniors, or chaperoning the marching band tour. You may even be rappelling with athletes or hiking mountains with students in South America. Injuries can happen. You will need to be prepared for emergencies.

When you're initially applying and interviewing for a volunteer position that is at a higher-than-average level of physical engagement, ask the charity about the risk. What is the history of injuries to volunteers? Does the charity have workers' compensation insurance that covers volunteers? What is the medical liability insurance coverage for volunteers? Are there on-site equipment and supplies in case someone gets hurt? Is there a staff person trained in CPR and first aid? Should *you* be trained in CPR and first aid? Is there an on-site AED (automated external defibrillator) and is someone always available who knows how to use it? What specialized physical conditioning will you need to do?

After you have this information, you may want to get a little extra first aid or CPR training on your own if the charity does not offer it. Depending on the charity's insurance coverages combined with the history of risk, you may want to check that your medical and medical liability insurance covers any gaps that the charity's coverage may have.

Insurance coverage is expensive, so don't take for granted that your organization is fully covered. In my experience, volunteers typically take care of their minor injuries themselves with their personal insurance. The nonprofit usually pays the volunteer's deductible cost to hospitals or doctors. For something more catastrophic, the insurance coverage may be a combination of the volunteer's personal medical insurance as well as the organization's medical liability coverage and/or worker's compensation coverage. In the best of all worlds, the charity will cover all the costs. Ask the charity about its practices and coverage.

Workers' compensation insurance generally covers employees of a business who have been injured on the job. It covers both medical expenses and lost wages. There are limits, based on the level of insurance for which the employers pay. In some states, the law allows coverage for volunteers. If covered as a volunteer, the coverage may be the same as a paid employee, or may be different than a paid employee. Insurance laws vary from state to state, so make sure you know how worker's compensation operates in your state, and confirm whether or not your charity has that covered.

Personal Liability for Direct Service

Serving clients one-on-one requires careful behavior. Volunteers can be unfairly accused of bad acts. Clients can also be in danger of being exposed to a volunteer who is in the wrong role. There are also very strict laws in place for the protection of most populations, whether or not they are considered at risk. You need to be aware that there can be personal liability vulnerability in providing direct service to clients.

Personal Physical Exposure

At the risk of being obvious, be sure that all possible protections are in place for your personal safety. If you volunteer late at night, make sure there is security to escort you to your car. If the clients have a tendency to be physically confrontational, make sure the organization is fully forthcoming about the situation and has processes in place to minimize any problems. Collect all the facts and make a fully informed decision about your involvement.

WATCH OUT!

Much of your liability exposure will be handled by your training and any certifications that might be required by your organization. Making sure you have the proper training is in the best interests of the charity as well as you when it comes to liability exposure. The charity's liability insurance would be the first coverage used, if it ever gets to that point. You should be sufficiently safe with that coverage.

However, avoiding getting to the level of litigation is the best. Be aware that wrong acts can be more perception than reality. Avoid even the possibility of doing anything that can be misconstrued. What those acts might be will depend on how you are volunteering. Examples would be to always count money with two people present, and both sign for the total. Never close yourself alone into a room, tent, or space with a client. Always have a door open and staff or other volunteers within sight. Fully and immediately report

Volunteer Liability Protections

In the United States, volunteers can be reassured about personal liability by the federal Volunteer Protection Act of 1997. Summarized, it states that volunteers for a qualified nonprofit generally will not be personally liable for harm caused if:

◆ they acted within the scope of their responsibilities;

◆ they were properly licensed or certified (if required under the circumstances);

◆ the harm was not caused by negligence and not willful or reckless misconduct; and

◆ the harm was not caused by the volunteer operating a motor vehicle, vessel, aircraft, or other vehicle for which the owner or operator is required to possess an operator's license or maintain insurance.

Note that while this act reduces the liability exposure for volunteers, it does not offer the same protections to the nonprofit.

Pure Genius!

anything out of the ordinary. Don't make verbal or written promises to clients. Always check with your supervisor if you have any doubts. Don't accept gifts of cash or of any value from clients. A picture colored by a child is fine. There are countless ways to find yourself in an unpleasant situation, so if there is any question at all, don't do it.

I don't mean to frighten you, but if you're aware, you can proactively avoid problems. An unfounded accusation of misbehavior can do immeasurable damage to a volunteer's life. (Hopefully, you will never be involved in a *founded* charge.)

You will likely never run across a situation like this, but know how to handle it if you do. In an immediate situation, report the problem to the on-site staff supervisor as well as the executive director. Follow the organization's stated procedures. Stay calm, honest, and don't speak to anyone except the supervisor or executive director until the issue is resolved.

Personal Liability for General Volunteer Work

In talking about general liability for volunteer work, we are talking about serving on boards, involvement in general staffing, direct fundraising, or special events—not direct client service. Liability in these roles would consist of causing loss or harm to the charity or to those it serves through deliberate or willful negligence or bad acts. This damage could consist of financial loss, damage to the reputation of the nonprofit, damage to a client or class of clients, or hiding wrongful activities by the charity, the charity's staff, or the charity's volunteers.

You're always personally responsible for doing your best work in good faith and in accordance with fiduciary duty, the law, and any applicable standards and regulations. Sometimes, however, you may find yourself inadvertently liable for acts of others. This is more possible during service as a board director. It can happen that a director or directors violate a law or fiduciary duty, and fail to notify the rest of the board of the situation. All directors could have some level of liability for not knowing or acting, depending on the details. To be held legally responsible for acts of others, you would have to know that these acts that are taking place are wrong in some way, and you failed to report or stop them.

Personal Liability Coverage for Volunteer Work

So far in my life, I have served on sixty-two nonprofit boards plus as a general volunteer for several other philanthropic causes. As a precaution over the years, I have put in place a total of $4 million in liability insurance. Coverages are held by homeowner's insurance, corporate insurance (I am self-employed), and liability umbrella insurance policies. Chat with your financial and legal advisors for options that will work best for you.

Incidentally, I have never come close to needing any of the coverage.

Pure Genius!

If you're serving on a board, the nonprofit should have directors and officers (D&O) liability insurance in place as well as liability coverage in the general liability coverage. These are not the same kinds of policies, so make sure D&O insurance exists. Volunteering on activities that do not include board service would be covered by the general liability coverage for the nonprofit. Additionally, most states afford legal liability protection for volunteers if the volunteers are acting in good faith and in a prudent and reasonable manner.

Although you will likely be fully covered when it comes to liability with the institutional insurance and state protections, you may want to consider carrying extra liability insurance on your own. If you own a house, you probably have some kind of liability insurance with your homeowner's insurance. If you rent, you should have some level of liability coverage in your renter's insurance policy.

Read your policy to make sure of any exemptions. It is unlikely that you will need to use any of these coverages, but it is better to be prepared and not need it than need it and not have it.

Again, most threats of liability litigation happen generally when there is a strong difference in opinion and someone is trying to force a particular agenda, so don't over react instantaneously. As a policy, do your best to avoid actions that can be viewed as unacceptable to avoid any negative consequences. Often, differences can be reduced to implementing more effective communication.

If the complaints and legal threats continue, try to mediate a solution either within the organization or with a professional mediator. If litigation is actually filed, there has to be a reasonable basis. This is rare, but typically ends up being very public, very expensive, and very damaging to all parties, regardless of the ultimate outcome. Consequences should be considered carefully prior to taking this litigation route.

On a positive note, understand that legal problems which this chapter discusses are extraordinarily unusual. It is important that you know what can happen in an adverse scenario in order to be protected and to avoid it. It will be surprising if any circumstance like this arises in your volunteer service.

Liability Insurance Options

There are several options and layers of liability protection for volunteers. Most states have legislation that protects volunteers who are doing their work in good faith. Most charities have D&O insurance that covers their boards, and may cover general volunteers. Charities customarily have general liability insurance as well (in addition to D&O) that would cover volunteers working on behalf of the organization. Be sure to check to make sure what coverage is in place with the organizations you serve. Your homeowner's insurance policy may have a liability clause that provides some level of personal protection for you. Contact your carrier to make sure what is and isn't covered related to any volunteer work you're doing. If you are driving while fulfilling your volunteer duties, the liability portion of your auto insurance may apply. You can also choose to purchase an insurance policy that covers personal liability only. These are fairly affordable, presuming you don't have any personal history that would prevent you from being coverable. Use your good judgment to figure out what you need.

To Summarize...

🔍 Personal liability in volunteer service is a reality.

🔍 Liability exists in direct service to clients as well as in general or board volunteer duties.

🔍 Ensure there is adequate insurance coverage in place, including medical, D&O insurance, general corporate liability, or your personal liability insurance coverage.

🔍 Most states provide statutory protection for volunteers to do their work professionally and in good faith.

Chapter 30

You're Needed and Appreciated

In This Chapter...

- Your volunteer journey
- Adventures abroad
- 360-degree view
- Thank you

Let's take stock. Since the beginning of human time, people have worked together for food, safety, shelter, and care for others in their families, in their communities, and in their world. Over time, how volunteering is defined as well as how volunteering is structured have become more evolved, formalized, and institutionalized. Different countries and cultures may approach volunteerism differently, but the Golden Rule exists universally.

As a volunteer, never underestimate the positive effect you have in the lives of people you may never meet. By the numbers, according to the National Council on Community Service (*volunteeringinamerica.gov*) 62.8 million residents of the United States in 2014 contributed 7.9 billion hours of volunteer work at a value of $184 billion. This translates into 32.1 volunteer hours for every man, woman, and young person. Additionally, 62.5 percent of the population volunteers "informally," such as helping your neighbor mow the grass or grocery shopping for a shut-in. These are big, intimidating numbers. It's almost too hard to comprehend. So, let's focus on what all the numbers really mean, and bring the picture into better focus for your life by reviewing where we have been in this book.

Your Volunteer Journey—Who You Are and What You Like to Do

Before you start more formalized volunteer involvement, know yourself. Know what you are interested in doing. Try to understand how you want to make a difference, and be honest about what kinds of activities with which you don't want to be involved. Understand your skills and experience as well as your lack of experience. Also, take stock of your personality quirks or amusing habits. You will want to make sure that all of these can be comfortably absorbed into the initiatives you are considering.

Taking the time to do this helps ensure the best effect and outcome for both you and the organization for which you volunteer. It is critical to be honest with yourself. Don't get involved for someone else's reasons or under pressure. If you want to leave your workday world behind, this is your chance to learn something new, have adventures, and expand your window to the world. If you choose to use the skill sets you have learned over your lifetime, enjoy sharing your expertise and experience to support the charity's mission in a substantive way. At the same time, know that you will be changing the world by changing people's lives one at a time.

Investigating Options and Choosing Your Involvement

The world of volunteer choices is your personal adventure waiting to happen! The options are nearly endless. Take the time to investigate. Do you want to be part of a socially or business-based service nonprofit? Are city, regional, state, or national governmental boards or commissions in your future? Are you happier being involved in your place of worship or school? Do you love politics? Is your interest more human services or more fine arts oriented? Do you like to travel or do you prefer staying closer to home? What about fraternal organizations? Do you want to be hands-on and work directly with women, men, and children, and possibly become a part of their daily lives, if only for a short time? Do you prefer organizing a special event or serving on a board? If you take a minute here, think of how many people you can touch just with this short list of possibilities. Let your imagination fly!

Adventures Abroad

Volunteering abroad is a special kind of commitment. The thought of traveling to another country, experiencing the sights, sounds, smells, and tastes of a place you have only seen in a book or movie can be exhilarating. This kind of travel will take time, planning, extensive research, and careful execution. For foreign volunteering, you will need to pay more attention to health and safety issues. Doing background investigation about the country, culture, and language as well as learning the job you will be doing might require more time and more effort than other kinds involvement. This option may also require a higher financial commitment from you. There will be a cost to the travel and for the program for which you are volunteering.

Foreign volunteering can be scheduled for almost any time frame depending on the program. There are volunteer vacations, school year, gap year, as well as child care to well digging to marine research choices. There are two-week to six-year project commitments available. You can go by yourself, take a friend, or take your entire family.

Don't forget the paperwork on the foreign country option. Plan now to get your passport and any visas that might be required. Become close friends with the project manager for your overseas nonprofit. This person will have all of the information you will need to be successful, from what to take in clothing to where to find a telephone when you arrive. The most important safety concern for you to be aware of is how to exit the country if significant problems arise. Even with the extra preparation, volunteering in another country will be a once-in-a-lifetime experience for you, as it will be for the men, women, and children you will help.

Expectations

Expect to learn. Expect to succeed. Expect to be excited. Expect to achieve. Be well educated before you make a commitment. Over the years, I have found that a successful charity/volunteer relationship generally can be attributed to excellent communication and passionate commitment. Before you begin any new volunteer endeavor, ask questions. Get as fully informed as you can about the charity, the job you will be doing, and how the charity expects you to do it. You should expect training, information, resources, and support from the organization. The organization will expect passion for the mission, your best work, dependability, confidentiality, and commitment from you. Then go forth with a happy heart and do good for as many folks as you can.

360-Degree View

As a volunteer, proactively decide what you're doing, why you are doing it, where you are doing it, and the difference it will make to those you serve. Millions of people do so much good as volunteers. As a volunteer, work hard and always plan for the best outcomes as well as the most positive experiences.

Remember that if you feel good about what you are doing and are having fun, those around you will as well.

Sometimes there can be concerns, so it is important that you're aware of conflict, risk, and liability exposure. In dealing with negative situations, try to stay focused on the system or process for resolution, not the individual, and your emotional reaction to the person. Take the high road; it will pay off in the end.

You're a Volunteer

The best way to not feel hopeless is to get up and do something. Don't wait for good things to happen to you. If you go out and make some good things happen, you will fill the world with hope, you will fill yourself with hope.

President Barak Obama

Quote

Thank You

Whatever you choose to do as a volunteer or however you choose to do it, you as an individual are changing, improving, helping, or making a difference in the life and well-being of at least one other person, over and over again. It is unlikely you will ever know these individuals. In your imagination, try to see that person smile, or feel safer, or experience success in school or work, or get the medicine his children need, or finally have a home, or get healthy, or be in less pain, or win the Olympics, or become a great opera singer, or to not be hungry, or take award winning photos, or finally graduate from school, or . . . and you will know that it is worth all the effort. That person's life is fundamentally changed for the better. So is yours. You are richer as a human being. You're important to your world. You are important to *their worlds.* And don't forget that in giving back, you will have a happier, longer life!

To Summarize...

- Now you understand the depth of volunteering, and are prepared for your personal, exciting, volunteer adventures.

- Make an intentional choice to make a difference in your neighborhood, in your country, or around the globe.

- Use common sense and kindness in managing adverse circumstances.

- Know that you're making a huge difference.

- On behalf of all those you have served or will serve, in recognition of all of the positive change you have or will bring to our world, and in appreciation for your giving heart, *THANK YOU.*

Index

For the GENIUS® Press is an imprint that produces books on just about any topic that people want to learn. *You don't have to be a genius to read a GENIUS book, but you'll sure be smarter once you do!*™ Here are some of our recently published titles.

ForTheGENIUS.com/bookstore

PRESS

Baking Bread for the GENIUS

Fast & Fearless Cooking for the GENIUS

Gourmet Breakfasts for the GENIUS

European Travel for the GENIUS

Cats for the GENIUS

Dog Care and Training for the GENIUS

Casino Video Poker for the GENIUS

Public Speaking for the GENIUS

ForTheGENIUS.com/bookstore

for the GENIUS PRESS

CPSIA information can be obtained
at www.ICGtesting.com
Printed in the USA
LVOW04s2257270317
528654LV00003B/13/P